Intuitive
Children

First published by O Books, 2009
O Books is an imprint of John Hunt Publishing Ltd., The Bothy, Deershot Lodge, Park Lane, Ropley,
Hants, SO24 0BE, UK
office1@o-books.net
www.o-books.net

Distribution in:	South Africa
	Alternative Books
UK and Europe	altbook@peterhyde.co.za
Orca Book Services	Tel: 021 555 4027 Fax: 021 447 1430
orders@orcabookservices.co.uk	
Tel: 01202 665432 Fax: 01202 666219	Text copyright Kylie Holmes 2008
Int. code (44)	
	Design: Stuart Davies
USA and Canada	
NBN	ISBN: 978 1 84694 165 8
custserv@nbnbooks.com	
Tel: 1 800 462 6420 Fax: 1 800 338 4550	All rights reserved. Except for brief quotations
	in critical articles or reviews, no part of this
Australia and New Zealand	book may be reproduced in any manner without
Brumby Books	prior written permission from the publishers.
sales@brumbybooks.com.au	
Tel: 61 3 9761 5535 Fax: 61 3 9761 7095	The rights of Kylie Holmes as author have been
	asserted in accordance with the Copyright,
Far East (offices in Singapore, Thailand,	Designs and Patents Act 1988.
Hong Kong, Taiwan)	
Pansing Distribution Pte Ltd	
kemal@pansing.com	A CIP catalogue record for this book is available
Tel: 65 6319 9939 Fax: 65 6462 5761	from the British Library.

Illustrations: The World Tree, Aura and Chakras by Robert Banbury

Printed by EPAC

Intuitive Children

Kylie Holmes

BOOKS

Winchester, UK
Washington, USA

CONTENTS

In Memory

In memory of my Nan, Phyllis Clara Holmes (Pearl), who taught me that the impossible is possible.

Memories of you stay within my heart,
So many stories I do not know where to start,
Here one minute and left the next,
Nan, you've gone to heaven for a rest,
To watch over us is what you intend to do,
Nan, will you still whisper the words 'I love you'?
If we could turn back time, what would we say?
Just spend longer moments together on our last day,
To share reminiscences of the past,
But how we want that day to last,
Nan you've always something to say,
Something to brighten up our day,
Laughter and smiles through our tears,
Nan, you made us grin from ear to ear,
Nan, you're someone to love, someone to hold,
Someone so strong and yet always so bold,
You were never afraid in what you had to say,
Which helped us to get through the day,
Taking you shopping was so much fun,
Queen Boudicca you've become!
Never pushing the trolley in a straight line,
Causing mayhem all the time,
On Grand National Day
You would telephone and say,
Look into your crystal ball
And tell me the winning horse, that's all.
Nan would smile with glee,
Because I helped her pick the Grand National Winner you see,
Every Horse crossed the finishing line,

And this was repeated time after time,
We smile at memories, remember you in our hearts,
Why is this the end, as we do not want a brand new start?
Sticking a feather in the ground for luck,
You would say, would help you come unstuck,
Family Tree Stories and Cowslip Wine
Will stay with us forever until the end of time,
Nan, you knocked on Heaven's Door
And you are with Granddad & Uncle Alan once more,
Nan, your Spirit is free,
Nan, you're the wind that blows through the trees,
In the sounds that I hear,
I know, Nan, that your Spirit is near.
God Bless, God Night, so the bed bugs don't bite,
As you used to say to us every night.
I miss hearing your familiar voice,
But that was not by choice,
Merry meet and merry part until we merry meet again,
I know life will never be the same,
Nan, give me a sign that you are ok,
Then I can move on to another day.

Blessed Be X

Acknowledgements

To my children, Jade, Amba and Leo. Every day you bring me laughter and joy in so many areas of my life. I love you so so much and cherish every day we spend together and more. You are all truly Old Souls that will encourage others with their own spiritual abilities. Lots and lots of love, Mum X

To my soul mate, Eric. Thanks for being there and encouraging me every step of the way. Love you always.

To my parents, Sharon & Terry, Sister, Kerry, brother, Matthew, and brother-in-law, Garry – A true Old Soul Family, that never forgets each other. Blessed Be X

To my nieces, Keeley, Holly, Eryn and Freya, for always keeping me on my toes.

To my step-daughter, Becks. You may live a million miles away with your own family, Steve, Chloe and Karmen, but you are always in my heart.

To my grandparents – Nan and Granddad Holmes and Nan and Granddad Odell. Thou you are in spirit, you never leave my side.

Ruth White – You were a spark of sunshine in such a dark area of my life. Thank you for encouraging my spiritual growth, shaping and changing my life. To Gildas, who I warmly welcome to the continuation of our work and contact. Thank you both for your love, blessing, healing and support at all times.

Keith Brazil – You are such an inspirational and quirky guy. You told me that all I needed was to believe in myself, and my natural gifts would unfold. I learnt such a lot in a short space of time and you became a dear friend. I will never forget you. You are an amazing person who had so much knowledge to share and a passion for life. Blessed Be X

Delphi Ellis – I have so much to say, but I do not know where to begin! You are a truly inspirational friend that gives more meaning to the word 'friendship'. You rock girl!

Angel Kershaw – A dear Old Soul who is always there for me. Thank you for the inspiration, chanting and friendship. Blessed Be X

George David Fryer – Thank you for your wonderful drawings and for opening me up to the possibilities that life can offer me. Blessed Be X

Keith Beasley – Thank you for sharing the energy of Reiki and allowing the energy to master me. I am never going to forget that you taught me that Reiki has no rules. Blessed Be X

Laura – A true Soul Friend. You are always there for me no matter what. If you never took me to see Janey, where would I be today? Lots of love to you and Bradley.

Karen – A true soul friend who is a rock and a shoulder to cry on. Thank you for everything. Lots of love to you, Jordan, Chloe, Mike and Joyce.

Emma – A true Soul Friend. Thank you for your support, love and friendship, the mad holidays we have had together, the tears we shared and the laughter too. Oh, to be seventeen again! Blessed Be, love to you, Nick, Adam and Holly.

Nina – Thank you for everything; looking after my kids and also the Pendulum sessions. Keep up the good work. Love you always.

Ann B – You a wonderful Soul friend who has a heart of gold and shines light and love to anyone. Thank you for your support, love and friendship. Blessed Be X

Thanks to Gemma Bailey for helping me with NLP writing. You're a true godsend who knows her stuff.

Thanks to Paula W for helping me with this book and continued friendship. Blessed Be X

Thanks to Australian Bush for allowing me to use their material; especially to Sallianne McGowan, whose knowledge on these wonderful Essences just blows me away every time.

Thanks to everyone, who took their time to contribute stories for this book to come to life, especially to all BBC Radio Stations and Cygnus Books.

To Trevor, and Hayley, the Editing Team at O Books, thank you so much for your time, patience in helping me bringing this book to life and help with my Dyslexia.

And finally to John at O Books who made this happen. Thank you for everything. Blessed Be.

The Unseen Playmate by Robert Louis Stevenson
From Child's Garden Of Verses

When children are playing alone on the green,
In comes the playmate that never was seen.
When children are happy and lonely and good,
The Friend of the Children comes out of the wood.

Nobody heard him, and nobody saw,
His is a picture you never could draw,
But he's sure to be present, abroad or at home,
When children are happy and playing alone.

He lies in the laurels, he runs on the grass,
He sings when you tinkle the musical glass;
Whene'er you are happy and cannot tell why,
The Friend of the Children is sure to be by!

He loves to be little, he hates to be big,
'T is he that inhabits the caves that you dig;
'T is he when you play with your soldiers of tin
That sides with the Frenchmen and never can win.

'T is he, when at night you go off to your bed,
Bids you go to sleep and not trouble your head;
For wherever they're lying, in cupboard or shelf,
'T is he will take care of your playthings himself!

Preface

Are children's imaginary companions scary spooks or a sign that your child is open to a whole other magical dimension of life? What can you learn about these other worlds to which your child may have a natural doorway? Many parents find it hard to bring up a child with spiritual gifts positively in a contemporary, materialistic society. However, parents in today's society really need to help their children to access such magical places so that their worldly experiences are accepted in everyday life and not frowned upon or mocked.

Any parent wishing to nurture the special nature of their child should know that they have boundless imagination and often glide into a little world of their own – one that exists only to them. They are very spiritually sensitive, which, if encouraged, becomes second nature to them.

Spiritual children know that you do not have to have any rigid spiritual values, and they challenge traditional, limited ways of thinking. Spiritual children can often surprise you by bringing new goals to the surface; they have great senses of humour, will thrive if you encourage their dreams and will learn more from direct experience than from intellectual pursuits. They respond very well to affection and are kind and sensitive to those around them, often trying to help out those who are suffering or in need. They can, however, experience a fluctuating disposition, so expect sudden bursts of anger, happiness, or sadness. A good schedule and steady affection helps them find their own sense of self-confidence.

These children are born with a positive outlook, which, in essence, needs to be encouraged for them to reach their fullest potential.

Angels Appear

I was at a real low point when the angels helped me open up to a more spiritual way of life. In 1991, when I was only twenty years old and told my boyfriend that I was pregnant, he walked out on me to be with another. The stress caused me to miscarry and I ended up trying to take my own life.

When I was in hospital, beings of light first surrounded my hospital bed and then my life. The angel who visited me told me that I would survive and that this experience would inspire others, rekindle their own faith in their lives and re-focus their life beliefs. Whilst in hospital, I initially put this experience down to medication, but in my heart I knew that someone was looking after me. Strangely enough, it was also a comfort. In those dark days, when I was coming to terms with my miscarriage, life seemed pretty empty. While others were carrying on with their own lives, I was trying to pick up the pieces of mine and slowly put it back together, but life seemed meaningless.

I now know from experience that when we have life crises, they strengthen our inner core, and this enables us to see the light at the end of the tunnel. When you are not afraid to step forward and state that you have no fear of the past, this becomes a step hold for the future; things happen for a reason whether you call it karma or fate, and the cloud of darkness and loss of both baby and boyfriend turned out to have an extraordinary silver lining for me.

Feathers Everywhere

From that point on, wherever I went, I would find white feathers everywhere: in the bathroom, the car, on my coat. I must have collected hundreds over the years and I know that this is a sign that the angels were with me and are with me still.

As this became more and more apparent, I decided, out of curiosity, to go and see a clairvoyant with my friend Laura and some acquaintances; no one in that group knew what I had been through. As Janey, the clairvoyant, spoke, she revealed what had happened to me. Silence fell, but I cried and rejoiced, as I had found someone who knew ME. She told me that I had a gift and that the angels would like me to work with them. And in that split second, I knew that she was speaking the truth. I gave up my office job and moved to London to work with the homeless.

London was a real eye-opener and it made me grow up fast. I had come home to myself and as I wanted to learn more about the world, I decided to travel around Europe. At my first destination, Italy, I met my future husband, Eric, and we are still together.

And the white feathers were still descending.

The experiences with the angels made me think about my childhood. When I was eight, I would spend many lonely nights crying in my room because of school bullies; I lived in fear of the next morning because the bullying started on the school bus and only ended when I arrived home, but during those lonely nights lights would often appear to me and make me feel strong again.

At that time, my granddad was in hospital with pneumonia and out of curiosity I went to Sunday school, with school friends to see what it had to offer . The things that I enjoyed the most were the stories of angels visiting people when they were in trouble or needed help. As my knowledge of angels grew I learned that if someone is ill, you should ask their angels to make them well again.

Whilst in Sunday school, I was told that praying for someone in need is a good way to call upon the Angels, and so as I began to pray every night and lights would illuminate the bedroom window. At first I was scared and wondered what on earth these lights could be. I would peer out through the curtains to see if anyone was in the back garden – Nothing! Not even a person shining a torch onto the windowpanes.

As I climbed back into bed, one light would sparkle and dart across the window. When the light came back, it would become bigger and brighter. The lights would multiply each time they left the window. They were a comfort; they took all my fears away and made me feel strong inside again by staying with me until I feel asleep, and when awakening on dark winter mornings, I could still see them.

It was the Angels who helped me get through the tough times.

Excitedly, I would tell my mum. She would say that they were car lights, but I would tell her that they were comforting and that they made Granddad Odell better.

As the bullying started to fade away into the distance, so did the lights at the window

Being born on Halloween has always made me feel that there is more to life. I always explore the possibilities of magic and bring it into my life and into the lives of others. Life is full of experiences, not mistakes. Find your own true authentic voice in this life; if you are open, you will allow the magic to take you on your journey and beyond.

Chapter One

Is Your Child an Old Soul?

The man who has no imagination has no wings.
Muhammad Ali

What is imagination? What would life be like without imagination? Your Stories, Dreams and 'The Shadow', Old Soul Children, Miscarriage, Earthbound Spirits and more of Your Stories.

I am in the company of my son Leo. I just watched him come rushing in, clutching a cardboard box; one moment he is talking to me, the next he is charging off to play because his friends have arrived. I sit down and watch the action unfold, which draws me in, but I see no one around; the three year old that I am watching is filled with excitement as I am told that his great mischievous friends Jack and Harry have arrived to play and a game of buses takes place with a cardboard box.

Leo is suddenly transported from our physical world and connecting with the spiritual world and this is not for the very first time. This is where Jack and Harry come from. Leo, like others that I have interviewed, takes you innocently into his world of imagination, connecting with the Universe and beyond.

What is Imagination?
The word comes from the Latin 'imago', meaning 'picture'. Imagination is, in general, the power or process of producing mental images and ideas. But imagination encourages creativity, focuses the mind, and increases concentration throughout

our lives.

Imagination is a hugely powerful tool for learning and a precious gift for children of all ages, which encompasses a wide range of activities.

Imagination gives children the freedom to follow their own ideas and interests; to thrive and grow in their own way. They can explore the world around them and make meaning out of it for their own lives.

What would life be like without imagination?

Life would not be a poignant drama without the use of imagination and we probably would not have the courage to follow our dreams and desires. Without imagination, we would be condemned to live a purely instinctive life. We would still be lacking in social compassion and empathy. We would have no thought of the great beyond and never contemplate our existence. There would be no pyramids, no Stonehenge, no cars, no aeroplanes and no people looking for new ways to tackle cancer, HIV and AIDS.

Imagination is a truly wonderful thing to have. It is truly an inner power and an ally. Great thinkers and inventors of our time relied on the power of imagination to solve problems and overcome obstacles.

We started using our imaginations in our childhoods, when the stairs that carried us to bed became our space rocket to Mars and we searched for alien life, along the way, to 'boldly go where no child has gone before'. This, of course, is also the time when we become companions with imaginary friends.

I was introduced to Children's imaginary friends when I picked up my eldest daughter, Jade, from nursery, ten years ago, and she announced that her brother – imaginary friend 'Sammy' – was going to live with us and sleep under her bed. Her mischievous playmate once persuaded her to clean the bathroom using toothpaste!

And so my adventure began. My Health Visitor told me it was just one of those things – part of growing up and she would grow out of it. This I simply did not believe and decided to do my own research, as there was not much available to read on the subject. It has taken me on many journeys, throughout the UK and around the world, and I have many stories to share with you of children  unaware of the real connection of their mystical and spiritual experiences.

Emily

I was on BBC Radio Birmingham being interviewed in the early hours, and whilst I began to talk about my research, a man called Alex rang in. Alex went on to tell us that the day before, at a family BBQ, his little girl Emily went up to the television and spooked the whole family!

They were watching a family video of his mum who had passed away before Emily, then four years old, was born. Emily went up to the television, kissed the screen, looked straight at the women and announced that "Betty comes to see me at night time. She reads me a story and then kisses me good night and then I go to sleep." The room fell silent because Emily never knew her name and Alex confirmed that his mum Betty had died before Emily was born. Alex also said that sometimes, late at night, he would walk past her room on the way to bed and hear Emily talking as if someone was with her. The day that they had watched the video, was the day that his mum had passed away six years ago.

From the research that I have carried out and the experiences with my own children, I truly believe that they can see spirits, angels and nature spirits. Any child has the ability to see a spirit of some kind.

Nicola

Nicola Stonehouse, who works for BBC Cambridgeshire, remembers her imaginary friend, Sean Betterby, who just appeared out of nowhere.

Nicola's mum heard her talking to someone, and then asked, Who you are talking to?

Nicola replied, "My friend, Sean Betterby."

Nicola was about three and her family had a good laugh. Her mum was studying Linguistics at university and thought it odd that Nicola's 'friend' had a surname.

Nicola recalls; "He was a young lad about six years old, with dark hair. He wore shorts – even in winter. Mum said he would come everywhere with us and they had to make space for him in the car, at the dinner table and on walks."

Sean Betterby also had everything that Nicola had – two biscuits for Nicola, two for Sean. They drew pictures together, and she would give him paper and pencils, and chat to him all the time. Her mum recollects that Nicola did not blame him for anything. He was "just my mate" says Nicola and he only appeared when she did not have any friends around to play with.

Nicola has one vivid memory of going to church with her grandparents and then going to have dinner with the vicar. The vicar was laughing and pulled out an extra chair and said, "This is for Sean." Nicola remembers looking up at the vicar and thinking, "How dare you laugh? You can't see him; he's just a joke to you!" Nicola remembers getting quite moody about it!

The only other memory that Nicola has is when Sean turned the light off for her. She was very young, but as Nicola remembers it; he put out the light one night, and her mum was shocked because she thought Nicola must have done it. When her mum went into the bedroom Nicola was fast asleep.

No one knows where the name came from. Her parents checked everything they could think of – neighbours, TV, radio, friends and so on, but found nothing. Sean disappeared when Nicola started school.

Nicola once talked about Sean on a radio show for a competition. She stated three things about herself and the listeners had to guess which was false. Nicola's statements included the fact that she had an imaginary friend called Sean. Every caller said that was the lie, but then they took a call from a spiritual healer called Dennis. Dennis told her that Sean is definitely true. His spirit guide had told him that Sean is also in spirit, and he talks to her through dreams.

Nicola was 'happily convinced.' With regards to Dennis, Nicola trusted him. He had travelled the world as a medium and healer, and was actually healing a dog at the time he phoned in.

Lisa

I first met Gordon Thorpe in 1996 when he visited me for a spiritual reading. Gordon later joined my meditation group and we became firm friends. Gordon learned of my quest for imaginary friend stories and I was delighted when he told me about his daughter Lisa.

Lisa, at a very early age, two or three years old, would cure headaches by voluntarily placing her hands on the affected person.

In 1970 to 1973, Gordon was stationed in Brügen, Germany, as a radar technician with the RAF. Peg, his wife, was pregnant with their second child Jason and, at that time, Lisa had an imaginary friend called Billy.

Billy appeared not long after they moved into an old, three bedroom house in Brügen, which was divided into two flats. Lisa would stand in the corner of the hall near the cellar door and seemed to talk to the wall. Gordon would ask her who she was talking to and she would always say, "Billy." Lisa would go to the corner and show Billy her new shoes and dress. Later on, Lisa would talk to him at night, but she would often shout "go away," "leave me alone," "I'm tried." Lisa would begin to cry and Gordon would go into her room and, when walking through the entrance, he would always feel a sensation like cobwebs being dragged across his face.

When Billy was present, Lisa's bedroom was always cold, and at times it would be the coldest room in the house. On one occasion, late afternoon, Peg smelt tobacco smoke and went into the lounge adjoining Lisa's bedroom. She saw dark blue tobacco smoke curling up from the high-backed armchair, but when she moved around to the front there was nothing there. Gordon was at work when this incident occurred and whilst Peg investigated she became nervous and would not enter the room until Gordon came home from work.

Hasan

"How could a four year old boy have a conversation with someone who had died the day before?" asked Irma, the shaken mum of Hasan.

Every Saturday, the Atkins family went to feed the ducks and then onto McDonald's for lunch. This had been a regular occurrence for the last five years until one day it was raining, and McDonald's was full that they decided to use the drive thru. Realising that they did not have enough money, they drove to the nearest cash point. On returning to McDonald's, Irma heard Hasan chatting away to nobody.

"Who are you talking to?" she asked.

"Elias," he told her, matter-of-factly. Great Uncle Elias was Irma's Uncle.

As they sped back towards McDonald's, Hasan shouted, "Bye, Elias!"

It wasn't until later that night that they discovered that Elias had died the night before. Irma then remembered that Hasan had been talking to him. They all brushed the incident off as a pretty amazing coincidence but maybe he had really seen Great Uncle Elias when they went to feed the ducks.

Hasan recently celebrated a birthday and I was one of the guests at his party. While the kids ran around the room and played party games, the adults sat at the table, sipping wine and talking about Hasan's newest imaginary friends. Hasan says they live at his house.

"My friends are all red," he would often tell his family. "They melted and I'm sad."

Knowing Hasan's history, his dad, Art, decided to do some research. When he looked into the history of the house, he discovered that the house had burned down in the 1800s and four people were killed in the fire!

Dreams and 'The Shadow'

When we tell our children 'it was just a bad dream', are we accidentally teaching them to mistrust what they may have actually been seeing? Some parents unknowingly start to teach and train their children, at a very young age, to block these images. This is carried out because of protection and misunderstanding of the situation. How many parents have tucked their little ones back into bed with the words that they thought were reassuring: "there are no such things as ghosts," "you just had a bad dream," "it wasn't real," "it was just your imagination."?

When we have a dream that worries us, we need to try to remember that usually dreams have a positive message in them.

Dreams may use symbolism of death, passing over and so on, but we need to see the symbolic meaning of this and not just the bleak, usual meaning. Death can also mean rebirth; passing over can mean that one stage is left behind and another embraced, and these probably have little to do with actual physical death.

And, for example, when we dream about trains it is usually

about direction. However, it is also, perhaps, showing or asking us what planetary energies or strengths we want to invite in to help us find and energise our sense of direction.

Spiritually orientated children often have nightmares. It is a way of dealing with 'the shadow'. In Jungian Psychology, Carl Jung developed his own distinctive approach to the study of the human mind and took a closer look at the mysterious depths of the human unconscious. Jung believed that 'the shadow' is a part of the unconscious mind. It may appear in dreams and visions in various forms, often as a feared person, and may act either as an adversary or as a friend. Interactions with 'the shadow' in dreams may shed light on one's state of mind. Also, it can be difficult to identify characters in dreams, so a character who seems, at first, to be a shadow might be represented in some other way.

Jung also suggests that there is more than one layer making up the shadow. The top layer is the rationally explicable unconscious; it contains material which has been made unconscious artificially and is made up of elements of one's personal experiences. Underneath this layer, however, are the archetypes which form the psychic contents of personal experiences. Jung described this bottom layer as "a psychic activity which goes on independently of the conscious mind and is not dependent even on the upper layers of the unconscious."

This bottom layer of the shadow is what Jung referred to as the collective unconscious. According to Jung, 'the shadow' sometimes overwhelms a person's actions, for example, when the conscious mind is shocked, confused, or paralyzed by indecision.

Having bad dreams is part of progressing through childhood. Cuddles and reassurance are a large part of the way forward in dealing with this. However, later in the book, I will be introducing Power Animals and how they can empower your child.

Old Soul Children

As part of my research, I have interviewed hundreds of children who have previous knowledge of being here, which indicates them being an Old Soul.

An Old Soul is a person who comes back and gains new understanding with each lifetime; an Old Soul Child has experienced many lives and appears wise beyond their years. The Old Souls found in young bodies, are returning to bring a much-needed change to the world, bringing the aspect of having a more laid back attitude towards their life.

For many young children, this is not their first visit on earth. 'Old Souls' are queuing to come down on earth, to encompass the human experience and rejoice in changing the world, which is seen as challenging.

Old Soul Children's imaginary friends are evidence of children's openness to the spirit worlds. They may also be the child's true self, helping to steer them through the world of conditioning that they have to encounter during their formative years. They are sometimes children that need companionship and cannot fully find it on the other side, because they have not yet let go of their, perhaps brief, incarnation in the present world. They are beings from the spirit worlds who also help the contact between different levels some Old Soul Children find their spiritual connections in their early years and begin to talk about it with ease. When they come into contact with people who have not woken up to spiritual awareness and energies, and are not heading in the same direction, these children find it difficult to understand why their peers are not supporting their spiritual education. This could be in schools, sport clubs and even in the families that they are born into, and so the lid gets firmly shut down on their spiritual aspects, which lay dormant until possible adult years, when they are awoken again. It is more acceptable for an adult to be psychic and spiritual than a child, but that is all changing at a rapid rate.

Some Old Soul Children come back to repeat learning patterns because of what they have disregarded in previous lifetimes.

17

Once back on earth, they have some powerful insights and start to undo the karma so that they do not repeat the same lessons over and over again. Earth becomes their 'knowledge playground,' and each day brings them a new experience for them to truly understand why they are here.

It is very clear to me that Old Soul Children are being born into families where the family has chosen to receive spiritual information and divine energies. These families do very well in encouraging their child's spiritual education and enabling them to use their spiritual gifts in every situation that is presented to the whole family.

As a past life regression therapist, I am very passionate about the journey of the soul, why we are here and why we choose experiences before we incarnate. Aristotle said "When the body dies, the soul passes onto another, leaving behind its memory but takes with it a higher realm of thought". Why are we attracted to certain foods, people and places and recognise, in an instance, our soul mate? The feeling that we get when that happens is called 'Soul Recognition'; when our souls becomes in tune with our soul mate, surroundings or emotional feelings, something just clicks inside of us that allows us to know that this person could be the one. We can also wonder why certain love affairs fail and why our stomach turns at the thought of coming face to face with a bully, tyrant or someone who makes our skin crawl. Could it be that karma has played a part in our life because we agreed that, at a certain time and date, we would encounter this being again in order to cross this off of our 'karmic shopping list'?

It takes such great courage and stamina to incarnate and live on earth that maybe we need to look at what happens to us with open eyes rather than remorse because if we see the bigger picture that is beckoning towards us, we would welcome it with open arms.

When a child is born, parents can wish that the child came with a set of instructions. However, parenting is about being a role model and setting up surroundings, which mix together spiritual growth, responsibility and delight for those involved. Choices are stumbled upon, whether they are good or bad ones, which are made at that moment in time. Yet, getting it right is something that all parents fret about. This can lead to us regularly feeling inadequate. But, if a newborn came down with a set of requests, then what would happen to free will? Free will gives us the chance to learn and grow from our experiences.

Before we incarnate, our soul makes a series of choices for the next incarnation and we choose our particular circumstances to help us to evolve as souls. The soul enters the body and the experiences are erased. This is because, if we were to remember what happened to us in a previous existence (for example, we were subject to a horrible death of the hands of someone else), we may seek revenge and, in return, it may alter our soul path lesson – the reason we decided to reincarnate. If the karmic lesson is not learnt at human level, we agree to come back again and learn the lesson again and again. We set out, whilst we are in the body, to begin to learn our earth experiences from our parents, friends and relatives. However, when the Old Soul Children arrive, they have not forgotten their soul path mission – what they need to do with their lives. As I said previously, it is only when we become adults that we may have a 'spiritual awakening', usually through a personal crisis, and we remember our spiritual awareness and calling. This is when we get back on the yellow brick road of enlightenment and our soul calls out to us and explains our 'calling' for this lifetime. The soul has many memories of past lives, which are stored away to protect us. Soul path lessons are involved in everything that we have to overcome to live more creatively, in a way that makes our hearts sing and to feel that we have taken control of our life and its direction.

Our personality may not have agreed to all these experiences, but our soul agreed it. That is why the soul and personality have to develop an alliance until the personality is a more willing instrument for the higher self or soul thread. You get the soul teaching from the being you have encountered, quite simply, by asking for it and then being open to receive it. It may come in short pieces at first, but will gradually expand.

The Old Soul Children are remembering this earlier on and talk of other lives, realising that their purpose is so strong that they cannot ignore it. Their 'calling' starts early and gets caught up with every day life. Most people have not woken up to what is really going on. As these children are born sensitive, childhood is not always easy, so, as parents, we can invoke the Angel of Delight, Angel of Protection and Angel of Sensitivity to help them whilst they are out of their normal environments. More information will be provided in Chapter Three on how your child can invoke angels for themselves.

Old Souls, whether they are children, teenagers or adults, feel isolated and lonely and are always unsettled in the physical world, whilst searching for spiritual truths and other Old Souls to share their experiences with. They have an inner knowing that pursuing fame and fortune is not on their to-do list once they have taken embodiment on earth; the knowledge they have collected through various lives is used for a bigger purpose. They become researchers, teachers and healers to feed their imagination as the yearning to learn more grows through learning from life's experiences.

Heath Ledger's family recognised that he was an Old Soul Adult; the devastated family placed a death notice in The West Australian Newspaper, which is based in his hometown of Perth, remembering him as 'the most amazing old soul in a young man's body'. His sister Kim paid her tribute: 'We were ultimate in soul mates', which gives proof that Old Soul Families recognise each other for their own talents and strengths. More information on Old Soul Adults and Old Soul Families can be found throughout this book.

Education

Since interviewing parents about their children's imaginary friends and spiritual abilities, many have expressed that they are going to educate their child at home due to the current failings of the education system. I am really pleased that my children, Jade, Amba and Leo, are thriving in their education establishments.

Many believe that children with special needs are at the front of the queue and are getting a lot of attention, which of course they need. Yet, the quality of care and education for children with no special needs falls below par, and these children are finding it difficult to struggle with a simple task given. Teachers are also under a great pressure to reach targets, with budget cuts and the lack of funding in education. Children in mainstream school often find it difficult to understand the concept of 'special needs'; all children, in my opinion, are special. However, children who do not fall into this group try and work out why they feel that they are not part of this special group. Occasionally, they may receive a special award for good behaviour and school work, but this only adds more confusion to the child. Labelling can be a dangerous thing and is rife in present society. It seems that everyone has to belong to a certain category or image; individuality is sometimes seen as threatening or frightening.

People use labels when looking for an outer authority and not relying on their own inner, instinctual wisdom. Too many people are looking to be 'nannied' and trust authorities that, in many ways, are questionable in their approach to power and wisdom.

They may sometimes have knowledge but all too often they are lacking in wisdom, which of course cannot exist if there is no heart quality. So, if we allow our heads and hearts to become one then we are working for the greater good and not from ego.

In these days of so many constraints, children are having a difficult time too and it is hard for them to not to get caught up in the negativity. As parents, all we can do is to stay calm as we state our cases, and be very clear on the outcome when we deal with authorities that have not woken up to spiritual awareness.

Right Brain, Left Brain Explanation

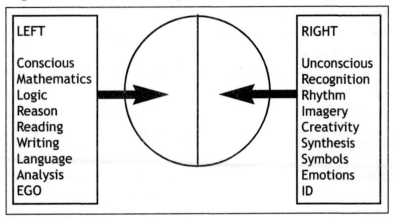

LEFT

Conscious
Mathematics
Logic
Reason
Reading
Writing
Language
Analysis
EGO

RIGHT

Unconscious
Recognition
Rhythm
Imagery
Creativity
Synthesis
Symbols
Emotions
ID

When we are born our right brain is dominant. All children rely more on an intuitive, creative approach towards life and process information in an instinctive and simultaneous way.

The education system in the United Kingdom is unaware that they are teaching children left-brain techniques in schools from the age of eight, which deal with logical problems, chronological events, rational thinking and analytical ways of dealing with everyday life problems. When this happens, it seems that the child's spiritual connection seems to diminish because of these complex strategies.

If the left brain is too dominant, the person can lack insight and imagination. If the person is limited in intelligence, they can be extremely stubborn. When the right brain is too dominant, the person can be too emotional or impulsive.

Generally speaking, women are more right-brain orientated and men more left-brain orientated. Right handedness is associated with the left brain and left hand with the right brain.

I feel that the curriculum in school needs to give equal weighting to the arts, creativity, and the skills of imagination and creation. Teachers, in their training, should be trained to use coaching skills that connect with both sides of the brain. They could increase their class' right-brain learning activities by incorporating more patterning, metaphors, analogies, role-playing, visuals, and movement into their reading, calculation, and analytical activities.

If this was achieved, the children of today would have a better grounding in education and be balanced in both left and right brain activities. Could this also help children with ADHD and other disorders?

Children's feelings are put to one side and they feel boxed-in when they demonstrate higher knowledge but are branded 'outspoken'. More and more children are remembering what they are meant to be doing here and as they set about changing and challenging rules and regulations, they get into trouble. They are challenging fear-based adults with what they already know from previous existences. Because of their own conditioning, they feel challenged because they do not understand what the child is talking about. Adults feel challenged by children who have no fears and just 'go with the flow'. Everyone seems to forget that they were once a child.

Our experiences create our reality – the way we see the world. This shapes children into adults.

There's an old saying: "What we know now is what we wish we knew then." But the soul part of us has requested the experiences that we're currently battling, what ever their shape or form. Some of us learn life lessons over and over again. The same agenda is repeated in different settings and those who are spiritually minded take heed that this is, in fact, a karmic lesson, which we can cross off on our 'to do list'. However, others stomp about and shout that "life's not fair" and attract other karmic issues in the process. The Universe presents us with magical ways for our life to unfold. Again, it is our free will that helps us to make decisions about what we are presented with. It is only when human judgment and conditioning get in the way that we start to stray from what we really know is our 'truth'. It is then that our confidence takes a nose-dive.

For some Old Soul Children, when they have encountered something that is wrong, they bounce back into reality and get on with it. Other children are not taught how to move on from negative experiences and may perhaps carry this into maturity; generally, as adults, we tend to mull over the smallest detail and create mountains out of molehills. Surely, we should all learn from a child's perspective and just dust ourselves down and put it down as a learning experience. When you have trust in yourself, you can put negative experiences aside and not always assume you are the one at fault.

Some children do feel that they have to carry a lot of blame as a child. When this is understood and recognised, they can see where it was unjust and realise that it was not because they were to blame, but because others did not know how to empower them or how to give true, unconditional love. It is only when this is realised and it is understood that that these things are not intrinsically true and that other people's opinions of you are related to their issues (even parents), that you can stop identifying with all the labels and set your true-self free.

At present, these Old Soul Children are responding to their own maps of reality. This sometimes means expressing themselves with unexpected behaviour. We have to recognise that each behaviour is the result of them making the best choice that they perceive to be available to them at that moment in time. Behind every behaviour is a positive intention and many parents are completely unaware they have expectations of their children that are contradictory to their own behaviours. For many, incongruent thinking is so unconscious that they do not know that they do it; so parents feel powerless, are unaware that they behave in this way and want a quick 'fix' to the problem that they contributed to in the first place.

As I begin writing this book, a change in this world is greatly needed. There are many wars already in children's lives because the world has forgotten to communicate verbally. Anger and violence seem, to some, to be the only primitive form of communication, and human beings will not choose the 'good' way of life, until they see clearly what their choice is. In these times, violence is seen and makes the news and so, gradually, humanity looks into a powerful mirror and it is only when they finally realise that they do not like what they see, that things will change; they will change by choice and that is important. Their own fears are highlighted to them in many ways, yet they may converse in anger rather than finding a way to resolve peace. It seems that when people touch the darkest point they can start healing; it is often seen negatively but darkness is needed for incubation and if humanity touches rock bottom, it is touching the crystal bed and will receive the energy to bounce back up again.

Miscarriage

It is very hard to believe that miscarriages are universal, like the common cold. I have experienced three miscarriages in my life and each one has been a devastating experience. With a miscarriage, people feel awkward around you, because they do not know how to react. Technically nothing is there for them to see, so cliché statements are often used to help you with your own grief. This may seem helpful to them, but it can be very annoying.

Each time it happened, however, it has lead me to find inner strength; to find peace within my soul and to find new meanings to why it was just not the right timing for this child to come into incarnation.

The experience of my miscarriages has opened up a lot of questioning of my life about why things happen and I have moved away from blaming myself – I didn't cause them to happen in any way.

It's a shame that they don't come with a little letter saying,

'Not going to get properly incarnated this time, just trying it out – might be back later!'

Mainly it is all a question of timing; it was just not the right timing for these Old Soul Children to come into incarnation. Sometimes a soul that is considering incarnation finds it valuable to experience what it is going to be like to gestate and form a body. They can then go back and take another overview of what their soul contract and task are going to be when they are born into the world. So, in some ways, I have been used by these souls for this purpose and as I let them go, with blessing, it seems more like a task that has been accomplished, rather than a pregnancy that has been unsuccessful.

At another level, these souls (and I don't feel that they are all the same soul), did not wait for a proper invitation to incarnate to my husband and I. It seems that we were not ready and my body, particularly, was not ready at that time. On a soul level, my Old Soul Family was not ready and that would have been known to the soul who, therefore, could only use this 'chance' conception as an opportunity to view the process of conception and incarnation.

At that particular time I was saying "Why me?" which is natural, but I tried also to understand 'why not me?' which was very helpful. I have an incredibly spiritual point of view, but my body and emotions were in such grief and confusion at that moment in time; eventually, however, I began to understand what had happened, and also I know that I can produce perfect children and already have three very precious ones.

Before we re-enter each lifetime, our Soul Path lessons are agreed. Sometimes many different souls are aware of our experiences. As souls, we come into this life to experience certain opportunities for growth and soul lessons. Through the sacred alchemy of our life existence, we come to transform our 'flaws' into strengths.

So, for me, part of the agreement at the soul level was to help sensitive souls find a way to incarnate. It is a work in its own right and because of war and violence and strife in the world, there are many souls who have had such a stressful previous incarnation that they need a lot of reassurance about the world and the processes of incarnation.

Mary

Mary, from Dublin, Ireland, contacted me after she saw my notice in *Cygnus Review*, asking for people to come forward and share their experiences with me.

Now fifty-two, Mary no longer remembers Rambla, the imaginary friend that she was told she had as a child. Rambla was around until she was three years and three months old – when her brother was born. Mary's mother went to a nursing home to have him and Mary stayed with a lovely kindly old friend, who was actually her cousin's granny.

Her mother had fortunately warned her about Rambla and she was very accommodating of Mary's friend from the beginning, when she came out of the bathroom and Mary complained that she had shut the door on Rambla. "Oh, I beg your pardon," She replied, kindly opening the door. "Come on Rambla," she invited and apparently Mary was satisfied.

This became a story to be retold and laughed about in a gentle way in the family, which Mary has always been grateful for because she might no longer know about her and somehow it's very important for her that she does. In fact, Mary would like to know more – to actually remember her.

When Mary first mentioned Rambla, her mother thought that her name must be Pamela, but Mary was adamant that it was Rambla. Curiously, Rambla disappeared once her baby brother was brought home, though Mary was told that she showed no interest in him as a baby, as she wanted a sister. Mary does remember wanting a sister.

For a long time Mary accepted her mother's description of her imaginary friend, but in latter years she has wondered if she was an angel, spirit friend, companion or guide; perhaps someone that Mary had known in a previous existence or lifetime, maybe someone to help her transition from the spirit to the material world in those early years.

Small children often retain a connection with where they have come from into this world and seem to be able to see spirits. It seems to be a transient phase of having that connection with where they came from.

Earthbound Spirits

Sometimes, when it is time for a spirit to pass over, they get stuck and become Earthbound Spirits. An Earthbound Spirit is unable to move on because of unfinished business and will try anything to reach out to a receptive live being, usually a child. The spirit, more often than not, wants to get a message to loved ones that they are ok.

When the message is given, the grieving process can began and the soul that has departed can go into the halls of learning and review their life. The newly departed cannot move on into the light because those left behind hold on emotionally, so they become earthbound once again. The people left behind often are filled with regrets of things not said and things that should not have been said. Guilt is another emotion that can tie the departed to the earth.

So what about the ghosts who rattle around in castles and cemeteries? What of their Soul Path Contracts? The ghost of a particular castle has chosen to stay earthbound because is too painful to experience life again. So, they choose to remain soulless, floating through our time and spooking every poor living soul that dares to enter their domain.

So, could your child's new imaginary friend be an Earthbound Spirit, stuck in the stubborn ways that served and supported them whilst they were on the earth plane? To a child, a ghost looks like any normal person and so they do not judge the new friend that has come to play. Again, a child does not judge their surroundings but they take on board what they see as their reality and get on with interacting with their new friend.

Emma

I have known my dear friend Emma since we were seventeen years old and met working at our local supermarket. She is my true 'Soul Friend' and is always there if I need her, night or day. She is married to Nick and is mother to Adam and Holly. We often get our families together; the adults eat and drink merrily, whilst all the children play together.

One night, at their home, Emma was telling us that the old man next door had died and since then Holly was not sleeping through the night, which was unusual for her. She began to explain that Nick had just spoken to him before he died and he had wished their family well. As she went into more detail of what had happened to her neighbour, he suddenly appeared in their kitchen. In my mind, I went back to an earlier conversation with my eldest daughter Jade; she had felt that there was someone watching her, a man, when she went to the bathroom. I told Jade that we would sort it out later, but did not say anything to Emma and Nick because I did not want to freak them out. However, it seemed obvious then that this neighbour of theirs, for whatever reason, really wanted to make contact with the family.

I suggested this to Emma and Nick and suggested that the man had not crossed over. The look on their faces changed in an instant and they told me that they didn't even know the man. I assured them that there was nothing to worry about and told them that if we do not know a ghost or spirit in life, yet they have entered our lives briefly, they can still hang round in death if they do not want to cross over. I decided to investigate and went outside into the garden with Jade in tow.

In a few moments, we both saw the spirit of a man. He told us that he did not want to go because he felt attached to this young family, who were so reminiscent of his own family when they were younger. He did not want to leave because his own family would argue over his possessions and will.

We both gave him reassurance that it would be ok for him to cross over to the other side and that his house and possessions would be looked after. The man thanked us and then walked to the light. Jade and I went back inside with beaming faces.

"Holly will sleep well tonight, Emma," said Jade and we explained what had happened.

I got a telephone call from Emma, a few days later, thanking me for helping Holly to sleep during the night again.

Emma and Nick use to run their own a pub called The George and you can find it in Spaldwick in Cambridgeshire. It's haunted by a Highwayman but that's another story!

Rachel

Rachel, forty, still thinks of the imaginary friend that she had for most of her childhood and wonders whether he was a spirit of some kind watching, or the overactive imagination of a four year old. He was an older man who wore a red velvet jacket; he was sweet and kind and very clearly said goodbye after her first day at school. Rachel remembers him sitting on top of her desk to keep her company and then, when it was break time, she began to make some friends. At lunchtime, she walked into the dining room with him by her side, he smiled at her, waved and then just disappeared. Rachel never saw him again.

Sandy

Sandy contacted me after seeing my notice in the Cygnus Review.

Sandy Tester has a three year old son. Since he was eighteen months old he has been referring to an imaginary being, although Sandy suspects he has been seeing him for a bit longer that that and only had the language skills at that age to say his name.

James is a highly sensitive, intelligent and articulate little boy with good communication skills and lots of 'real' friends. Sandy actually thinks the boy that he sees is the spirit/soul of her next child, which is due in April/May.

Before Sandy became pregnant, in the summer, she was talking about having a second child and James started to talk about the little boy he could see around the house. He followed this imaginary being around the room with his eyes, so Sandy believes that he was definitely seeing something. The little boy used to appear in Sandy's bedroom first thing in the morning when James came in to wake her up; when asked where he slept, James would say, "In mummy's bed."

The little boy liked to go in the garden a lot and tidy up, so Sandy thought that it could be a reflection of James' own character, as he is very conscientious, tidy and loves helping in the garden himself. The little boy gradually appeared throughout the day, every day, especially during June and July, although he never played with James' toys or seemed to play with James at all. Sandy asked James whether the little boy would like to play with his trains; James pushed a toy over to him, but the little boy obviously didn't want to play with them, so James never offered him again, and snatched back his toys if Sandy offered them.

James likes a dummy and again the little boy didn't have one and did not want one, according to James.

The little boy always appeared when they were walking upstairs, especially when it was bedtime and nearly always seemed to be able to come if Sandy asked James where he was today. He would, however, disappear as quickly as he had arrived; they would be in the middle of something and James would ask where the little boy was going, or start waving goodbye when Little Boy was 'off'. That was just the way things were and James learned to accept the little boy's way of drifting in and out of their activities.

After a few weeks James announced that the little boy was called ITN, which Sandy assumed was his version of the name

Etienne. This completely surprised them, as they had no idea where he got that name. It wasn't from the ITN News (UK) either, as he was never up that late and he never watched adult TV.

Sandy always believed that she would have two boys and started to sense a child feeling around her. Her 20-week scan confirmed that she was having a second boy. They took James with them and from that moment onwards, they believed ITN would disappear completely.

They have decided to call the new baby Adam, but James insists on calling him ITN. James has started referring to Sandy's stomach as ITN and refuses to call him Adam. On questioning him James about ITN, he confirmed that the little boy was now inside Mummy's tummy. James loves him, kisses him and hugs him and is eager for the birth now.

But what about ghosts who have just left their bodies?

There are a lot of adjustments for them to make which can be alarming even for the newly departed; especially when the spirit of a person is a result of something that they had no control over, like a murder or car accident.

When this happens the spirit is usually disorientated, unaware that they are about to pass over into the light that is beckoning them, which they usually ignore because they are filled with confusion. My children have witnessed this when driving past a fatal car accident; Jade told me that the man standing in the road had just gone to heaven, whilst Amba asked why the lady standing by her car looked so sad.

These spirits do not go to the light for reasons such as the fear that their existence will end, fear of the unknown, fear of going to hell or being judged for past deeds. These spirits are bound here because of their own fears and are also sceptical about the light. This may be because they may have been burned to death in a previous incarnation and the brightness of the light re-stimulates the fear. If the person died with feelings of anger, revenge or resentment, these will persist in spirit and keep them secured to the earth plane.

Guilt can also be a reason for an earthbound spirit being stuck here. They may feel like they have left the family or loved ones too soon and that they feel uncared for, or that they have not achieved their life's work because their life was cut short. These souls will eventually return to the light once they come to terms with their passing. The earthbound spirit is often fixated in the death trauma. With the knowledge of having died, the spirit will move on.

Ann

I first met my very good friend Ann Brady on a Karuna Reiki course, in Margate, in 2001. We have become very close, talking on the telephone regularly and seeing each other when we can. Ann is a Reiki master and holistic therapist and lives in Liverpool. Her two grandchildren, Daniel who is ten and Mia who is five, also live in Liverpool, informed me of her spiritually aware Grandson.

Daniel is a full of confidence and Ann believes that he is very advanced for his age, calling him 'old in the head'. He can be a bossy type but in a kind way and his character shows that he is a born leader, especially with other children of his own age.

Ann says that you could take Daniel to a party full of children that he does not know, but he will make contact with everyone and be their friend by the end of the party. He is natural and gets on with everyone.

When he is with adults he will stand up to them and say that he cannot understand why he can't do different tasks. He is a child who does not take no for an answer, thinks that he is always right and does not act like a child of his age but more like a young adult.

On one occasion, Daniel accompanied his parents to put some flowers on a grave. Whilst they were there he decided to play a game with some children that he could see. For half an hour he played happily in the sun, while his parents attended the grave. When they had to go home, Daniel became upset and said that the children he was playing with are going to a party and he wanted to go with them. Daniel's parents insisted that he come with them, and he screamed, "I want to go to the party. I want to stay with my new friends." However, as they looked around, they could not see Daniel's new playmates, but Daniel was still insisting that his new friends wanted him to go.

As his parents walked back to the car, Daniel ran over to the graves that he first saw when he arrived. "My friends live here, in the churchyard," explained a tearful Daniel.

Both parents looked in amazement at each other. The graves that Daniel was looking at were of five children that had died two years ago. If they had been alive, the day Daniel had met them would have been their birthdays.

Throughout these remarkable ten years, the research that I have carried out has led me to believe that children, unlike adults, have not had many years to adjust their thinking and so have not had the time to train their perception of reality. As adults we can programme our thinking and consequently dismiss certain images, noises and feelings simply because, in our minds, we cannot accept the impossible, but Old Soul Children can.

Chapter Two

Empowering your Spiritual Child

Imagination is more important than knowledge.
Knowledge is limited. Imagination encircles the world.
Albert Einstein

What is Shamanism? Totem Animals, Power Animals,
Using Power Animals To Empower Your Child, Our
Stories, Children's Aura's, Chakras in Old Soul Children,
More Of Your Stories

What is Shamanism?

Shamans have been around for over 50,000 years. These wisdom
keepers only pass their knowledge orally from generation to
generation, from father to son, mother to daughter.

Today, they still thrive in many parts of the world such as
Native America, Siberia, Mongolia, Tibet, Hawaii and Africa.
Before records began, Shamanism was an ancient way of taking
care of natural, spiritual and physical welfare.

The word Shaman comes from Turkic-Tungus word, meaning
'he or she who knows'.

Shamanism is an ancient trance technique, in which the
Shaman acts as a mediator between the spiritual worlds and the
inner self, and can also open the door to the inner and outer
world of nature. Information about ourselves, in the form of
spiritual guidance, lies hidden in these other worlds and is accessible to the Shamanic Practitioner.

In many cultures, the calling to become a Shaman may occur
because of a personal crisis, resulting in severe trauma or a near

death experience. Dreams or visions may also occur before they answer the call.

A person aspiring to become a Shaman will have to undergo many years of strenuous training before they begin to practice as one. During their apprenticeship, a Shaman learns about the soul and other techniques to incite trance-like states. Today, Modern Shamanism is becoming very popular and is often practiced in groups and lodges through workshops and classes. This is because it can be shaped to suit the individual needs and weaved into modern day living.

Shamans have the ability to connect with the elemental energies of Mother Earth. With these abilities it helps them to access their own personal healing spirits for empowerment and protection, and gain the confidence to succeed in developing their abilities to cross between the worlds.

The beating of the drum or the use of a rattle allows the Shaman to achieve an altered state of consciousness, enabling them to get in touch with spirits. The drum is referred to as 'horse' or 'rainbow-bridge' between the physical and spiritual worlds. Shamanic drumming is very powerful, as it resonates with the heart frequency and beat of the drum carries you into a non-ordinary reality, which unlocks sacred knowledge deep within our souls. Shamans are conscious of everything that transpires on their journey and are not limited by the constraints of time in their quest for ways to help and heal their community.

Shamans have travelled on the World Tree, for thousand of years, meeting and working with their spirit helpers. The World Tree can be divided into three realms: the Lower World, Middle World and Upper World.

These three worlds are not separated by time and distance, but are separated by visions because they have more dimensions than the physical world. Each path to enter the individual worlds is completely different. Different cultures have different interpretations of the significance of these different worlds. Hawaiian

culture, for example, compares the Lower World with memory, the Middle World with the reasoning mind, and the Upper World with the highest aspirations of the mind.

The Lower World

To enter the Lower World, some find a hole in a tree trunk and travel down deep into the earth; others enter under a waterfall or into the deep earth through a cave. This ancient world has a complete landscape and can look much like our everyday world with ground, sky, grass and trees and is inhabited by Power Animals and teachers that guide and protect us from harm. Our

Power Animals are usually found waiting for us when make our entrance into this world.

The Middle World

To enter the Middle World, you connect through the spirit of the mountains, trees and springs. The Middle world is similar to our own world, but is the spiritual parallel and this realm co-exists along with ours in current time.

The journey to the Middle World is to help find lost objects. When the Shaman arrive in this world, they could be in the past, representing a time in the past that their client is stuck in. The Middle World is the centre between the Lower and Upper Worlds and it is in this realm that fairies, devas, elementals and dragons are encountered. The Shaman's journey to this realm is also to help spirits that are stuck between worlds to cross over to the Upper World. This may happen because of a sudden death and can cause a spirit not to cross over naturally. The Shaman also will find answers to questions about the world we are living in.

The Upper World

The Upper World is full of bright colours. This ethereal place is accessed by flying on a cloud that takes you to an uplifting place. In this world, angelic forces, our ancestors and our guides can be found. The Upper World has powers of knowledge, enlightenment and creativity that can be used to enhance everyday living. This is also the world where people have been when have experienced a near-death experience.

The World Tree is the bridge that connects these three worlds; it is the axis mundi about which the universe of the Shaman extends and it is on the tree that the spirits pass from one world to another.

The World Tree is a common image in accounts of shamanic experiences from both traditional societies and in modern shamanic groups. In fact, it is theorised that 30,000 year old, shamanic cave paintings described what they saw in the three worlds of the tree, or even acted as portals to access them.

The World Tree forms an integral part of the shamanic cosmos, linking the world of humanity with the world of the spirits. Its appearance, in numerous tales of shamanic ritual, reflects the importance to the Shamans themselves. The World Tree also acts like a bridge between worlds, which allows the shaman and spirit helpers to travel from one world to another.

Shamanism is gaining popularity with many who yearn for a more mystical life. The objective of Shamanism is to bring ancient techniques, healing, sacred teachings and spiritual guidance for themselves and other people.

The Old Soul Children that we meet today are born natural Shamans. Their relationships with Faeries, Devas and Elves are natural for them, which brings enchantment into their lives. They will look after their own 'inner child' as they watch and learn about their unfolding magic, which will help others in their families and communities.

Soul Retrieval

Soul Retrieval has been practised in many different cultures since antiquity. A Shamanic belief is that pieces of our soul can leave our bodies if we do not protect ourselves from traumatic experiences. The technique of retrieving these pieces is still used in Shamanic communities around the world.

When we experience any kind of trauma, a part of us dissociates to survive. This manifests itself in different ways: depression or gaps in details relating to the past. In Shamanic terms, part of the soul becomes lost.

From the Shamanic point of view, the place that the dissociated part goes to is essential to the healing process. By contrast, with hypnosis and other psychotherapeutic processes, the dissociated part is perceived as being buried somewhere in the subconscious.

Before the Shaman makes the journey, an intention is stated, which serves as a point of focus. When the Shaman makes the journey to the Lower, Middle and Upper Worlds, they usually know which world to travel to and will ask their Power Animal what has happened to the missing part of the soul and for assistance in looking for it.

When the Shaman finds the missing part of the soul, they blow it back into the person's body, but a therapist would reintegrate the past. When a soul part is returned, the individual has more power to draw on in their lives.

At this present moment in time, I am training to be a Shaman. The training is intense, but it has helped me to let go of what I no longer need and to move forward to a new experience.

Some Old Soul Children naturally feel that a part of them is missing. This could be because they have, in fact, given their own power away; for example, if they are in a situation where they feel powerless – this is usually connected to any form of bullying. This feeling can then become a fear-based, endless cycle which is reinforced by themselves, because they start to believe that they cannot do anything to change the situation. In these situations, we need to encourage our Old Soul Children that they are powerful, precious, individual beings that can achieve anything that they put their minds to. They can change the atmosphere wherever they go, and their attitudes, personalities and actions influence the environment that they are in. We need to tell our children not to give their power away.

Totem Animals

An Animal Totem is an animal or group of animals that a person identifies with spiritually and can also be an animal guide. Some believe that you choose your totem but they also choose you. The Totem Animal tradition goes back many thousands of years, and can be found in Norse and Celtic mythology, Australian Aboriginal teachings and Japanese folklore.

Totem animals can be any bird, insect or animal, and each animal offers you wisdom and can teach you about inspirational power. My belief is that they are different from Power Animals because they can be found in the Astral World and come to us when we need to learn a new aspect about ourselves.

Many believe that their Totem animal is, in fact, their four legged friend that has passed into spirit. Some feel the presence of their cat or dog staying by their side, still protecting them, even though they have crossed over. Others see a shadow walk by, or feel them jump on the bed to wake them up for breakfast and some hear the sound of their collars tinkling throughout the house, or see the same dips in their chairs in the place where they used to sleep. We should really encourage these animals to stay around and become our protector in every sense.

Power Animals

Power Animals are animal spirits that reside with each individual and act similarly to a guardian spirit or angel; adding to their power and protecting them from illness and harm. Each Power Animal that you have increases your power so that illnesses or negative energy cannot enter your body and the spirit also lends you the wisdom and medicine of its kind. For example, a hawk spirit will give you hawk wisdom, and lend you some of the attributes of hawk. An elephant spirit, can teach us about communication in relationships and about gentleness. A badger is a Power Animal with many aspects and supports you in taking charge of your life and your talents.

A Power Animal can stay with you and your Old Soul Child. It's a little similar to Philip Pullman's fantastic and spellbinding book, *Northern Lights*, where heroine, Lyra, has a 'daemon' called Pantalaimon who is her dearest companion and the embodiment of her soul.

Power Animals are used as a guide for inner journeying and are a likened to an aspect of the Shaman; a source of inner strength and intuitiveness. Shamanistic journeying can be very helpful and is another dimension of the spiritual worlds, in which you can find comfort and adventure with the Power Animals, Spirit Guides and even your ancestors. The Shaman can, at any time during the journey, share in the consciousness of the animal guide and experience its natural aptitude. He/she can also, at any time, call upon the strength and nature of the Power Animal energy to enhance their life. Just imagine, for a moment running with a leopard, swimming with a family of dolphins and soaring the skies with the eagle; the Shaman is truly being at oneness. Whilst journeying into the spiritual realms there is a profound shift in one's awareness, at a very deep level, when the experience becomes very real and with that comes a truly deep understanding.

Power Animals are an essential component of shamanic practice. Shamans believe that animals are messengers of the Great Spirit. It is the Shamanic belief that everything is alive and carries with it power and wisdom. They are the helping spirit, which add to the power of the Shaman and are essential for success in any venture undertaken by the Shaman.

Using Power Animals to Empower your Child

Power Animals can help children stand up to bullies. I know, first hand, the serious impact of bullying. I survived bullying throughout my school years and, even though the bullying was subtle, my confidence plummeted. Self-esteem can hit an all time low and the effects from the ongoing taunts can stay with you for a lifetime.

When my eldest daughter, Jade, was bullied at just six years of age, I decided to help her gain the confidence she needed. Power Animals helped her feel empowered to move forward with issues that she found difficult in solving. For many, childhood can be a lonely and frightening experience. It's easy to feel isolated but, by finding your Power Animal and staying in touch, you'll never feel lonely again.

Ask any child to name their favourite animal and they will choose a domestic pet, a wild beast, an insect, a reptile or a mythological creature. Most children love at least one animal and most children love to play imaginary games. Based on such factors, it is extremely useful to draw children's attention to the concept of Power Animals to help them overcome life's challenges and obstacles. They can also help parents' self-confidence and self-control as, often, parents feel powerless when they know their child needs help. The techniques can also help you and your child get better at considering other people's feelings.

I have seen the benefits of this ancient technique empower children facing problems such as bullying. These children are taught to draw strength and comfort from visualising a favourite Power Animal standing beside them, and each time they confront a fear or anxiety – such as bullying – a child imagines that their animal is protecting them; whilst the bully is taunting the child, the animal frightens the bully away.

I have assisted many parents and children to help choose a Power Animal. Getting a soft toy to represent it in the outer world helps too, but I tell any child that the magic is that the toy becomes their real friend, pet, protector. In the inner world, it is alive and can talk to them and help them with anything that they want to do. Allowing children to choose a Power Animal beside them in their dreams who can deal with anything for them can also help with bad dreams, nightmares and night terrors.

My work is very important to me and I believe that if your child chooses a Power Animal on a daily basis, it can contribute towards helping children lead positive, healthy and happy lives. Working with Power Animals is extremely rewarding, as it helps to increase a child's personal power and sense of oneness. There are many Power Animal techniques for children and/or teenagers to explore through many different genres: art, music, writing, playing interactive games and numerous other fun activities.

It does not matter what Power Animal the child chooses, as it is often based on what your child needs at that moment in time, and each animal has its own message and special power. You and your child can think about what animals you are drawn to and ones that you really do not like. What animals present themselves to you when you are in nature? What animals do you see in your dreams and meditations? Each animal has a message for us; keep a diary of what animals you call upon for their assistance and you will begin to see a pattern in which animal can assist you in your daily life.

It is interesting and important to consider the significance of your child's choice of power animal. For example, if we look at the camel, this may signify all of the burdens that the child is carrying. Is there some way, perhaps, that you need to encourage your child to open up? Does this animal, itself, open up the opportunity to do a little ritual together of dropping off the burdens, i.e. writing them down and burning them or burying them? In this way, there could really be a lot in these animals, not just as a delightful thing for children to feel around them, but as a support and an aid to magical parenting.

Exercise – Turning Buts into Butterflies

I give great thanks to Keith Beasley, my Reiki Master, who taught me Reiki without rules. His book, also titled *Reiki without Rules*, explains how we can use Reiki not as a therapy on others, but on ourselves and as a path to our own self awareness and spiritual growth, which is a truly great concept. Keith also taught me that when you have a BUT in your life it can be turned into a BUTTERFLY, and here is my version:

When you and your Old Soul Child have your life filled with ponderings that sound like this: 'If I do this, this will happen, BUT if I do this, that could happen, BUT...' It interrupts the flow of life because we are questioning everything.

Imagine and visualise the BUT forming beautiful, but very

large, butterfly wings. Place your BUT thought onto your butterfly and imagine, visualise and believe that it will fly away.

Keep repeating, 'Turn BUTS into BUTTERFLIES' as a mantra everyday, to help form a positive belief that BUTS do turn into BUTTERFLIES.

When we see butterflies in our dreams it means transformation; your unconscious mind is pointing positive parts about yourself.

Butterflies are a powerful symbol in myth, legends and religion; the early Christians believed that the butterfly represented the soul itself. In China it symbolises conjugal bliss and joy. The Native Americans would call upon butterfly medicine for guidance in changes in their life and greater freedom, self transformation, reincarnation and magic. Another superstition is that if see a Butterfly among flowers it indicates prosperity.

When a Butterfly enters into our life, it is telling us that we do not need to take things so seriously.

Nikki

Nikki, who lives in South Yorkshire, was sceptical about imaginary friends, but used to see things as a child. She also went on to tell me about one of her four children; when Oliver was eight years old (he's now eleven) had an imaginary stripy tiger called Jin Jin. This surprised her because Djinn is an Asian spirit and she felt that this was a bit of a coincidence. Oliver loved to talk about Jin Jin and told her that he had hundreds of siblings and travelled all over the world. Jin Jin went to see his father in India and loved to visit Spain and Russia; the family had never been to any of these places. Jin Jin liked to drink Martini and fix clocks for other people, which was his day job. Nikki had no idea where he got that from, because they have never had Martini in the house and not one in her family tended to drink it. In fact they didn't drink any alcohol at home.

Nikki feels that she was not particularly spiritually aware, and when growing up she experienced quite bad bullying as a result of being a little 'different' to her peers. This resulted in her shutting a lot of things out. It was only whilst her parents were going through a divorce that she found out that her brother, mother and grandmother had similar experiences of visions. Her Grandmother had things that move around her. Her mother continues to receive flashes of insight to help others and is always developing her skills; already an aromatherapist and currently undergoing training in Reiki, she also runs a small bed and breakfast from her home.

Knowing that it runs in the family has helped because, although she could not see who/what her child was talking to, she could approach it in a non-judgemental way and not isolate him. Nikki certainly would not want her children to experience bullying for having 'over-active imagination'.

Her daughter Alice, four, and is quite a sensitive soul; she has very unusual green eyes that many people have commented on when they have been on the bus and in the street. A few people have said that she is 'one of the faeries'. Quite recently, Alice kept talking to 'Sebastian' and talking to us about him. At first, Nikki thought she was talking about the son of a friend they had not seen for some time. He was the only boy of that name that they know, but Alice was adamant that Sebastian was a man. Alice described him and said that he always wore a hat or scarf on his head and he talked to her about all sorts of things. This became rather perplexing, and when Nikki spoke to a close friend about it, the friend turned rather pale. Alice had described her dead brother, right down to the fact that he always wore a hat or bandana on his head. On the way home in the car, Nikki suggested to Alice that Sebastian really should go home to his sister and not stay with them, so she asked out loud for him to finish what he had came to do. Alice has not really mentioned him since.

Her children have a bit of a history of chatting to all sorts of things, although Oliver does not do so much now. When he was younger, however, there was much to see and hear, to the point that he would complain that he could not get to sleep at night because 'they' kept giggling in the corner. He also told his parents about some very tall things which he described as having wings, but no faces, or changing faces that used to talk to him sometimes. Out of the blue, Oliver also talked about living in Spain, in the mountains, on a farm with three dogs and whilst growing up he mentioned it on many occasions.

With being a Mother to four children and using her experience in the early years field, Nikki is running her own business, Ninny Noodle Noo, which stocks a range of heirlooms and high-quality toys, including beautiful hand-crafted Ostheimer toy figures, toys from Spiel & Holz, Kinderdram, Erzi and Haba, Barefoot Books, organic children's clothes and toiletries.

Nikki is committed to trying to be as environmentally considerate in her approach to life as possible and feels that, perhaps, when her children are older, she will come back to nurturing her special gifts.

Just listening to this incredible old soul family story shows how united they all are and both parents are really making sure that childhood stays magical by supporting their spiritual gifts in any way they can. Oliver's imaginary friend is, in fact, a Power Animal, which for an eight year old is remarkable because it takes Shamans years and lots of intense training to connect with their own. It is also very clear to me that Sebastian was an Earth-Bound Spirit who had unfinished business to clear up with his family, before he could finally cross over and say goodbye to his grieving relatives.

Jade and the Unicorn

Jade was just six years old when severe bullying began and it lasted for eighteen months. Knowing how she felt, and with the school she was attending not addressing the issues and blanking

our pleas, I decided to find other ways to empower her and Amba. In order for both girls to feel better about the situation that they were in, on a daily basis, I decided to get them both to choose a Power Animal to walk with them at school.

The Power Animal chosen was a unicorn and it went everywhere with Jade: to the supermarket, swimming lessons and even to bed. Jade believed that during break times, if the bullies came too close to her, the unicorn would chase them away and for her it worked.

With Jade's birthday approaching, we planned to take her whole class bowling. I asked her what she wanted for her birthday and she replied, "A real unicorn!" Well, I thought that would be pretty hard, because pet shops do not exactly sell live ones, put that idea to the back of my mind and got on with organising the bowling party. The party arrived and it went really well. Jade began to open her birthday presents from her guests. I watched her face light up with everything that she was given. Jade got to her last present and begin to open it and squealed with delight. I turned round and watch Jade hug a multicoloured soft toy which was a unicorn!

"See Mum, I told you I would get one for my birthday!"

Exercise – Choosing a Power Animal with Your Old Soul Child

This exercise will teach you how to choose a special Power Animal to help you and your Old Soul Child feel positive again. This animal can stand by your side and help you all day long. You do not need to have any particular belief in order to benefit from a Power Animal and feel strong again.

Firstly, ask your child what their favourite animal is.

If your child is great at visualisation, they will find this part easy.

Ask your child to visualise and imagine their animal standing by their side. Get them to imagine that the animal is magic and that they are the only ones that can see them. When they feel frightened, sad or even happy, their new friend will always be with them. They may want to give their magical friend a name so they can call them in moments of distress.

If they cannot visualise their Power Animal, then get them to draw or paint their animal. Put their masterpiece in the kitchen or their bedroom and it will act as a reminder that their animal is not very far away.

Go to the library to find out more information about its habitat and how it protects its own family.

Visit a zoo, farm or aquarium to watch their chosen Power Animal in action to empower your child further.

Why not buy your child an animal T-shirt to give them a much needed extra boost of confidence, comfort or healing.

Your child may even come across there much needed power animal in a magazine, newspaper article. Collect facts and help your child make collage of their chosen animal. Why not encourage your child to write a story or poem about their chosen animal.

Your child may want to carry around with them a crystal that symbolizes their chosen animal. For example, if the chosen power animal is a dolphin, they may choose to carry a piece of coral to symbolize the seas of the world. A Tiger's Eye crystal could be used to represent any member of the cat family. Buy a gemstone and crystal animal to place in their bedroom. The Wisdom of animal kingdom is represented in carved animal pendants, wearing this can also aid a child's self esteem and development.

There are many popular Power Animal card decks available to buy in bookshops and on the internet. You would need to pick a deck those appeals to the both of you. If you cannot find one suitable, why not make up your own set with your child? With the combination of your child's imagination, you can both use your intuition to inspire and guide what animals you both feel a strong connection to.

Children's Auras

Auras can be found around all living people, plants and animals. Auras are made from our own electromagnetic energy field,

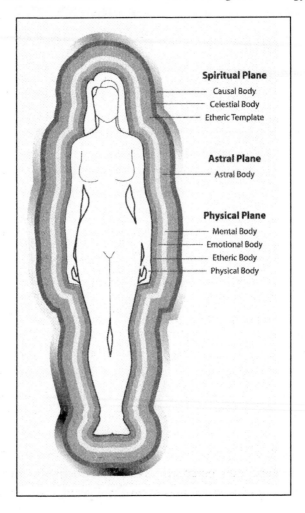

Spiritual Plane
Causal Body
Celestial Body
Etheric Template

Astral Plane
Astral Body

Physical Plane
Mental Body
Emotional Body
Etheric Body
Physical Body

which is made up of atoms, molecules, vibrations and many different, beautiful colours that form an egg shape around our physical body. The aura, like our chakras, gives us indications on how we are feeling and thinking and reflects our physical, emotional, mental and spiritual experiences. The aura is  composed of seven layers, which are: physical body, emotional body, mental body, astral body, casual body, celestial body and ketheric body.

I believe that the first auric layer, the physical body, is actually the skin. It is associated with the physical aspects and awareness of our bodies and relates to health and our own security. Physical signs of illness and injury are detected in this layer. The physical body layer is also related to the base chakra. Working with this layer encourages you to deal with basic needs that you require in your life. This is the easiest and first layer seen. We may not be able to sense it in the beginning but if we brush our skin on our arms, and hold our hand directly over where we have just brushed, we can, in fact, feel our own aura.

The second auric layer, the emotional body, is related to the emotions that we have for others and ourselves. It also holds our human emotions as we experience them and is connected to the sacral chakra, as we process our inner thoughts, feelings and our sensitivity to those who come into our lives. The colours of this layer will alter according to our emotions and what we are inter-acting with. When certain situations trigger specific emotions, we sometimes find difficulty in expressing our feelings because of the fear we may be holding in our bodies.

The third auric layer, the mental body, is related to our belief system, intellect and personal power. Our thoughts, ideas, and understanding of who we and others really are, are stored here.

This layer expands and radiates as we concentrate on a particular issue to empower ourselves. This layer links with our own minds as well as others. Connecting to the Solar Plexus, it also holds the beliefs that we develop from birth.

The fourth auric layer, the astral body, connects to the heart chakra, and helps us to pinpoint our ideas about relationships. From working with energy healing, I believe that the heart chakra and auric layer form a bridge that helps us, whilst we are on the physical plane, to connect with the higher vibrations of the spiritual planes. Our astral bodies link to the astral plane when we are sleeping, dreaming and when we astrally project. This layer also holds our individual personality, has a direct link to spiritual sources and holds soul path contracts between people.

The fifth auric layer, the casual body, connects with the throat chakra, and aids our everyday communication and creative expression. It also aids us in opening up to other dimensions and helps us to make a commitment to speak and follow our own truths, expressing and bringing them to the outside. The fifth layer also helps us to listen and develop our own intuition, which can guide us to create endless abundance with the Universe's help.

The celestial body is the sixth layer and connects with the third eye. This is associated with our communication, our spiritual friends and processes of enlightenment, and gives us access to manifestations. The sixth layer also helps with choices and consequences with the truth of universal love and reflects our individual view of our choices, surroundings and views.

The ketheric body is the seventh layer and connects to the crown chakra. This layer records all of our soul's experiences and contains our soul path plan, reflecting current life experiences and events. Again, within this layer, we can communicate with our spiritual friends. It also extends to conscious and unconscious planes; it grounds us to our life purpose and helps with our own life purpose and tasks.

From any age, Old Soul Children can sense and see auras

naturally and can read them without any formal training. This is because they have natural auric sight, which changes as they learn more and more left brain activities during their school education.

I have noticed from a young age that my children, when drawing people, pick up different colours for the heads and bodies. They choose the colours that reflect subtle energies that they see around many people. The chosen colours can often indicate how they are feeling towards that person and also what they are sensing from them.

Old Soul Children's auras are stronger and clearer than adults because they are free from conditioning and negative thinking. Every Old Soul Child is an individual, and their auric fields will be different because their own auras are filled with colours that reflect and depict every facet of them. Their auras will also show how they are feeling physically, mentally and spiritually at that moment in time.

Different colours do have different meanings, but for Old Soul Children, I would not put any strong emphasise on this because they are still learning, growing, thinking and connecting to different things at different rates. Their auras can change constantly from one minute to the next according to what influences are with them. If you take four children from different families and look at the auras you will see what strong influences they have in their lives and the type of the personality they are developing.

I cannot label any colour to describe Old Soul Children because I think it is important not to; a child could grow up being told that there is, which can affect them greatly, especially when they reach adulthood. For most, when they reach adulthood, they find it hard to reach out into the world because adults react differently to 'misfits', and so they find it hard to fit in to normal day living.

When puberty kicks in, and their bodies begin to mature biologically, psychologically, socially, and cognitively, the auric field starts to change. This is because of hormones, growing up issues and outside influences that really take hold of their lives. Girls and boys mature in different ways, and the individual's personality is also a major contributor in this. For all teenagers, their emotions seem all over the place and the aura will change again at between sixteen and nineteen years of age. For example, at this age, affairs of the heart for girls are important and the aura may be filled with the colours of various pinks greens and golds because they are listening to their heart chakras and following their own hearts in pursuing love. For teenage boys, they could be intensely into sports at this age, whether participation or watching; their auras may be filled with various red and browns and deep greens as they can become goal oriented and embark on an intellectual use of their own will power.

Isabella

Isabella is ten years old and has been reading people's auras since she was seven. This extremely bright and gifted young lady told me that, first, she can see faint colours around people's heads. Isabella tells me that she has not read any books on auras or done any research on the internet, but she knows that different colours have lots of different meanings.

When she has to go to the doctors for an asthma check and waits to be called, she often sees people with a gap in their aura because they are not well. Isabella knows intuitively that if they have dark yellow, they are feeling very tired and dark green means that they are feeling jealous about something. In the super-market, doing the weekly shopping with her mum, she says that purple means that fairies work with them and silver means that angels are with them all the time, but they may not be aware.

Isabella sees three layers of aura around adults, two layers around children and one layer around animals and plants. Her school teacher always has a golden light around her head, because she is always thinking when she is teaching.

When she was younger, she clearly remembers talking to a woman at school, in the playground, that no one else could see and her teacher told her off for talking to thin air. After that incident, the family moved back to Northern Ireland. Isabella tells me that she is happy there, because many fairies live there and can teach her about how to help the environment that she lives in.

How to See Auras

On daily basis, look at the tops of trees, with the sky as a background, without any harsh light. Do not stare at the tree and when you are relaxed enough, you will begin to see a soft haze around the tree. In time, you will be able to see colours, and as you practise more, you will be able to see several colours at once. If you do not see anything for the first few times, please do not be discouraged; it takes practise for the skills to develop, but by working with trees, you will gradually be able to observe the auras of other people and animals. This exercise will also help you to train your eyes to have natural auric sight.

To Help You to See Your Own Aura

First, place your hands in front you, again with no harsh light. Slightly spread your fingers and look directly at them. When you are relaxed enough, you will begin to see a soft haze around your fingertips and hand. Again, practise makes perfect, and in time, you will be able to start to see colours. In the beginning, you may only be able to make out one colour, but as you get better, you will be able to see several at one time. Again, do not be discouraged if you do not see anything the first few times.

Feeling Your Own Auric Field

When you naturally rub your hand together vigorously, you begin to build up the body's own natural heat. As you begin to do this, place your hands apart and in a few seconds, you will begin to feel heat building up between your hands. Put your arms wide apart, and bring your hands together slowly, noticing what you are feeling when you do so. Start to move your hands backwards and forwards. You will begin to feel the energy between your hands is like a soft ball which can become intense, thicker and thinner as you move your hands apart.

Rebecca

Rebecca is thirteen years old and is extremely creative. She was diagnosed with ADHD when she was very young. Since Rebecca was a baby, her mum, Cathy, had heard her in her room having conversations with people that weren't there and laughing and playing, so she asked her if she ever saw people that others couldn't see. Rebecca told her mum that she did, all the time.

Rebecca said that she could often see people, leaning against the wall or sitting next to her. She gave vivid descriptions about one of them, who was about forty years old; another is a teenager. When Rebecca is bored, mostly when she is alone, she will see them and they will make her laugh or comfort her. Rebecca also told Cathy that they sometimes have rainbow colours around them like a vibration coming off of them. This caught my attention, as it sounded like she was describing auras. Cathy's main concern is that her psychologist thinks that Rebecca has bipolar rather than ADHD. The psychologist was the one who prompted Cathy to ask Rebecca if she hears or sees things that are not there. She is reluctant to tell the psychologist because scientists tend to explain these things as being 'just in your mind' or a some kind of disorder.

I truly do believe that this Old Soul Child is open to the spiritual realms around her. It is sad but true that many psychologist are not in tune with their spiritual connection, and are very quick to put a label on their patient before really looking at the wonder of a gifted child.

In time, I do believe that Cathy will nurture these gifts and Rebecca will be able to use them in her life.

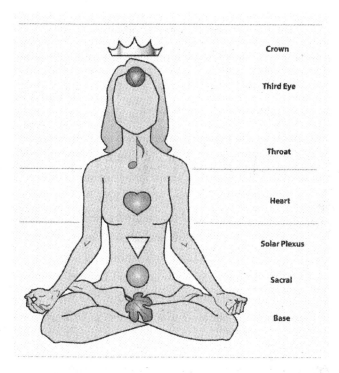

Chakras in Old Soul Children

Chakra is a Sanskrit word, meaning wheel or vortex. Indian Yogis first wrote about these powerful centres, explaining that they allowed the universal life force energy to flow through us.

The seven main chakras, which are located along the spine, start at the base and finish on the crown on top of our heads. Each chakra is related to particular organs in the body and each main centre is connected to several different areas of life, which are: physical, emotional, mental and spiritual. There are also chakra points in our feet and hands. When you place a crystal into the palm of your hand, and it begins to tingle, you are activating the hand chakras. By doing this, we develop the ability to feel subtle energies.

When you step into a hot bath or a cold sea, the foot chakras send a message to the rest of the body. These are essential, as they enable us to ground our energy system to Mother Earth; this works as a stabilising force for our entire auric field.

Chakras are like wheels spinning at different rates, with the lower chakras much slower than the higher, which is normal for everyone.

As I close my eyes, I see my own chakras as spinning sticks that turn in a fast, clockwise direction. If they are slow moving, in an anti-clockwise direction, I begin working with a pendulum to identify which chakra is out of balance, so I can make the appropriate movements to restore my own inner healing.

The function of the chakras reflects decisions we make concerning certain situations in our life. The chakras open and close when we decide what to think, what to feel and what we choose to experience.

Even though they are developed as souls, they still have to re-learn what life on earth is all about. Our chakras will develop in logical sequences as we grow from children into adults. When chakras are well-balanced, we feel fit, healthy and harmonious and when not, we tend to feel disorientated, lack energy and feel uncomfortable in our familiar surroundings. When the chakras become out of balance, the energy of our bodies will not be balanced and free-flowing.

There are many books written about chakras. The information below will help your Old Soul Child thrive in their own environment.

The Seven Major Chakras

CHAKRA	COLOUR	BODY	LOCATION
Base	Red	Physical Body	Base of Spine
Sacral	Orange	Emotional Body	Below Naval
Solar Plexus	Yellow	Mental/Intellectual Body	Above Naval
Heart	Pink, Green, Gold	Astral Body	Centre of Chest
Throat	Blue	Etheric Body	Base of Throat
Third Eye	Purple	Celestial Body	Centre of forehead
Crown	White/Clear	Ketheric Body	Whole top of head

Base Chakra

For an Old Soul Child, the base chakra is where information is stored about their biological family and previous, past life families. It is connected to their survival instincts, how they ground to the physical plane and how they feel at home in situations. It gives them power to achieve goals and energy for achieving purpose in life, enabling them to feel stable and secure. It is also connected to their basic drives and helps their instincts when they become adults for things such as eating, protecting their family and staying safe. If this chakra is unbalanced, then it may be due to feeling insecure, fearful or nervous and feel unwelcome in new surroundings. The base chakra also holds onto negative experiences within their own family, especially if the family is dysfunctional. A dysfunctional family will reincarnate together over many lifetimes so their own family karma will become resolute.

Sacral Chakra

The sacral chakra is connected to feelings and sexuality. When it is open, your Old Soul Child's feelings flow freely, and they can nurture their connection to the elemental worlds. They will also have a sense of pride in who they are, have positive relationships in their lives and draw on your love and support for all their needs. It is linked to their own creativity and interpersonal ability to empower themselves. If the sacral chakra becomes unbalanced, your Old Soul Child will lose their own inner power, begin to feel that the world does not love them and begin to feel rejected by friends and even their own family. Jealousies will surface and sibling rivalry will become unbearable. Creative blocks arise in feeling stuck in situations that they feel that they have no power over. A child prodigy connects to this chakra by connecting and unleashing their past life talents, in their current life, to help them adjust to working in the adult world. When they start to question their own talents because they feel that they do not fit in, this chakra becomes out of alignment and faith is lost in their own abilities.

Solar Plexus Chakra

The solar plexus chakra is connected to an Old Soul Child's personal power. This is where they store their feelings of self esteem and confidence. It also holds their judgements, opinions and beliefs. The solar plexus chakra helps Old Soul Children to maintain strong personal boundaries. When this chakra is healthy, it brings energy and sufficient self esteem. When we use the term, 'gut feeling', we are actually taping into the energy of the solar plexus to help us make decisions. If resentment is held onto and anger is stored in their bodies, they tend to become aggressive, resulting in lack of self-confidence and low self-esteem. Your Old Soul Child may also manipulate others and situations to gain approval in situations that they have no control over.

Old Soul Children connect with the solar plexus when meeting other Old Souls. Soul Recognition takes place and the awareness of others becomes greater as they connect to their soul friends and soul mates throughout their journey on the earth plane.

Heart Chakra

Some cultures regard this as the centre of the human body and indicate that you can not move forward in your spiritual journey without working with the energy of the heart chakra. It is the centre of relationships, love and compassion and helps your Old Soul Child to balance their connection between the physical and spiritual worlds. The heart chakra is about love, kindness and affection and helps your Old Soul Child to become compassionate and create harmonious relationships. Your Old Soul Child will begin to lose energy when they hold onto past negative experiences and resentments that stop their spiritual growth. It will also hold them in the past when they do not open up and express their true feelings or allow others to love them, resulting in them becoming cold and distant.

Old Soul Children store the energy of past life, feelings and emotions within their heart centres. In their early years, they may be filled with anger towards someone that they have met for the very first time and not know why. However, because generations of souls carry emotional suitcases from one life to the next, it is sometimes held onto for the next reincarnation to be worked through again and again. Just a simple trigger can ignite such memories in all of us, and we act out the same memories because we need to encounter the learning experience as Old Souls.

Throat Chakra

The throat chakra is related to self expression of your Old Soul Child's desires and the area where they say yes or no to situations in life. It is related to communication, creativity and generates the power for the child to speak up and define their own needs. It is their centre of will and choice and enables them to exercise the self control to empower others and themselves. When they begin to lose energy from this chakra, they begin to have non-assertion and unexpressed emotions. This chakra is often most affected if a child is being bullied because they let others define their needs and wants. Your Old Soul Child may also begin to tell lies because they are afraid to speak honestly because of confusions. If your Old Soul Child says there is a blocked and feeling in their throat, or they have many severe sore throats, this often is an indicator of unexpressed words and emotions. When your Old Soul Child states what is really bothering them, they will recover from having a sore throat.

Old Soul Children may not be able to speak, which is connected to a past life connection. The reason for this is that they could have been ridiculed because of speaking in public or even hanged for a certain belief that they adhered to. From an early age, encourage your Old Soul Child to speak their truth as this will aid their own creativity.

Third Eye Chakra

The third eye chakra is related to concentration, imagination, intuition and dreaming. It gives an Old Soul Child a much larger viewpoint of the world that they live in and helps them to connect to others on a much deeper level. Your Old Soul Child begins to hold trust in their own abilities and intuition, and learns through life by having creative awareness of their world.

When Old Soul Children experience ESP it is because energy is flowing through this chakra. This then allows their inner senses to work in harmony and they can deepen their perception abilities and spiritual awareness.

When energy is lost from this chakra, your Old Soul Child will be filled with feelings of confusion, and will experience headaches, poor eyesight and lack concentration on school work. They will feel less imaginative and shut off from the rest of the world. Any fears that your Old Soul Child may have will also come to the surface, as they are not trusting their own inner sixth sense, are unable to focus on their own thoughts and find it hard to solve their own problems themselves.

From a past life connection, Old Soul Children may not want to connect to their spiritual side and so shut that part down. This may because of persecutions that may have happened, which clouded their own judgements and belief system.

Crown Chakra

The Crown Chakra is related to spiritual energy and higher knowledge: wisdom, intuition and sensory perception. For Old Soul Children, this energy centre brings them knowledge from their past lives to use in their present incarnation and is often passed onto others.

When your Old Soul Child loses energy from this chakra they begin to reject any form of guidance, unless it comes in a form they approve. They also lack faith in their own abilities; life seems meaningless, they can experience depression and become ungrounded due to a lack of inspiration. They also mistrust everyone in their environment and feel that others may have hidden agendas. If your Old Soul Child feels isolated and not connected, the crown chakra may be closed and the child may have a strong desire not to learn anything. Learning disorders also occurs when this chakra is permanently closed.

For every human being, the crown chakra is connected to the Akashic Records. Unfinished business is recorded here and also future soul path plans. The Old Soul Child connects to this innocently, which influences a positive or negative outcome in their life. When Karmic lessons have not been played out, they are stored for future life incarnations that support and feed their spiritual awareness.

A Simple Way

To help your Old Soul Child with chakra balancing, a fundamental way to boost your child's energy is to place a rose quartz crystal into their hand. By doing this, it will give each chakra a boost of its own vibration, restoring energy and harmony once again. Awareness of the Chakras may, in fact, help your child immediately to release how they are feeling.

Exercises for Chakra Balancing – Colour Breathing

When using visualisation and meditation techniques, people often go into fear and panic mode because they do not know how to use those skills. They can begin to put up blocks within themselves, before even attempting a unique experience that will restore mind, body, spirit and soul harmony. Do not worry if you are not able to do it straight away. It takes practise.

Sit in a comfortable position and relax the body. If any thoughts come into your mind, then visualise a waste paper basket in front you and allow yourself to place any thought, person or situation into the waste paper basket. This helps you to dissociate yourself from day to day things and empower yourself with your own thoughts. Start with simple and easy steps before embarking on a meditation.

When breathing in the colours, it will energise your whole being and can be practiced anywhere.

When you are ready, begin with the colour red; breathe in the colour for one breath and then breathe it out. If you are unable to see the colour, please do not worry, you can use other ways, like feel, sense or touching the colour red. Some of my clients visualise a red post box to give them the colour red. For the colour yellow, they may sense the warm sun on their face. There are countless ways in order to help you enjoy a simple visualisation.

On the next breath, breathe in the colour orange for one breath and breathe it out.

On the next breath, breathe in the colour yellow for one breath and breathe it out.

Continue with green, blue, purple and, finally, white – breathing in the colour for one breathe and releasing it.

As the weeks go by, you can increase the times you breathe in the colour, allowing the body to re-new and balance. This simple practice will cleanse your chakras and invigorate the body.

Wearing the colours of the chakras will also bring balance and harmony to your Old Soul Child. When you embark on arts and crafts activities in your own home, painting colours in different rooms will help stimulate the family environment and help everyone to balance themselves

Christopher Robin Milne

Christopher Robin Milne received a small Alpha Farnell stuffed teddy bear on his first birthday. He named him Edward Bear. Christopher loved and played with this bear throughout his childhood. Edward Bear was later renamed Winnie, after he saw a real bear at London Zoo, and the name 'Pooh' belonged to a Swan. He also had an imaginary friend called Binker.

This eventually became the inspiration for Christopher's

father, A.A. Milne, and an artist named Ernest H. Shepard, to decide that his son's two imaginary friends, Owl and Rabbit, would make fantastic characters for a bedtime story. Piglet, Eeyore, Tigger, Kanga and Roo were based on stuffed animals belonging to Christopher Robin.

Winnie the Pooh was first published by Methuen on October 14th, 1926. Pooh and his friends have had many adventures in the 100 acre wood. These stories have been embraced by millions of children and adult readers for more than seventy years and can be found in dozens of different languages.

Chapter Three

Working with Spiritual Energies and Other Dimensions

It is the imagination that gives shape to the universe.
Barry Lopez

Past Life Regression, Children with Past Life Memories, Life Before Birth, Angels, Angel Kershaw, Angels and Children, Children with ESP, Fairies, George David Fryer, Undines, Sylphs, The Fairy Kingdom.

Past Life Regression

When you hear certain music are you called into a past? Do you dream of another time or place? Have you met someone you felt you have always known and yet it is your first meeting? Do you feel drawn to some people and not others? Have you ever been somewhere new and are certain that you have been there before? Have you got strong interests for particular places that cannot be explained? Do you have a desire to visit certain countries, and not know why? Do you feel completely at home when arriving in a different country, where you have never been? If so, then you have already begun to draw on your soul's memories of previous incarnations. These interests serve as reminders that we have been here many times before. Many people believe that we exist in a cycle of life, death and rebirth and that, in each lifetime, we come into the world to resolve emotional problems and learn karmic lessons.

Past life regression therapy is a holistic psychotherapeutic tool, which fits into the transpersonal psychology category of therapy, dealing with the emotional, physical, mental and spiritual aspects of a person's makeup.

Past life regression therapy is the recalling, reliving and re-experiencing of past life memories. This therapy is frequently successful in tracing the past causes of present day stress.

Sometimes we find ourselves repeating behaviours that are not productive, sabotaging career opportunities or having relationships that seem damaging. Through hypnosis, past life regression can open windows to the unconscious mind where memories of past lives are stored.

Uncovering and confronting a long-buried trauma can release the emotional blocks around it, relieve the emotional pain, and enable one to see the present in perspective. Through the process of reliving and releasing the original memory, it is possible to let go of its emotional content.

Spontaneous past life memories are always just fragments of a life: scenes picked out in the spotlight of memory from a story that seems to have no beginning and no end, which often seems to come from nowhere. A series of past lives can create a tangled skin of emotional, physical, spiritual and mental problems in the present.

A phobia may be accompanied by a physical symptom. For example, if a person was hanged for speaking out against authorities in a previous life, this could result in chronic neck pain and a fear of speaking in public. This actual happened to a client of mine, Christopher, who hated public speaking. When regressed, he found himself in Ancient Egypt, speaking out his true beliefs and was eventually hanged.

Another client, Steve, was a middle aged, single man, and had never truly committed to anything in his life. He had many uncompleted tasks and unhappy relationships and when regressed, he found himself as a young woman living in Italy, escaping a man that she did not love. She was forced into marriage by her overbearing father, because of the huge family debts that her father incurred. This gave Steve incredible awareness as to why he had never completed relationships and tasks; his heart had been committed to marrying for love, and not money, a very long time ago.

The memories of previous lives run in sequence because they are a continuation of the same essential soul or person. The many levels of the self are like the many skins of an onion; we peel these off as we look into our past lives or connect to our dreams.

The unconscious mind will almost always produce a past life when invited in the right way. If encouraged to see the story as now, we can finish a pattern that need not be repeated.

A past live personality is not single, it is multiple. One person may have several theme-related past lives that will have common psychological issues, which have responded to past life regression therapy.

I have found, through experience, that when clients have their first past life regressions, they rarely get violent or horrible memories. As a rule, the unconscious mind, which carries past life memories, as well as forgotten childhood events and archetypes, will only send us past life memories that we are ready to deal with, which we are able to integrate into our conscious personality structure.

Past life regression is a safe process. The unconscious mind, where past life memories reside, is selective in what it releases to the conscious mind. It will allow the person to go as deeply and as far as they need to go and no further.

For me, past life regression has given me a new purpose. Re-experiencing my past lives has released the grip of the past and given me a fresh start in the present.

Past life regression can, therefore, serve many purposes. By revisiting your past lives you can begin to see and understand how you are influenced and what lies at the root cause of repressed fears and phobias, or patterns of negative thinking and behaviour. This understanding can then bring release and allow you to move forward with your life. It can also show us why we have such close or difficult relationships with those around us. Again, this understanding can allow us to understand why we feel the way we do in our current life and help us to make choices.

We also learn and evolve between incarnations. During past life regression, some of my clients automatically go to the 'Interlife', which is the in-between state for souls to wait before they incarnate again. From the sessions, clients have found it particularly beneficial when the purpose of their current life seems unclear.

Through past life regression, answers are found to questions that the client has been trying to solve. Meetings with spirit guides and groups of souls from various incarnations, in the Halls of Learning, help them to understand their current Soul Life Journey. They also have reported a great sense of peace, understanding and higher awareness. Feelings and experience at this level have a very profound effect and there is often a reluctance to leave this state.

Accessing memories from your soul's many lifetimes is a very enlightening process. Whether you are just curious or looking for some therapeutic value, a journey into your soul's past is an amazing experience.

Lucy

Lucy, eighteen, came for a past life regression, as she wanted to know why she struggled with becoming independent and self-sufficient, and why she was always desperately seeking her parents' approval.

During the session, it emerged that, in a previous lifetime, Lucy's parents had abandoned her. She had spent a whole lifetime searching for her parents and wanting to learn why they had discarded her. When we spoke about the session, Lucy began to realise why she had chosen her parents in this lifetime, why she so wanted their approval and most of all, their unconditional love.

The sessions also gave insight into why her parents behaved in certain ways towards Lucy and why it would not have been easy, on their part, to give her the approval that she so obviously wanted. I worked with Lucy to show her that the only approval she needed was her own inner approval and approval from her own inner authority.

No one needs permission to be themselves – just the courage to do it. Once we cut the puppet strings, so that we are not seeking others' approval, we stop being their puppet, under their control.

Children with Past Life Memories

As a past life regression Therapist, I have noticed, when interviewing children about their imaginary friends, that many children remember their past lives without being encouraged by their parents. It seems that playing with their toys or friends, talking to their parents, doing drawing or even reading a book, helps them to recall 'another life' with ease, and when questioned and challenged further about what they are talking about, they will talk about something completely different. As soon as they learn to speak, some children are able to tell remarkably detailed stories of people, places and events that happened in their past lives.

Your Old Soul Child will go through similar experiences as their soul develops. They chose you as parents, with all the wisdom of their higher selves – all you owe them is to be yourself.

Everyone's soul path is different and children choose parents because of significance of the experience that they know they will get by being born to those parents.

From my interviews, I have seen that Old Soul Children are incarnating over and over again to gain more knowledge, not just the human perceptive but also from the soul's. The soul has a consciousness and retains what has been learnt and experienced. This is carried forward to the next incarnation as our subconscious.

The positive things that Old Soul Children learn in previous incarnations helps them to progress and move forward in their current life but, equally, the negative things that they have learnt and experienced can hinder them and hold them back; many Old Soul Children are displaying seemingly unexplained negative behaviours or have supposedly irrational fears and phobias, which have their roots buried in past lives. Even for the Old Soul Child, this is confusing. Some of their experiences will be positive and some negative but together they will give each individual a balanced perspective.

We re-incarnate with those we have known before, not only so we can enjoy being with one another again – for example, your husband or wife in a previous life could be your grandmother or grandfather in this life – but also to learn from a different perspective with them. The Universal Laws of Karma also govern our reincarnations. If we had issues with another soul in a previous life, we will reincarnate with them again to work towards a balanced conclusion. This could take one or more lifetimes to achieve.

Meredith and Toby

My husband, Eric, has had many jobs since we have been together. At one time, he was recovering broken-down vehicles and driving the client home. My husband met Meredith in Raunds, Northamptonshire. Her vehicle was recovered from Raunds due to a head gasket. Eric explained to me that she only had the standard AA cover and that meant that he could only take her ten miles to the nearest garage or home.

Meredith lived in Great Yarmouth and worked in Oxford. She travelled two days a week; her husband was an engineer and worked in Birmingham.

As they travelled to her home in the thick fog, the journey took four hours and they spoke non-stop. Eric explained that I was writing this book and she began this story, which is retold in

Eric's words:

One day her only child Toby, five, was being really cheeky towards her. Meredith said, "Don't be cheeky to your mummy."

Toby replied, "You're not my first mummy, you're my second mummy. My first mummy was killed and I saw it happen."

Meredith said that a cold shudder filled her body; she stopped dead in her tracks, sat down straight away and began to ponder what Toby had just said.

Later that day, as Toby played with his toys, Meredith began to quiz him gently about what he said and he began to come forward about other relatives. As Toby liked to draw, Meredith asked him to draw his first mummy. Meredith began to look through history books and she discovered that the clothes he had drawn looked Victorian.

Tracie and Noah

Tracie contacted me after I posted this subject on a forum. Her middle son, Noah, had an imaginary friend for three years and always talked about another life as a boy with brown skin. When he reached six it stopped. Noah would talk about walking a long time to get food and water for his family and that the sun was always hot when he walked. His mum had died and he had to help his father look after his younger sister and brothers. Noah said that his friend was his brother and that he died before he got some food home. When Tracie heard this, because Noah explained it with so much conviction, it made her cry.

Lisa

When I met Lisa, four, for the very first time, she insisted that her name was June and got very upset when people didn't call her that. She told me that Lisa was her friend and was 8 years old. Lisa was still there, she insisted, but we cannot see her because she is invisible and only people with special magical powers can see her. Lisa left the other family because her parents were not very nice to her.

This went on until she started school the following year and then her imaginary friend was not mentioned ever again. When I asked Lisa where her friend was, a blank stare was given in return and then, five minutes after, I was informed that she had gone on holiday and was not coming back.

Jade

I went to pick Jade up from nursery one day and found that she already had her coat and shoes on, waiting for me to collect her. I was informed by nervous staff that she had been telling all the staff that Mummy has colours around her. When she is happy they are pink and purple and when she is sad, they are brown.

The manager of the nursery told me that they could not tolerate this kind of behaviour and because it was scaring staff and other children, Jade was, in fact, not welcome at the nursery anymore. I was told that it must be because of the work that I do – I must be encouraging some kind of witchcraft at home! Driving home in bewilderment, I was wondering how to respond to that kind of statement, let alone find another replacement nursery for my spiritually aware daughter.

As I approached our village, still clouded with what had just happened, Jade came out with a statement that I shall never forget, which nearly made me crash into the telegraph pole.

"Mummy," said Jade.

"Yes, darling," I replied.

"Do you remember the time when I was the mummy and you were the baby?"

I was stunned by what she had said, and then she went on to say, "We had a pram with big wheels and I took you for walks. Do you remember?"

I pulled the car over and turned around. "What pram with big wheels?" I asked.

Jade replied, "What's for tea, Mum?" and gazed out of the car window.

As soon as I got Jade and Amba from the car, I searched Victorian prams on the internet and within seconds pictures emerged onto the screen.

"Jade," I shouted. "Quick, come here." Jade walked towards me and I lifted her onto my knee. "Is this what you had?" I asked, pointing to the computer screen.

Jade nodded her head, told me that it was not white, but dark, and then jumped down from my knee and went to play with Amba.

The Guynn Family

The Guynn Family live in Bedfordshire and Becky, the mum, has shared many stories with me about her children's incredible past life tales.

Her eldest Son, Decclan, is eleven and has talked about at least two past lives. When he was about two, his mum brought a new painting of a lady dressed in Victorian/Edwardian clothes with a large hat and a feather in it. Decclan got very excited and said that his mum before was called Deedee and she dressed like that.

Another time, the family were watching a programme about the pyramids being built and Decclan became extremely upset, so upset that they had to turn off the television. He said that he did that (building the pyramids) and that daddy was not his dad then, but had hit him to make him work. Becky's husband was also very distressed by this. A while later, Becky and her husband had a reading by a medium who said that they had both lived before and amazingly that he had lived in Egypt – he had been a task master! This upset her husband even more.

Decclan has also seen, sensed and heard spirits and angels, and dreamed about people that he has never met and subsequently meets.

This is not happening as much now because he is getting older, but when Becky told him about me and my search for stories, he began to tell her some amazing stuff. Decclan had been seeing a huge cloak with a large hood, but couldn't see the face, so he was not scared of it. At that moment in time (and he didn't know this), Becky was asking Archangel Michael to protect the family. She envisioned his cloak surrounding them and the home, with it reaching all the way to the floor and the hood completely covering the face – exactly as he described.

Decclan also said that he had seen scary looking monster faces but knew that they were not monsters who would hurt him – like gargoyle-type figures. Oddly, her husband, Michael, also had similar visions when he was a boy. Again, their son did not know this.

Becky's eldest daughter Aimee, who is six, is a very intuitive child and would often tell Becky what she was thinking so accurately that it left her wondering if she was thinking it out loud. Aimee has also told her parents many things about when she lived before. She told them once that she wanted to be able to look out of her bedroom window and see the tigers, elephants and monkeys again. When asked where she lived, she said it was not in this country, and Becky wondered if it was India – the only place she could think of with those three types of animals together.

Another time, Aimee got very emotional and said that she never wanted her mum and dad to leave her on her own. They assured her that they wouldn't and Aimee explained that her other parents had left her and she was very scared by it.

Aimee talks about her 'Pink Heart Angel' who comes and visits her at night, takes her to fun places and tells her things she would not know. Her Angel told her that we all have two hearts, a pink and a green one, that work together. Becky thought she had been watching too much *Dr Who* until she found out that in chakra healing they do use both pink and green for the heart chakra.

Her imaginary friends, Kane and Shannenous (both of which

are names that she has not heard anywhere else), have whole life stories and personalities.

Connal, her younger son, also speaks to Kane but when he wants to say anything to Shannenous he asks Aimee to say it.

Becky asked Aimee's school teacher if there are any children with those names at school and there were none. The family does not do not know anyone with those names or any programmes or films she watches with those names in them. Becky has the sense that Kane is really Connal's guide, but he does not know it, and Shannenous is Aimee's.

Aimee also tells her mum that she sees different coloured lights sometimes around people and places, which is the auric field. Becky works a lot with angels. On very few times, she has seen them as the winged beings that we see in pictures, but mostly sees them as flashes of different coloured lights around the room. However, Aimee was not aware of this information.

Becky's younger son Connal, who is four, has told her of when he lived before and was a man. Strangely, it seems that Connal may have lived in the same town as they do now because when they go to places they seem to spark off the memories. For example, when they went to the park, he pointed to a tree and told his parents he fell out of it and did not wake up again. Could this be how he died? Connal spoke with such emotion and detail that it just didn't seem possible that a two year old would know that sort of thing. When they were driving down a street, Connal was even able to point out where he used to live.

Connal also has memories of another life that he has lived; Decclan, his older brother, was talking about learning French at school and Connal recalled a previous life when his name was Tim Cavalin. He explained that there was a battle on a ship and someone had their head cut off and thrown into the water, which wasn't very nice. The family looked up the name on the internet and although they could not find much detail, there was in fact a Tim Cavalin around in Napoleonic times.

Even though the older children are quite spiritually aware, Connal seems to be more aware and has a very powerful spirit. When Becky was pregnant with him, but did not know, she was asked by a friend if she would let her do a Tarot reading and agreed. Becky pulled out the Page of Pentacles, which apparently is a boy who is very impish and can be trouble.

All of her children have also had a spiritual naming ceremony and at Connal's the Medium told us that he would be a handful, but would be extremely psychic. He is a handful, but Becky thinks that this could be because he doesn't understand himself and his abilities. She also thinks that his large soul feels trapped by his small human body.

On numerous occasions he has proven his abilities and has many stories to tell. Perhaps one of the most compelling stories happened when he was only tiny. We were all watching TV one evening and he was playing with his cars on the floor when he looked up and said, "He's coming."

When we asked him, who? he said it was Lee. Lee was her husband's best friend of nearly thirty years who had died not long before. We told Connal to say hello from us, then he smiled and went back to playing with his cars. A while later he said, "He's gone now, he said he'll be back later."

Later that night, as Becky and her husband got into bed, her husband yelled and jumped back out again. Turning on the light and pulling back the covers, they found lots of little screws on his side of the bed. They laughed because that was what he and Lee used to do to each other's beds when they were kids, and presumed that one of the four children were following in their dad's footsteps. They pulled the cover right off, cleared the bed, turned off the light and got back into bed, but once again he yelled and jumped out. Pulling back the cover and turning the light on, they again found more screws and knew that there was no way that it was the children – it had to be Lee 'coming back later', as Connal had said. They told Lee to behave himself and finally got to go to sleep.

Another time, Becky was desperately racking her brains to think of a person's name but just could not remember it. She described the person to her husband, but he too could not remember. Minutes later, Connal walked into the room and asked, "Is her name Kerry?" The name was correct, yet he had never met this person or knew anything about her. Becky asked how he knew; he shrugged and asked if he done wrong. Becky told him that he had done nothing wrong but, in fact, he is an amazing kid.

Connal talks an awful lot about magic and says that we can all do magic if we want to. If they are running late for school, or the traffic is bad, Connal says, "We say we won't be late because the time will go slow." Nine times out ten, if this happens, they are never late! Becky believes that this is because time is a manmade concept and not real, so if we tune into the universal time wave instead, we can work with that to manipulate it.

Becky's youngest Daughter Maddison, who is two, has yet to tell us about her past lives but does see things, as she will often point at thin air and say, "Look at that." When the phone rings she will say the name of the caller before they answer and gets it right every time.

She has also started talking to 'someone' called Jordan and although they do know a Jordan, she says that it isn't him! She goes off for ages and plays games with little dolls or cars and always reserves one for Jordan.

She is the complete opposite of Connal; where he seems to be in battle with himself, she is so calm and accepting. She gets very excited by pictures of angels and fairies and likes to carry round a little confetti angel with her. She also has an affinity with crystals; she recently climbed up on to the wall unit, which she had never done before, took down all the crystals and carried them out into the back garden. When asked what she was doing she said, "They want sun, they want to play."

Maddison also has a wonderful bond with animals. They have

a pet bird (a Cockatiel who is rather shy and hides from the rest of the family whenever they go near his cage.) Whenever Maddison talks to him he comes to her and even lets her stroke him. They also had a wild Jay bird in their garden who just wouldn't leave Maddison alone; it kept hoping along next to her as she ran around giggling. This also happens with the sparrows.

When her younger son was a baby, his first trip was to the park. They were followed by a whole flock of birds, an old lady even commented on it. Maddison often says that animals are talking to her. When she sees dogs, cats or birds, she says "I heard him/her in here," and points to her head.

One day Becky caught Maddison trying to catch the fish in the tank with a net and told her to stop. She got very upset and said the baby one had asked her to rescue it as the others were hurting it. When Becky looked carefully at the fish, the larger ones were actually pecking at the baby one, so took it out and put it in a separate bowl.

Maddison was very happy that the little fish was safe and sat talking to the bowl, telling the fish that it would be ok now. It seems that the Guynn family have their very own little Dr Doolittle!

Old Soul Families

Old Soul families incarnate together at the same time, to support one another and to grow spiritually. So, it's completely possibly that our children, who have been here many times, are, in fact, our great, great, great grandparents from another lifetime.

Our current parents, brothers, sisters, cousins and grand-parents all help with the lessons that we have to learn by connecting with our soul family. This, I feel, is what the Guynn family are; each family member is made up of: Old Soul Child, Old Soul Teenager, and Old Soul Adults.

Old Soul Children are born into the same families over many lifetimes because of the soul agreement they all make, as a family, in the Interlife. Reflection on what they have achieved as a family and where they want to direct their new family energies is agreed and they review their family karma to clear up unfinished business between themselves.

In my family – and you may want do this with your own family – every New Year's Eve and New Year's Day, we all write down, as a family, what we want to achieve in the coming year. We write them down as an 'intentions', rather than New Year's resolutions because, from experience, we tend to beat ourselves up when we fail at the first hurdle. As our thoughts create our world, we support one another by empowering all that is possible.

The famous Kennedys and also Marlon Brando's family are just two of Old Soul Families that I can mention to give you an example; incarnating together and meeting in the physical realm, their souls reflect the challenges needed for their family karma to learn how to live in harmony as a unit.

Working through personal karmic memories can also be triggered when choices and actions have to be made. Family karma can be passed, not just from generation to generation, but also from one lifetime to the next until the desired goal is reached.

Old Soul Child, Old Soul Teenagers, Old Soul Adults

Old Soul Children are in touch with their intuitive feelings because they are in tune with their heart chakras up until the age of eight. This begins to change because of learning left brain activities within school. These souls do not get bogged down with Karma – they develop more in the Interlife, which liberates their learning experience on earth enabling them to grasp new experiences. They mature fast on the earth plane, reflecting back to themselves their life experiences and they come across as very wise for their age.

They work with their spirit guides, planning their soul path and what karmic issues to work on for their next incarnation. Their visual perception is the same, as they connect to their imaginary friend/spirit guide, who will draw close to them to help them to readjust on the earth plane.

An Old Soul Child will create confidence in animals, adults, their teachers and their friends. As they are very open to all energies around them, they often feel other people's pain, fear, and emotions as well as their own.

Old Soul Teenagers tend to get confused in which path to take, especially if they are pushed into a direction or career that they are unsure of. They formulate their true selves and are easily distracted and wonder away from their goals. Their love and romantic life is often difficult, filled with much pain and disappointment. They also suffer lots of jealousy, because they give their hearts to everyone that they meet. Not sure how to make the right choice and action in their own life, because of feeling very unsure and unsettled, they can often feel disempowered by the society they have chosen to live in as a soul. They are not bothered about any consequences that happen, and the ache of loneliness is also a memory that can stay with them until early adulthood. When this is the case and Old Soul Teenagers feel lost in life and that things are not going right for them, they are given nudges in life in their present incarnation about moving in the right direction of life. Their paths interact with others to help them get back on their chosen soul path and to keep up with their soul growth. Soul development helps them to understand their personal, family relationships.

It is only around seventeen that they begin to choose a course of action and have in mind some goal that they like to pursue, as not wanting to miss out on what life should be giving them. Memories are ingrained deep within their souls from current life experiences and if they feel that there family is dysfunctional, they will step away from it and start a new beginning for themselves.

From my own experiences, I have met many people that I feel I have known for eternity, and as you get to know each other, you discover that you share the same beliefs. With others, however, there is just no connection – no vibe to really affirm to. Often enough, an Old Soul Adult has a spiritual awakening, or a near-death or out-of-body experience that helps them get back on their soul path. When the soul incarnates it does not worry about the concept of time. It is only when human embodiment takes place that they feel that they have wasted their life because their spiritual awakening happened late in adult life and instead of getting on with it, they spend time fretting about what time they have left.

As souls, we forget that this has already been agreed – planned in the planning stages, whilst being in the Interlife. It is only when that is recognised that they let go and move to a more spiritual way of life.

Before seeking healing and spiritual wisdom, they may have felt that their life is filled with work that is unpleasant and undemanding; their own individual power to carry on in life diminishes and the desire to keep on going starts to fall to the wayside.

Their choice of medical care tends to be alternative and holistic. Old Soul Adults are here to teach others their spiritual understandings. Their philosophies and writings are simple and easy to read

To find an Old Soul Baby, Old Soul Child, Old Soul Teenager or Old Soul Adult, their eyes are the windows to their Soul.

Announcing Dreams

How Jade Choose Her Own Name

Two days before I gave birth to Jade, I just did not know what to call her. As she was our firstborn, I must have bought every baby name book I could get my hands on just to find a name that would be perfect for our new arrival.

On awakening, I heard the name, Jade, very clearly and

thought nothing of it, as I often tend to hear names when rising relating to clients and their pregnancies.

That day, however, I had no clients close to giving birth. I came downstairs for breakfast, and as I waked downstairs, I notice a crystal on the floor. I picked it up and noticed that it was a piece of jade. I put it back in the crystal box and muttered something to myself about the kittens removing it from its place.

Eric was working away and so I went to make myself a cup of tea and switch the television on. In channel hopping across the television, I stopped when a presenter was talking about crystals and jade was centre to the talk. He went on to say that people believed that jade was the expression of the most beautiful stone and had been in China for at least 4000 years. To be honest, I thought it was telling me that I needed to buy a jade crystal to help with the pregnancy. When looking up the meaning, it said that it would help with worry and tension, which I was not feeling at that time.

I went to the supermarket and met friends for lunch. To my amazement, they were wearing jade jewellery. After battling with the crowds, and feeling full from lunch, I decided to grab a couple of hours sleep. I begin to doze and the thoughts of the morning and the crystal jade were in my mind, helping me drift off to sleep. I awoke a few hours later feeling refreshed. As I lay there, I heard the word, jade, again and decided to look up the meaning of the name in my baby book. In an instance, when reading the meaning, I knew that I had found a perfect name for my newborn.

The experience I had is called an 'Announcing Dream'; these are very common in pregnancy. Announcing Dreams are believed to be the announcement of an individual's rebirth. For me, I feel that Jade wanted this to be her name because it will serve as a further purpose that will be announced to her when she is older.

Leo Did The Same Thing

This happened again when I found out I was pregnant with Leo.

I was extremely happy, but also stunned and fearful, because thoughts of miscarriage doomed my every waking thought. When I reached twenty weeks, I breathed a sigh of relief because I knew then that this child wanted to be with us.

In the middle of the night, I awoke to a voice. Eric was working away that night and so I rolled over to go back to sleep. I shot up in the bed, because I could hear the name, Leo, being shouted at me several times. I tried to go back to sleep but the name got louder and louder, so I dived under the duvet because it scared me to hear it so strongly.

As I lay there, hiding under the duvet, I thought about how stupid I was being, because I spoke to spirits on a regular basis. I pulled back the duvet and shouted, "God bless. Turn to the light," and as I begin to fall asleep, I thought that Leo was a great name to use if I was having a boy. I told Eric about the name when he returned from Spain and we both felt the name was the correct one. Again, going through the baby name books seemed an endless waste of time because we just could not agree or even find the appropriate name.

The name Leo stayed with us until the moment he came into the world. Our eyes both filled with tears, as the long wait was over for us both to have a son that we named Leo.

My Name is Baby!

I had several names for Amba when she arrived and we just could not decided what to call her, as the names chosen just did not suit her. For a few weeks, my husband and I called her 'Baby' before we registered her birth. When she was growing up, she would disagree with Eric and say that her name is not Amba, but 'Baby'. The reason for her protests did not occur to me until I found some photographs with 'Baby' written on the back – then it clicked. This went on until she started school at five. Could Amba, in fact, remember and recall, in those few weeks, what her first name was? As she has grown up into a beautiful, well-natured, caring young lady, she has earned the name 'Pixie'. She adores being called Pixie. Amba has elfin like features and huge blue eyes that are always smiling and filled with mischief.

Angels
What is an Angel?

Angels are beings of energy that are composed of ethereal matter. Angels are androgynous, which means they are neither male nor female, and cannot take on human form because they are from different streams of consciousness.

The word 'Angel' is derived from the Greek word 'Angelos', which means messenger. Christians, Muslims and many other religions believe that angels deliver messages warning us of impending danger, and give instructions about what to do in a particular situation.

Angels have such a high vibratory rate that most people cannot see them, so they show themselves to us in whichever physical form best suits our immediate needs. They appear to us when we have lost our faith and trust is broken, and carry the essence of purity and integrity.

The angelic realm surrounds us on a daily basis and are working in close contact with mankind to help us raise our consciousness so that we become aware of their presences and divine guidance. As they wish to raise their profile, angels are inspiring others to write about them in books and on television, which has been successfully done in series such as *Highway to Heaven* and *Touched by an Angel*. They have even hit the big silver screen with films like *City of Angels* (1998) with Meg Ryan and Nicholas Cage, *Michael* (1996) with John Travolta and *It's a Wonderful Life* (1946). Robbie Williams, Abba and also the Eurythmics sang about angels. So when Christmas comes around and you are in the shops, surrounded by angels on the shop counters, just believe that they are really with you, by your side, every step of the way.

My Experiences

After my first Angelic experience in 1991, I always know that the angels are consistently by my side. I believe that working with angels came at a time of great change and transition in my life; the discovery of angels gave me a sense of being in a non-dualistic place where thinking and feeling were not separate or dominant. The great sense of peace that comes during working with angels helps you become open to divine guidance and helps me to have a smoother path in life. You do not need to be deeply religious or do any particular thing; many of them have chosen to serve mankind and are available to help, support, heal and guide us – all we have to do is ask.

There have been hundreds of times, when I have seen an angel and here are a few stories to share with you:

My sister, Kerry, got married in September 2001, at Wellingborough Registry Office in Northamptonshire. The happy couple walked in to take their vows and a huge angel flew over them and began to play a trumpet. I will never forget what I saw and my expression of "Bloody Hell!" got the whole wedding party glaring at me. I sat bolt upright, looking straight up with tears falling down my face and watched the angel fly around the room. I was still looking up as my sister exchanged her vows, and the angel explained that is was a 'marriage angel'; it was helping the union by connecting these two Old Souls together. Throughout the whole service, I just cried with joy because of what I had just witnessed. It was a truly magical experience that just took my breath away.

Another experience I had was at my mother in law's house in Peterlee. I had gone upstairs to lie on her bed because I had a raging headache that I just could not get rid of, and decided that a cat nap would do the trick. As I began to fall asleep, a gold light came through the window and changed into the form of an angel. The room was filled with a glorious golden light and as I lay on in the bed, again with tears in my eyes, the energy of this beautiful being just took my breath away. The angel told me not to be afraid and that I was going to be OK, moments later my headache just disappeared.

When I was training for my Hypnotherapy and Past Life Regression Diploma in London with the European College of Hypnotherapy, I witnessed two angels in Birbeck College, in December 1999 and January 2001. The December angel was a healing angel and appeared behind a Russian lady when she was being hypnotised.

The angel explained to me that it was giving her healing and the lady slumped down one side of the chair; the energy in the room was so intense from the healing that she was receiving. I became very excited, turned to my tutor and explained what I had seen. I was greeted with a blank expression as he told me that he couldn't see anything. After that experience, I learnt that there are times, when witnessing angelic presences, to be quiet and just enjoy it for myself.

The January angel was for me and I can tell you that it was a 'Bloody Big One!' It was my turn to be hypnotised and I was very lucky because the person carrying out the exercise also believed in angels and brought them into the session. A spectrum of colours emerged into a 7ft angel, which told me that my life direction was about to change and should be embraced. If I were to fight it, my path would not be an easy one and I cannot thank them enough, because it was right.

The 'rainbow angel' is my guardian angel and I am now able to call it to assist me whilst I am teaching. Working with my guardian angel helps other students to connect with their own angels.

I can also remember watching *Richard and Judy* (UK morning television presenters) when they were on *This Morning*, interviewing someone about angels. It had been raining outside and the grey clouds just filled the sky. Just as I was going to switch the television off, a silver angel appeared to me in my lounge, and the whole room was radiated by sunlight which became very intense. I sat down in the chair and looked up at the silver angel. Gently, it gave me some much-needed healing for a reoccurring tonsillitis infection, which just wouldn't leave my body. After receiving such an intense healing energy, I recovered very quickly from the infection.

In my work, as an Intuitive Angel Therapist, I teach out of my own experience of angel contact and have built up my own school. Diploma courses in working with angels and your guides, as well as other spiritual and personal development courses are available to people from all walks of life. Please visit www.touchedbyanangel.me.uk for more information.

Angel Kershaw

Angel Kershaw was born in the North of England and has been a natural healer and 'sensitive' from birth. As a small child, she informed her grandmother of the 'pretty lights' that she could see around people and the 'shiny people' that she often saw. Although no one knew or understood what she was talking about, Angel knew that there was more to life than the base, mundane world she was forced to live in. She was consciously aware from her primary school years onwards that she had abilities to heal and to sense more than just the material world we see, often communicating with ethereal beings we know as angels (whom she called her 'shiny people). She would often say things about people or events that happened before she was born, and which she could not possibly know.

Angel's early life was difficult and traumatic, and her abilities helped comfort her at the darkest times of her life. There were times when only her 'shiny people' comforted her. Although her maternal grandmother and Granddad loved her, they were not aware of the abusive situation that she was living with – abusers are, by their nature, good at hiding their abuse, and intimidating their victims into silence.

Angel is Dyslexic, and struggled with schoolwork except for one subject – art. Angel loved to draw and paint, and was recognised as having talent from early on in her school career. Her mother, however, had no intention of letting her follow her heart, and did everything she could to restrict her artistic endeavours, not allowing her to be creative at home. She often gave her household chores when she showed signs of 'creating' anything, and ridiculed and mocked any art work she brought home.

Angel had a close connection with her grandmother (her beloved 'Grandma') who often seemed to understand how people were feeling, or what they needed without ever having to say a word. Grandma may have been psychic but, in a Catholic working class family, such things were not spoken of.

At such an early age, Angel did not understand terms such as 'the angelic realm' but she found that what her beautiful shiny people told her was true. At night, after all the lights in the house had gone out, her mother, stepfather and sisters were in bed, and she felt safe, at last. She would sit up in her bed and calmly invite them to come close to her. Usually these beings took on a human form of great beauty, and were surrounded by bright lights. Sometimes, these lights shone pink or bright turquoise; other times, they shone bright gold and silver or white, shimmering in the dark. Angel learnt to talk silently to these beings, so that her sisters would not awaken. Although their voices sounded like gentle breezes, her sisters never woke, and she would fall asleep feeling calm again, even after a day that had been filled with fear and tension.

When walking in the park one day, at about six years of age, she found a bird on the ground, hobbling and flapping its wings, but unable to fly. Afraid that a cat would find it, she picked the little brown bird up, and held it gently in her hands. She felt a warmth emanate from her hands, and saw bright turquoise light build up around the little bird. The light shone for a few minutes then slowly dimmed. She opened her hands and the bird looked up at her, gave a little twitter and flew out of her hands, souring into the sky above.

On another occasion she was sitting on a bench in the same park, watching other children play. She wanted to join in, but was too shy to go and ask. A man and his dog walked by, and suddenly the dog did a U-turn and came bounding up to her. She leaned forward to pat the dog, and he sat down in front of her. As she touched the animal and looked into his face, she could feel that he was in pain, and instinctively ran her hands down to his back legs and hips. Her hands grew warm; the bright turquoise light began to emanate from them, and was absorbed into the dog's skin. The owner of the dog looked on in amazement then explained that the dog never let anyone touch him there because his hips were too painful.

"Yes, he hurts in his hips," Angel replied, as the turquoise light began to fade. "But it's going to be alright now."

The man looked warily at her, but decided that he would not discourage a little girl. The dog stood up and wagged his tail, then turned and walked away with his master, looking back just once, as if to say "Thank you." He seemed to have a new spring in his step.

Unfortunately, Angel's abilities were not always welcome. She knew when people were lying, and could sense their discomfort when they were hiding their feelings. If she mentioned this, it could cause an argument, or cause people to turn on her, so she often kept her thoughts to herself.

In her mid-teens, Angel began to realise that her gifts could help others, so she decided to begin to use them to assist those around her. Angel was painfully shy, and was nervous about declaring her abilities. When she eventually did this, the response was very mixed. However, it was soon realised that Angel could indeed 'see' into people's lives, as well as help them heal physical and emotional illness. Over several years she developed a reputation as being reliable and able, and clients came to her from all walks of life.

In her twenties and thirties, whilst living in Edinburgh, Angel continued to develop her abilities, and her clients were often senior business executives and VIPs, as well as ordinary working people. Angel treated them all equally, charging the same reasonable fees (except when she chose to waive the fee altogether). Angel trained as a psychotherapist, and was frequently recognised for her insightful ability to pinpoint a client's issues. For this reason, Angel was able to achieve profound results in a short space of time.

Angel was given an opportunity to go to Hollywood, where her abilities were soon recognised. In a town where most of the population are, in some way, involved in the entertainment business, it was not long before Angel's presence was requested on film and television sets. This work, however, was not particularly fulfilling, as Angel felt that, while she could certainly help people, many of her clients wanted her to sort out their problems, and were reluctant to take firm action to change any life patterns themselves. Angel moved briefly to Chicago, where she continued her work, working alongside others who were attempting to tackle many of the difficult issues faced by society. She facilitated in workshops and seminars, appeared at conferences as a guest speaker, and continued to see private clients for healing and therapy sessions.

Angel eventually returned to the UK and lived in London, where she spent some time re-evaluating her life and her goals. She began practicing Nichren Diashonin's Buddhism and became a member of SGI. Angel returned to her first love of art, and through a series of blessings and fortunate circumstances, was able to attend college; she then went on to university and gained a Bachelor of Arts Honours Degree in Art for Public Space in 2005. Angel felt that much contemporary art was aesthetically barren, and difficult for the general population to access and understand, and had always dreamed of manifesting images that would inspire and provoke the viewer to consider the higher functions in life – offering hope and encouragement to the world. She wanted to create art that uplifted the spirit, and spoke to the deeper being of humanity. We live in such difficult times that Angel feels that the only way we can change this world is by connecting with the deeper essence of all humanity. Many of her paintings are of angels, or incorporate angels within them, as they symbolise the very highest attainable good.

Angel also writes poetry, which is often inspired by the same events that inspire her to paint. Many are moved by these images and the poetry that accompanies them. Angel calls this work 'Etherealism'.

Angel now lives in South Yorkshire where she continues to create artwork to inspire and uplift. She is currently working on further projects which will bring these images even further into the public's awareness. Her aim is to touch the hearts of those who see it, and to encourage them to create the best lives possible for themselves and for their communities.

She believes that we are all one, that there is no such thing as separation and that it is our duty, as human beings, to make the best of ourselves, and encourage others to do the same. Please go to www.angels.me.uk for further information.

How Angels Can Help You and Your Old Soul Child

You and your child have probably experienced some angel signs already, maybe finding white feathers, which is a sign that they are near. On numerous occasions, I have asked the angels to send me proof that they were with me, and fluffy white feathers have drifted down in front of me on my walks with my dog, Max, and even when I am driving in my car. Feathers just float down from out of nowhere and I have found hundreds inside the house; I even found one in the bank before I went to see to the Bank Manager.

I am always finding angel feathers in the garden, in the car, in

my bag, and also in the strangest of places like
cupboard. When you find an angel feather, it's your a
of leaving their calling card behind, to let you know tha
with you. I am also finding five pence pieces on my trave , which
is another gift from the angels, telling me that abundant things
shall come my way.

If you start with baby steps in bringing angels into your life on
a daily basis, you can then move on to explore further.

Angels can provide constant divine guidance but due to our
own fears and doubts, we sometimes do not always receive the
messages. I believe, from my own experiences, that you do not
need to have special abilities to connect with the angelic realm, or
go into a deep meaningful meditation to experience a connection.
Every human being is fully capable of connecting and receiving
messages. Because of the free will, angels will help you when you
ask for help.

My experience in working with angels has allowed me to
understand that, as they get closer to working with our earthly
energies, angels are eager to help us in a range of mundane tasks.
The 'Car Parking Angel' is the best known of the angels that help
us find a parking space when we arrive at our destination. Angels
are always with us, and as we connect to the angelic realm, we
can anchor our own energy to helps us with our day to day living.

So, what Angels can you call upon to help you with everyday
things? I am currently writing another book, *The Angel Journeying
Workbook* and this can assist you in how you could make more use
of angels in your life. A useful starting point would be to list the
different angels that you can think of and just call on the name to
let them know that you want help. Please remember, when you
invoke angels, that the outcome will almost always be successful,
but they are catalysts and the journey to the outcome may not
always happen as you might have imagined it would. The more
you are able to detach yourself from the outcome (and this
something that you can never control), the freer you will become.

As you begin to create an environment that allows you to become more creative, true happiness will come from gaining a new perspective from what you really need in your life.

I teach this aspect in many angel workshops and students find it a great way to connect with angels without meditating. For some, meditation is a great way to alleviate stress, anxiety and enhance self esteem. Yet, others find it hard to meditate, and find this technique to be a great way of unwinding and really connecting with the angelic realm.

Cheryl

Cheryl, sixteen, wanted to say something to her tutor at college and did not how, because he was the type of person who just did not really listen to what his students were saying. In the angel workshop, she asked for help and called upon the Angel of Communications help her find the confidence to say that she was having difficulty in grasping the lessons, and for her tutor to listen to her. Monday morning came, and I got a telephone call from her at lunchtime, thanking me for introducing her to the angels. Her tutor finally listened to what she had to say, which resulted in her getting extra tuition.

When invoking the Angels, say your request three times out loud and give thanks for listening. Here are some examples to help you get started:

Invoke the Angel of Success to give you a blessing and to help you with your fear of success.

Invoke the Angel of Money to help you to manifest what you want and need.

Invoke the Angel of Healing to help you through a health crisis.

If you have a problem with money and you need a new car, invoke the Angels of Manifestation to get to work on it as powerfully as they can.

Ask Archangel Raphael, who is the Angel of Families, to help all the members of your family that you feel so deeply about and wish to be awakened and helped to a smoother path.

Ask Archangel Michael, who is a Protection Angel, to look after all the members of your family.

Ask the Angel of Loss and Bereavement to help you to come through your loss and to understand and deeply release.

Ask the Angel of Release to help you to let go of anything that may still be 'sticking' around you.

Ask the Angel of Courage to stand alongside you when you have to meet someone for the very first time.

When you have to go on a long journey in the car, ask the Angel of Travelling and the Angel of Clear Roads to assist you when you travel.

For Old Soul Children, childhood is not always easy; invoking the Angel of Delight will help them.

Open your heart to the angels, but never expect to be told exactly what is going on in your life, or what to do about it; in a sense, if they did this, your life would no longer be your own in the same way any more, would it?

Angels and Children

A guardian angel is born at the moment that the soul has decided to incarnate. The guardian angel stays with the being through birth, life, into death and back to the learning halls to valuate their life once again. Babies' eyesight for things in the material world is not very well developed when they are first born, but they can still feel and sense other worlds and their guardian angels.

When a child is about to be born, ask the child's guardian angel to be specially near to him/her and ask the family guardian angel to be near to them all, to bring the newborn safely into this world. When a newborn arrives, the whole family goes through a transition. This is only because the baby has arrived to take their place in the family, so a family needs to remember to emphasise their love for all the children as individuals and to focus on things that are special in each one of the children. Teach them, as much as you can, to celebrate difference instead of being in competition. Invoke the Angel of Transition to help the family unite as one.

I have often seen and wondered at babies staring at certain places away from our faces, smiling at nothing, or perhaps attempting to talk, so it could be possible that they are actually seeing someone (something) that we are not attuned to.

Babies and children see their guardian angels through their own loving eyes. I can remember placing Jade in her travel cot for a nap when she was twelve months old. I went to the kitchen to finish clearing up and after half an hour I heard Jade crying. I went flying into the lounge and stopped in mid-flight at the doorway. It was a strange experience because the clouds were grey outside and full of rain, and yet there was, what I would describe as, a beam of sunlight pouring threw the window. Jade had stopped crying and I stood watching from a distance. I heard Jade giggle and she was smiling a beautiful smile at this little beam of light. When I kept on watching, I saw that she was standing up with her little arms stretched out like she was asking someone to pick her up. When I stepped into the room I asked her who she was talking to and picked her up; she began to laugh and pointed towards the window.

Alice

Alice is five years old. She is a very bright child with a sunny disposition. Alice told me that the angels sing to her at night time to help go to sleep. When she is asleep and has bad dreams, the angels sing again to make the bad dreams go away. Alice tells me that the gold angels go to school with her and make everyone in the class be friends. An angel also sits on top of the car when her mum takes her brother and her to school.

George David Fryer

For most of his life, George David Fryer has worked as a commercial illustrator and taught illustration in further education colleges and Blackpool University. He also carried out children's book illustrations for encyclopaedias.

He felt drawn to spirit in early 1996 and went along to Manchester Metaphysical Society, to watch a demonstration about psychic art. While he was in the audience, he began to doodle faces on an envelope. A women looked over his shoulder and said, "That's my spirit guide." He also drew four of the six guides, which the demonstrator had drawn before she revealed them to the audience.

This moved him into working with spiritual energies for over eleven years. Since 1996, when George first had his experience with Godan, his spirit guide, he has been able to contact to the spirit world on a continual basis.

George draws spirit guides and channels readings from guides. The readings contain advice and wisdom to help people understand their life patterns and why they have created the life experiences that they have.

The guides reside on the higher planes of reality and they have a unique overview of you and what you have chosen to experience in this lifetime.

He has since been taught by many guides how to bring their love, wisdom and truth into the physical world, to help and assist souls in the fulfilment of their life quests. The guides that he brings through are usually of the next level of mastery and are here to help us move to a higher level of experience and understanding of life, so that we can connect more deeply to our true soul purpose.

He remembers his dad saying, when he was a child, "I love your drawing son, but you keep drawing these bloody faces! Can you draw anything else?"

George draws what he sees and gets a sense of what they are

and what they have come to tell us. George does not draw for many children but when he does, he draws what he sees and gets a sense that they are different energies. Mostly, they are undines, which are water spirits, and sylphs, which are air spirits. These nature spirits are explained further on in this chapter.

Children are open to them all the time and nature spirits are not fearful of children; they want to be mischievous, naughty and make you giggle and yet they show themselves only when appropriate. George could see spirits around children but wasn't allowed to draw them for many years. Now he is allowed to and has drawn over a dozen portraits for children, but he isn't allowed to give them a reading.

George was working at a Mind Body Spirit Fayre in Ilkey and created a picture for a young woman, who had her daughter, Ellie, with her. After he completed the drawing, Ellie wanted one too and would not stop asking until her request was granted. George began drawing the hair, which felt like it was water. As George began to draw, her got the name 'Elspeth' and wrote it down. Ellie was adamant that George was drawing her, but her mother told her that he was drawing her guide. However, Ellie still insisted that George was drawing her. George explained that he was drawing Ellie's true essence, which the mother simply did not understand. He also drew a waterfall in the picture and Ellie's mother told him that she loved and was fascinated by waterfalls. On leaving, George was told that Ellie's real name was, in fact, Elspeth.

Sylphs and Undines are showing themselves to us all but because children are still more tuned into these subtle realms, they see them more than adults do.

Adults often use their minds to objectify and quantify their experiences, based on what they have been taught through logic, whereas children just express what they see and experience until they lose this ability. This is usually because the adults around them dismiss their accounts and call them mistaken or even foolish. The child then starts to believe that their parents know more than they do and start to see from their parent's mental, logical level, thus, losing some of their natural intuitive abilities.

Undines

Undines or ondines are water elementals and are etheric in nature. They have appeared in British Folklore, the Middle East, Indonesia, Germany and other European countries. In eighteenth century Scotland, they were referred to as the wraiths of water. Derived from the Greek figures, known as Nereids, attendants of the sea god Poseidon, they were originally recorded in the Aegean Sea, off the coast of Greece.

Paracelsus first mentioned Undines in his writings. He put forth his theory that these spirits inhabit and exist within water. Necksa is their ruler, who they love, serve and honour unceasingly.

Undines inhabit waterfalls, ponds, seas, lakes and rivers and coral caves. They can also be found in fountains, marshlands and underneath lily pads. They are able to control the course and motion of water, as well as the tides, and care for plants above and below the water.

Human in appearance and size, they are beautiful, emotional, and graceful beings who dress themselves in a shimmery substance looking like water, with the colours of their surroundings being predominant in their appearance.

They can be seductive and can take the shape of beautiful maidens. They were also said to be able to gain a soul by marrying a human and bearing his child. Undines are emotional, very friendly and love to help humans. However, they possess a strong influence upon your own emotional well being, and great care must be taken when working with them.

Undines work with you to honour your own truths, help you understand love and bonding, and experience loyalty. They have intense healing energies that you can tap into, which help you to understand your own emotions and aid work with your heart chakra.

They show themselves to children and help them to become sympathetic and more loving. Undines are helpful in matters dealing with emotional issues, such as love, friendship and having fun, especially when the children are swimming in the sea, as they will ride the waves with them and support them if they are not strong swimmers.

In German mythology, Undine was a beautiful, immortal. Yet, if she fell in love with a human and carried his child and he fell in love with another mortal, she would lose her gift of everlasting life. Undine did, in fact, fall in love with Sir Angus; they exchanged vows and he pledged his love and faithfulness to her. A year into their marriage she gave birth to Sir Angus' son and then began to age. Undine's beauty began to diminish and Sir Angus began to lose interest in her. One day, late in the afternoon, Undine was walking by the stables when she heard her husband snoring. As she entered the stable, she found Sir Angus lying in the arms of another woman. Undine pointed her finger at Sir Angus and rattled off her curse: "You swore faithfulness to me with every waking breath, and I accepted your oath. So be it. As long as you are awake, you shall have your breath, but should you ever fall asleep, then that breath will be taken from you and you will die!"

In 1962, Severinghaus and Mitchell coined the term 'Ondine's Curse' to describe an inability to have spontaneous breathing during sleep states.

My Encounter with Undines

It was September 2007, and the whole family picked up the boat from Holyhead, which was heading for Dun Leaoghire, Ireland. Eric and the children went to explore the boat on crossing and sat down to watch a film. I really needed some fresh air to wake me up and since getting up at 1am to travel, it was starting to really get to me.

I made my way to the back of the boat, where the smokers were puffing away and fighting against the high winds. As I watched the waves at the back of the boat, I began to notice faces in the seas and I thought that I was seeing things because the tiredness in my body was taking over. My first reaction was that someone had fallen into the Irish Sea and panic filled me. I stood with my back against the boat and closed my eyes and opened them again. When I looked out into the sea, there was no one there.

I breathed a sigh of relief and walked towards the mental railings that were surrounding the back of the boat. I could smell the sea air and the spray began to wash my face. As I looked again, I saw faces bobbing up and down in the sea, and they were riding the waves from the boat, as it sped towards Ireland. It was amazing to watch, and I really did think that I was seeing things and had to take a double take. However, I was in no doubt when I looked back. These magical creatures, who were white, were swimming up and down, around the back of the boat, blending into the sea. I sensed that they were female, although they were not mermaids. They had long hair that covered their middles and were very beautiful to look at. I thought that they could have been sirens, but I can remember my Irish grandfather telling me that sirens were the ones who called sailors and fisherman to their death by singing and calling out their names.

We both knew that we could see each other, yet they were not miffed by me. There were several, blending perfectly into their watery surroundings as the boat glided across the water, yet only one was brave enough to swim higher and higher. Even as I write about them, I'm still in awe about what I experienced and find it incredibly powerful to write about them.

On arriving at our holiday home, we all sat and watched television before going to bed. Just as I was going to switch it off, an advertisement caught my eye and I had to watch it. It was of a white being blending into his environment and being at one with nature. This was the confirmation that I needed to understand that what I had seen earlier on that day was, in fact, real and that I was not hallucinating because of the tiredness.

Sylphs

Sylphs, which are also known as Sylphids, were described by Paracelsus as invisible beings of air. The word 'Sylph' comes from Greek word 'silphe', which means butterfly or moth. Sylphs are known to be the winged protectors of the Garden of Eden and become visible to those without clairvoyant abilities. They were first named by the Rosicrucians and Cabalists in their folklore.

Sylphs are highly-evolved etheric beings that are small, winged, transparent, light creatures that float in the air for long periods of time. They are very beautiful beings that have huge, feathered wings sprouting from their backs, large eyes and sharp, angular faces. They never seem to get old as they live for hundreds of years.

The winds are their vehicle to work, as they manage the worlds air. Riding the currents of the wind, they race on storm clouds, and call in the soft breezes of day, yet they are loners and will fly with the birds. Content to soar the skies with the eagles, they are very regal in manner and are timid and flighty, only associating with their own kind and defending their homes. When it is a truly windy day, you can hear their voices in the winds.

When Buddhism was just beginning to take hold in Ancient China, Taoism held teachings that Sylphs were elementals that could help highly advanced practitioners who had awakened their consciousness. Sylphs have also been mentioned in China's early histories in various literatures. For example, William Shakespeare, in *A Midsummer Night's Dream*, refers to a slender girl as a 'Sylph'. They have also been associated with one of the world's oldest romantic ballets, *La Sylphide*.

My children and I often lay on the grass and 'cloud watch'. High up in the skies, the clouds move at a rapid rate, and you witness how many shapes and objects the Sylphs have created. They are truly artists, creating wispy, think and thin clouds with their trail, which almost look like feathers in the sky.

One day, when my children and I were at the park and did our usual cloud watching, we saw a long trail that turned into a series of dashes that were equally-spaced. It really looked bizarre. I went back to throwing the ball for our dog Max and when we all checked again, a few minutes later, the whole trail was now gone.

They care very little for the other fairy folk and do not interfere with the grand order of things. However, sylphs form bonds with children that last for lifetimes and inspire them to be creative, free spirits – like themselves. Their function is to inspire children and in return, they receive inspiration and are drawn to them because of their creativity, especially with those who are interested in the arts. Children's minds are also why sylphs are drawn to them because they are deep thinkers with a connection to the fairy kingdom, but they pose no threat to them.

When they show themselves to adults, it is to help them to find a deeper fulfilment and meaning in their own lives. Sometimes it can be very intense, as humans want answers without looking within. The first step is recognition of their presence and then asking what is needed for you to understand how they can help you and how you can work together.

The Fairy Kingdom

When Jade and Amba used to take the school bus in the morning, we were able to take time to be aware of nature, the elemental, nature spirits and the flower fairies; this helped them to combine the spiritual element of themselves with everyday issues, without having any fears of being ridiculed.

Fairies, pixies and elves, also known as 'the little people', have been part of our culture for centuries and come from a place where magic really does exist; where wishes are granted, but please be prepared for mischief! Fairies are not just confined to the bottom of your garden.

The stories that we heard as small children were usually folktales and fairy stories – tales that our parents and their parents heard when they were young, passed down through the generations.

Folktales were stories of hopes and dreams, of encounters with giants, wicked witches and goblins that inflict chaos. However, we also must not forget the kind fairies and dragons that restored peace and order.

These stories are often our first experience of life's changing patterns and through them we begin to know good from evil, kindness from cruelty, and the difference between ambition and despair.

William Shakespeare used the enchantment of fairies in *A Midsummer Night's Dream* with the characters Oberon, Titania and Puck taking centre stage. Chaucer mentioned that the United Kingdom was occupied with fairies before the time of King Arthur, so with those teaspoons and socks that keep going missing, could this mean that a house fairy has moved into your home?

Fairy lore is older than Christianity. The term 'fairy' comes from the Latin word 'fata', or 'fate', which refers to the fates of mythology. 'Fairy' originally meant 'fae-erie', or a state of enchantment. The word 'fairy' came into usage in medieval times and was often used to refer to women who had magical powers.

Fairies occupy a middle realm between earth and the heavenly spiritual planes, and are associated with the concerns of earth.

Our psychic abilities in childhood are more perceptive to the invisible kingdoms of where these little people come from. Children have no boundaries, yet question every thing that happens to them and take it in their stride. The little people are very aware of adult human hidden agendas (e.g. greed) and so children are the perfect solution to appearing without feeling threatened.

Angels appear to mankind to help with human evolution, as well as providing consolation in the heart of our dilemmas. The fairies are appealing to us to help Mother Nature restore her natural beauty before major concerns rear their ugly heads in the environment that we live in. With regards to the whole nature cycle, it seems that mankind is not really seeing the bigger picture of what it is really creating. For example, building on flood plains for cheaper housing and extinguishing the earth's minerals to heat our homes, which is causing more harm than good. Perhaps in time, when maybe it's too late, mankind will see that it is really creating dis-harmony rather harmony with its own environment. I feel that I am one of the lucky ones that the little people have shown themselves to me to help them to restore the environmental needs and I would like to this opportunity to introduce you to them:

It was my grandfather who first told me tales of the little people as a child; this was my introduction to the fairy realm. He would weave his magic as we sat by the open fire, leaving us spellbound as he told us tales of the leprechauns of Ireland, who would help people in need and play tricks on those that were full of gluttony.

Many years later, when I had my own family, I was re-introduced to the fairy realm by my two magical daughters, Jade and Amba.

We were on holiday in Great Yarmouth, Norfolk and one morning I awoke to a fairy sitting on the end of my nose with her arms crossed and looking at me very angrily. The beautiful green being, with gossamer wings, introduced herself to me as Thistle and told me that they needed me to work with their kind because human folk were destroying their worlds. Thistle went on to explain that by introducing children to fairies, the environment, in years to come, had a better chance of surviving.

So, what better way for my girls, Jade and Amba, to learn about the countryside? But, little did I know, that they knew more than me!

Amba, who was then five, would explain that the fairies can be naughty, especially the red and blue ones, because they tickle her when she is asleep. However, the sliver fairies are the best because she dreams about them all the time and the gold fairies help her find money in the street for sweets.

Jade, at the time, was seven, and was totally devastated when her godmother told her that there is no such thing as fairies. With her hands on her hips, Jade replied, "You need fairy dust to believe and then you will see one," and marched off to her bedroom. At that age, Jade always told her friends at school that you need to put the rubbish in the bin, because the fairies will not like it in their home. She also told them to be kind to the countryside, because we need to look after the environment.

She still tells people off when they try and put their rubbish out of the car window. "How would you like it, if I put rubbish in your garden?" she would say. "The fairies don't like it, so please do not do it."

On another occasion, I can remember being awoken by my husband's snoring. He was fast asleep, oblivious that he had woken me up. On awakening, I noticed a fairy asleep by his side, dressed in white, unaware that Eric was snoring. So, I tiptoed out of the bedroom, in order not to wake them both.

From my experiences in connecting with the fairy realm, I decided to help other children throughout the UK to connect with their own fairies. I truly believe that fairies can help children learn about nature and the environment that we live in. Children have always had special relationships with the fairies and for that reason will love these parties. Parents and other adults can also have fun participating within these parties and these workshops can show everyone how to connect.

Most people have heard of flower fairies, but have most people heard about household and garden fairies? Fairy parties will show children, teenagers and adults how to connect with the fairy realm. Once these fairies enter your life they can show you the beauty of their worlds.

In the workshops, I teach the children and their parents how to recognise fairy messages in their dreams, how to call upon them for assistance and how to unearth the truths hidden within fairy tales and folklore. We also teach the children about 'The Countryside Code'. I tell the children that the fairies would like us to take this into consideration when they go to the countryside with their families and that they must be safe, plan ahead, follow any signs, leave gates and property as they find them, protect plants and animals, take their litter home, keep dogs under close control and also consider other people.

There are many inspiring stories that I tell the children and their parents. One that seems very popular is that they can invite the fairies into their own garden at home and they can help look after the plants and vegetables. I have completed this task many times with my own girls and found results amazing; plants flourish and vegetables grow at an amazing rate, and the crop that we receive is magical because it also teaches the children how things grow when you look after them. It also teaches children that there is magic in the simple things of life and that magic can help things to grow.

These workshops really help children and their parents to learn about nature in a fun and magical way, whilst also looking after the environment that they live in. Hundreds of fairies work and play in every garden, wood and meadow, caring for flowers and trees. They only reveal themselves to those who believe in them. So, leave your disbelief behind, and prepare to enter the secret world of the Fairies.

It is truly amazing how many people come up to me, young and old, and confess that they still believe in fairies, do you?

Peter

Peter was three when he was very much into his imaginary friends, a couple of years ago. He had a zebra who went everywhere with his family, in Cardiff, South Wales, and had to be included in all games. There was also Dot and the fairies. Dot seemed to be just the light reflection from a watch and the fairies just dust in the sunlight. However, could it be – because Wales, like Ireland, is abundant with fairy folk – that Peter was seeing much more?

Peter seemed very convinced by his playmates until they went shopping for food. His mum asked if there was anything else that they needed, such as food for Zebra. Peter put his hands on his hips, looked at her exasperatedly and said, "Don't be silly, Mummy. He's a pretend zebra. He only eats pretend food." That told his mum!

Susan Bevan

Susan Bevan had seen my advert in Cygnus magazine and decided to respond with this poem, which is based on a true experience:

The Pearl Flower

I had an invisible friend who was a dancer
She loves to try any dance and was a Prancer
She loved folk dancing at a country fair
She did aerobics on the floor or with a chair
If she danced a ballet she jumped graciously in the air
Other times she did magic tricks with her hair.

Everyone called her a figment of my imagination
She told me in a song she would prove them wrong
She claimed she was my spiritual guide
The following night she danced a ballet in my dream
Her dress was turquoise and cream
First she danced with a small team
Then danced on her own by a small stream.

She used to wear a silver chain
It had a delicate pearl flower pendant
She danced near a white stone
And quietly placed her necklace under it
Once everyone was gone and we were alone.

The next day I had to travel away
Everyone was amused by my tale
The constant walking made me weary
I looked for a good place to rest
An area with a stream and stone was best.

Then I recognised the lovely place
It had such tranquillity and space
Under the stone was her pearl flower
It glittered after a quick shower
It's elegance gave it charm and power.

Faerie Rings

Faeries dance in circles and leave behind faerie rings, which are
dangerous to humans who mistakenly tread within them. A circle
of mushrooms most often marks a faerie circle. If you become
stuck in a faerie ring make sure you have fairy cake in your
pocket, as this is the only bargaining tool that can get you out of
the fairy ring in one piece.

How to Attract More Fairies in Your Garden

The fairies tell me that in nature, gardens are actually wild. It is only us humans that come along with a lawn mower to have the perfect lawn and flowerbeds, so encourage a wild garden in your own garden and let the fairies work their magic. Plant a rowen tree in your garden or plant an area of your garden with an assortment of wild flowers and let them do their own thing each year, so that fairies can come freely.

Here is a list of flowers that will help you to invite the fairies into your garden: Bluebells, Roses, Thyme, Primroses, Daylilies, Cleomes, Coleus, Gaillardias, Cosmos, Impatiens, Oenothera, New Guinea Impatiens, Obedient Plant, Coreopsis, Butterfly Weed, Verbena, Celosia, Columbine and Zinnias.

In addition, place rose quartz crystals in your flowerbeds, as fairies adore crystals. The crystals help a fairy to recharge their energies once they are asleep between the fallen leaves, grass and flowers; it also makes them feel safe and comfortable.

Water features also attract fairies into your garden, as the sound of running water soothes away their worries of how the environment is changing on a daily basis.

How to See a Fairy

You simply have to believe! Have an open mind, open heart and if you find yourself laughing at everything then the fairies are around you, as they just adore laughter. Ask the fairies to sprinkle some fairy dust over you before you go to sleep and wait and see what unfolds – you'll be surprised!

So do you still believe in the little people? I do!

Chapter Four

Raising your Old Soul Child

Live out of your imagination, not your history.
Stephen Covey

How Reiki can help your Old Soul Child, 'Emotional
Intelligence', Flower Essences, Aromatherapy,
Homeopathy, Other things that may be of use to you,
Weleda, Steiner Education, Baby Mozart, Affirmations,
What foods are best for your Old Soul Child.

Reiki

For those who do not know what Reiki
(pronounced 'ray-key') is, it is an ancient energy
healing system, which channels natural healing
energy through the gentle placing of hands. Reiki
energy flows through the Reiki practitioner and is
drawn into the receiver, bringing a unique state of
deep relaxation, a feeling of peace, well being and
spiritual growth.

Reiki is a Japanese word. 'Rei' means 'universal wisdom' and
'Ki' means 'life energy'. Reiki is, therefore, vital life energy
guided by universal wisdom.

Reiki is also a powerful tool for physical, mental, emotional,
spiritual healing and balancing, whilst greatly enhancing
personal growth. The 'Ki' energy is the vital flowing life force
contained in all life. It is a whole and complete, unlimited energy.
All that is needed to receive the Reiki energy is the desire to
receive it.

Reiki can be used to treat anything on any level and is an effective method of maintaining a balanced well being. As Reiki is universal and is not connected to any religion or belief system, it embraces and enhances the 'all' and is constructive in bringing about a greater awareness of self. Reiki can help to bring a clearer understanding and in giving clearer direction.

Most cultures and religions have a term which corresponds to 'Ki', as listed below:

Chi	Chinese
Light or Holy Ghost	Christians
Prana	Hindu and Yoga
Mana	The Kahunas of Hawaii
Jesod	Jewish Cabalists
Wakan	Sioux

You do not have to believe in God or an equivalent to be able to practice Reiki. Reiki works on the unconditional love principle and is channelled as opposed to given. Therefore, Reiki is directed to where it is needed by the recipient.

When you are attuned to Reiki energy, your channels are opened to universal life force energy. Reiki attunements are much like tuning a radio to a desired station. The attunements that you will receive, tune you into Reiki energy so you can channel it for yourself or others at any time, for the rest of your life.

All of us have universal life force energy, essential for health and life. We all have some amount of healing energy coming from our hands and that energy is directed by intention and taken exactly where it is needed.

Reiki, for me, is a journey of spiritual self-discovery, in more ways than one. As I am interested in energy healing, I was lucky enough to train as a Reiki Master, Karuna Reiki Master and Sekhem Master Teacher. I use Reiki, Karuna Reiki and Sekhem everyday in bringing up my three spiritually aware children.

I first introduced Reiki to Jade, Amba and Leo when I was pregnant; I did daily treatments throughout the nine months to connect with my unborn children. Then, using my intuition, I attuned them to Reiki when they where still in the womb. So, you could say that my children are natural born Reiki Masters.

During the Reiki attunement process, the Reiki symbols are used to permanently restructure aspects of your energy bodies to:

Allow you access to a reservoir of Reiki energy set up by Reiki Masters of the past.
Increase the flow of life force energy through your energy body.
Access a consciousness factor that connects to the symbols.
Implant the symbols for the rest of your life.

As parents, we always want the best for our children and go to great lengths just to achieve that. Raising spiritually aware children can sometimes be very challenging, as they question everything around them and strongly assert their point of view. This can sometimes leave you flummoxed as to where you go from here.

I can remember my early days and I was not a confident child. For my children, I wanted to make certain that they felt self-assured in what they set out to achieve. Empowering them to always feel balanced and grounded, and reassuring them that they could come and talk to us about anything that troubled them was very important to my husband and I.

I wanted my children to be able to help themselves when they are hurt, feel sad or even afraid. Feeling that they are always safe and protected with Reiki would empower them to live life to the fullest. It would also act as a self-empowerment tool that would always serve them throughout their lives.

Children are still so much in touch with all that there is between heaven and earth that they pick up on energies quite naturally.

Some would argue that I should have waited until they were old enough to understand, so that they had a choice in whether they wished to be attuned, claiming that I have taken away the children's free will. But, I do not feel that this is the case. Before we re-enter each lifetime, our soul lessons are agreed sometimes with many different souls to be aware of our experiences. As souls, we come into this life to experience certain opportunities for growth and soul lessons. I believe that, as a family, our soul contract was decided to incorporate Reiki in our everyday lives.

I really do sense that they gave me their permission for initiation to Reiki whilst in the womb, so it will always play a part in their lives.

Reiki Principles

Dr Mikao Usui, the founder of Reiki, developed the five principles of Reiki which are listed below. Dr Usui created these because he wanted his students to become a clear channel of Reiki and considered that, if these were recited in the beginning and end of each day, it would bring about happiness into their lives and bring life more in sync with the universal source of light, love and harmony, that is Reiki. It is also my understanding that he wanted these principles to be a way of life:

Just for today, do not worry.
Just for today, do not anger.
Honour your parents, teachers and elders.
Earn your living honestly.
Show gratitude to everything.

You will find many variations of these on the internet and in many books about Reiki. I really do feel that selecting one you feel drawn to is always a deeply personal and individual experience.

I have found that adopting the Reiki principals and entwining them into my children's upbringing, has helped us, as family and as individuals, to strive and find our greatest assets.

With regards to 'Just for today', this means living in the moment, as the past has gone and the future will never actually arrive. The Reiki principles can also be used as affirmations. I will be honest with you, they do look really easy but when you get into living your life by them, they are very challenging and also rewarding at the same time.

Just for Today, Do Not Worry

If my children do not feel comfortable with something that is disconcerting them (for example, being bullied at school), we sit down together and talk about what is troubling them. We also discuss the best way forward in dealing with the bullying. Worry is a usual response when we are unsure what to do for the best and can cause a lot of unnecessary stress. To be able to let go of the past and what might happen in the future, you must do your best for today, and live in the here and now.

Just for Today, Do Not Anger

We can all feel angry and agitated and get caught up in the drama of the day and forget about the peace with ones' self. We can also be hard on ourselves at every given moment for not being at our best and then worry when we suffer major setbacks. Holding onto it can manifest itself in other dramatic ways. My children know that if they feel angry or someone is angry towards them, it is best for them to speak about this emotion, instead of holding onto negative thoughts, which make them feel unhappy. We have chosen, as a family, to learn to deal with this emotion in a constructive way, rather than having the anger being mirrored to us. By using meditation, we can also learn where our feelings of anger come from. You can use this Reiki principle as a manta every day to help generate a better understanding of yourself.

Honour Your Parents, Teachers and Elders

We choose our parents, teachers and elders before we born and they help us to grow spiritually, once we are on earth. As people come into our lives, each one offers messages and lessons for us to learn. I am a great believer in that 'what goes around, comes around'. If you honour your parents, teachers and elders, it will be returned.

Earn Your Living Honestly

Do you meet people in your life that are takers and givers? Do you wish that you could break the cycle that you are always are the one giving? When we live life honestly, we are facing our own truths in all matters and can live in harmony and find life is much easier. We have chosen our path in accordance to what lessons are required by our soul.

Show Gratitude to Everything

When we are comfortable in our lives, we tend to take everything for granted, especially when it has been a busy day and it seems that there are not enough hours in the day. If we begin to send out a signal that we are living in poverty, we then become a magnet and attract that type of interaction in to our life. What we fear is usually what we attract into our lives. When we show gratitude, we experience a great unity with everything and then attract abundant things. We are all part of the universal life force and if we fully trust in this, believe that we are looked after and remember to give thanks; many blessings will come into our lives.

Teaching our children from a young age the five Reiki principles can provide them with life enhancing ways to deal with things such as stressful situations. When said often, the children, from early on in their lives, have the effect of transforming the mind away from the ego-based fear, anger and worry. As a result, they have a greater focus on their soul path mission and have gratitude and compassion to all.

Most Reiki students then begin to see a pattern. As adults, we are habitual in our reactions to things and these reactions are based on the ego and its conditionings.

When the principals are practiced more and more, they begin to become a part of our consciousness, and then, when something adverse happens, we may still react in the same way, but during conflicts, we start to remember the principles and begin to stop the reaction earlier and earlier in the cycle. It does take time to break free of that conditioning; yet, responding to a situation in kindness will have much more effect on others you come into contact with. This really is the basis of how the principles can work in your lifestyle.

For those who are Reiki practitioners and Reiki masters, I would recommend that you could meditate on one Reiki principal each day before doing your Reiki healing or self healing. From this, you will find more understanding of the Reiki energy.

Growing up with Reiki creates a greater world for children to reside in. I am finding that, by doing it this way, they will learn to love and respect for themselves, the people they come into contact with and the environment that they live in.

My three children can do Reiki anytime, anywhere. For example, when they watch television, they are giving each other a very effective Reiki session. Or even when they are reading a book quietly on there own, they can do a self-treatment. Jade and Amba like to give Reiki to their dad when he has a headache. My husband states that their energy is, at all times, strong, even when they move their hands to different positions. Jade and Amba always feel the Reiki energy leaving their hands as a tingling sensation.

Amba likes to give Reiki to our cats, Kassie, Bracken, Salem and Murphy. They all just purr away with contentment. Our dog, Max, just falls asleep every time they perform Reiki, and Max does demand regular Reiki treatments. We have also noticed that trips to the vets have been reduced as well.

As a family, we like to spend a lot of time in our garden. When Jade, Amba and I plant bulbs for spring, the girls place their hands around each bulb and they ask the bulbs if they would like some Reiki to help them grow year after year.

We also grow our own vegetables from seeds and when we plant them into the ground, Jade and Amba ask Mother Nature to look after the seeds and perform Reiki to help the seeds grow into healthy vegetables. Jade and Amba also like to water the vegetables and watch the changes in them on a weekly basis.

As we spend a lot of time in the garden and I am always bringing in new plants home. Each new plant, tree and shrub gets a full Reiki treatment before entering of the thriving plants. In 2008, the plan is to grow a herb garden and we are all very excited as to what we can grow.

In the Playground - In Jade's Words

"When my best friend Georgina fell over in the playground, she hurt herself. Her knee was bleeding and I put my hand over Georgina's knee and she stopped crying. I said that I was doing Reiki and Georgina asked what Reiki was. I told her that Reiki helps people to feel better when they are sad. Georgina said that she felt heat and warmth from my hands and that her knee stopped bleeding. Georgina told a few friends from our class that I was doing Reiki. They then pretended to do Reiki themselves on each other."

Jade and Amba do Reiki on themselves before they do their homework. When they feel unsure of a new project at school, they place their hands on their hearts to give them courage and confidence to move forward without fear, so they can accomplish the task to their best ability.

Jade tells me that she feels the heat from her hands when she places them on her school friend's back and her friend stops crying. As a family, my husband (who is not attuned) feels that Reiki does benefit family life.

In the Classroom - In Amba's Words

"My best friend is called Jack. Jack comes to school in a wheelchair and I like to help him whenever I can. I place my hand on Jack's back so that the Reiki can help him learn. Reiki also helps Jack to stay at school all day so that he can play with us at playtime. When Jack is sad, I like to give him a Reiki hug to make him feel better."

I love the school holidays. It's a chance to put routine to one side and explore the United Kingdom in our caravan, as well as spending quality time with my children.

We often visit zoos, aquariums and butterfly parks, as we know that animals enjoy Reiki.

It seems that when we visit these places, the animal residents enjoy the children's company. Simply patting, stroking and touching the animals draws them to experience Reiki and they will not leave the children's side or even go to anyone else.

On a regular basis, Jade and Amba like to go horse riding. Before they start their ride they like to stroke the ponies head. When they are sitting on their ponies they like to give their ponies a Reiki hug at the start of the lesson. At the end of the lesson they give their ponies another Reiki hug and also a Reiki pat and say thank you to their ponies for their time.

Jade likes to do Reiki on her guinea pig, Poppy. Jade informs me that, when she is giving Reiki to Poppy, she squeaks and squawks in a happy way.

Amba likes to give herself Reiki when she is learning her spellings. Amba says that when she cannot sleep at night she will give one of her favourite toys Reiki. Amba then cuddles her toy, which helps her go to sleep.

Amba also likes to help me bake cakes, biscuits and also family meals. When Amba is putting the ingredients together and mixing them with a spoon, she tells us that the special ingredient goes in last, which is Reiki, to make us feel better when we are eating them.

Leo is still learning about this wonderful energy for himself and likes to watch and copy his big sisters. Rocket, his rabbit, gets Reiki everyday after he has fed him his carrots. Leo comments on how his hands get warm when he is doing it and that Rocket likes it.

The nature of the Reiki energy is intuitive; there is no right or wrong way of using the energy; it can do no harm and flows where it needs to go. Many people try to save the world in some attempt to save themselves and set themselves complicated set of rules and beliefs; that really is not what Reiki is about. Instead of tying ourselves up in spiritual knots, we need to simply 'be' Reiki, and 'do' Reiki, let go of what we cling to about it and be free of concepts and beliefs.

To give you a clear example, a group of blindfolded children at a party, playing 'Pin the tail on the donkey' are responding to what is in that moment. They do not worry about where the tail might end up. At that moment in time, they simply 'be' their natural selves no matter what the outcome may be. They have trust in themselves and the universe.

Reiki Symbols

With regards to your Old Soul Children using the Reiki Symbols, I would go with your intuition as to when you would want to introduce them. The Reiki Symbols do not contain power on their own, but when empowered by the individual, they can be used as tools to help us direct energy.

The symbols of Reiki are transcendental in nature and will change the way the Reiki energy is working. All you have to do is think of the symbols, visualise them or draw them and they automatically affect the energy – like putting a key in a lock.

Before my children go to school, horse riding or even to a party, I visualise the power symbol surrounding them for extra protection. When they are feeling low, or unwell, I tend to use the mental/emotional symbol to help them with their own inner healing. When Jade was being bullied, this symbol helped her feelings and helped us to heal as a family. The symbol can help in relationships, with family members and your friends, and can work for the highest good for everyone.

I would like to make it very clear that my husband and I do not force the children to do Reiki. To be honest with you, Jade and Amba use their intuition in finding new ways to use Reiki to help with family life, their friends and themselves.

Emotional Intelligence

Psychologist, Daniel Goleman, achieved worldwide recognition in 1995 when he wrote the international best seller, *Emotional Intelligence* (Bantam Books).

EI, as it is known today, is having the ability to understand and be aware of your emotions, the emotions of others and your ability to act or behave based on this understanding.

The characteristics of an emotionally intelligent person are that they can monitor their own and other's feelings and emotions, they can tell the difference between them, and use this information to guide their thinking and actions.

In the workplace, individuals high on emotional intelligence will be happier in their roles, perform their jobs more effectively, and lead and motivate others in an effective manner.

I often met and worked with people that have a high IQ and collect degrees for something to do. Yet, their emotional intelligence is very low, and they do not know how to encompass other feelings, especially when someone cries or is a very emotional person. Their response to the emotion is to make it about them, read the signs wrong and then react in anger to the situation. Receiving a negative comment produces a non-desirable outcome and we do not do well in response to it.

The Key Features of Emotional Intelligence

Awareness of your own emotions by having a well-developed

emotional vocabulary and from experience of being able to say how you are feeling.

Managing your own emotions by creating and maintaining positive emotions for yourself. When you are feeling angry, sadness, hurt, rejection, boredom, anxiety, you know how to handle the situation without resorting to behaviour that is harmful to you and others.

Motivating yourself by setting goals, learning to identify what you do best and challenging yourself to do better.

Recognising emotions in others and being able recognise the situation and the feelings from another person's perspective.

Handling relationships effectively. Creating positive interactions with others and managing conflict well.

Emotional intelligence tools can be used with Old Soul Children to assess their personal strengths. Their own emotional intelligence will change from time to time and it will help them identify areas that require more focus. It will also help them to improve their awareness and understanding of their own emotions, and communicate more effectively with others.

Emotional intelligence contains four key elements: self-awareness, self-management, social awareness and relationship management. It can be used as an essential part of bringing up your Old Soul Child, as they learn from us, as parents, about emotions and how to display them. If it was used in schools, especially between the ages of three and ten, and carried on in teenage years, it would save years of heartache and anguish for so many children.

Emotional intelligence, taught to teenagers, would help with leadership skills. Instead of having children that are depressed, despondent and becoming more violent, why not teach children more about anger management? This would enable them to find resolution in conflicts, reduce violence, crime and the 'hoody culture' that is growing day by day in the United Kingdom.

This new idea of EI should be adapted in the coming years in the education system, in this country, to enhance the emotional aptitudes and helping young people to understand the strengths and limitations of their emotional intelligence, and also ways to improve it.

Good Mental Health should be flowing in every child, which also acts as a great contributor to having emotional intelligence. My nan, Phyll, would tell me when I was feeling really despondent, that "the impossible is always possible"; that saying has stayed with me all my life. It would kick-start new ideas again and get the adrenalin flowing.

Old Soul children have great empathy, which enables them to have insight into other lives and of their own, and have a great connection with family and friends. They take their time listening to others and making sure everyone's needs are met, including their own.

The author suggests five competencies in which we can manage ourselves and can really help our Old Soul Children:

Self awareness – emotional awareness, self-assessment and self-confidence.
Self regulation – self-control, trustworthiness, adaptability and innovation.
Motivation – ambition, commitment, initiative and optimism.
Empathy – understanding others, developing others, service oriented and political awareness.
Social skills – influence, conflict management, leadership, catalyst, building bonds, collaboration, cooperation and Teamwork.

Old Soul Children still have plenty of room for emotional growth. They can continue to be introspective as they grow up, if we can continue to communicate with them and encourage them to work on their goals.

Emotional intelligence never stops growing. We are always

evolving as people, and emotional intelligence is something that must be nurtured. If it is not cultivated, it will disappear.

Flower Essences

Australian Aborigines and Egyptians used flower essences to bring about emotional balance; this was also very popular in the middle ages.

Hildegard Von Bingen (1098-1179) was a composer of music, author and mystic, and used the medicinal qualities of plants, animals, trees and stones. She had a sickly childhood, experienced visions from the age of three, and soon realized she had a unique ability. However, she hid her gift for many years. She wrote about how she collected dew from flowering plants to treat health imbalances and continued to receive heavenly visions.

Paracelsus (1493 -1541) was a Swiss doctor, alchemist and practicing astrologer. He collected dew from flowering plants and diluted it to treat his patient's emotional states. He believed that good health came from having physical, emotional, spiritual and mental harmony, which were the four elements that needed to be balanced to heal the soul. A true Alchemist, he believed in natural healing of the magical world he lived in and, as a doctor, he did not go along with conventional treatment of wounds, rejecting Gnostic traditions. Astrology played an important part in his medicine, and he truly believed that when you treat emotional imbalances, the disease and physical conditions are cured.

Flower essences are powerful and deep-acting healers needed for Old Soul Children living in the 21st Century, to help them adjust to the fast pace of their life on earth. Flower essences can help with the constant change in their lives and also enable them to stabilise easier. In addition, they help develop self awareness and responsibility for life's lessons and challenges. This simple and natural method of healing, by means of using wild flowers containing the energies of nature, works well on their energetic fields – balancing and strengthening subtle bodies. If we strengthen these qualities in our children, we allow them the opportunity to move forward in life.

I use flower essences regularly on my children, as I always treat any situation, illness or accident holistically. It is a safe and simple process and any flower essence will enable your Old Soul Child to have courage and strength, and develop inner love and self esteem. They also stimulate creativity and enable them to have fun in all their activities.

These remedies are a tool, but they are particularly good for children. Children are sensitive and open to the subtleties of the remedies, so they really can work magic. I always say that it is important to be open and the right solution will come to mind.

I use Bach Flower Remedies, Australian Bush Essences and Findhorn Essences and have narrowed down what will be useful for your own Old Soul Child. Please note: flower essences should not take the place of emergency medical treatment. With serious conditions or situations requiring medical attention, a doctor should be notified immediately.

Bach Flower Remedies

The Bach Flower Remedies were developed by Dr. Edward Bach, who practiced for over twenty years as a prominent consultant, homeopath and bacteriologist in London. Dr. Bach gave up his lucrative Harley Street practice in 1930 and moved to the English countryside. There, he spent the remaining years of his life developing his thirty-eight flower remedies, which have been proven to restore balance and vitality. Bach, in a lecture shortly before his death, said that the real purpose of the remedies was to "bring us nearer to the Divinity within". Indicating that it is the divinity within which heals us.

Bach Flower Remedies do not treat specific physical or medical conditions. They are not meant to take the place of any other medical or holistic treatment. Bach Flower Remedies work at the emotional and mental level. They facilitate the release of negative emotions in a gentle and safe way, and bring the body back to balance. In order for true healing process to be successful, the practitioner seeks to treat the client, not the symptoms. This allows the individual to further take charge of their own process and to heal. Each treatment lasts up to three weeks when taken as recommended and normally lasts about two weeks

There are thirty-eight remedies and you cannot say one will be good for this or one will be good for something else, as it all depends on the individual's personality and how they feel about any given situation.

The thirty-eight flower remedies can be divided up into twelve healers, seven helpers and nineteen 'backer uppers'! The twelve healers are personality types, and everyone should fall into a type. For example, clematis types are dreamers. The Centaury types are over-anxious to serve others and are the ones who tend to be bullied at school or at work. The seven helpers represent the way we tend to cope with life and our emotional way of dealing with situations. For example, Oak is the type who struggles on, never giving up, even if all seems lost and Gorse is for those who have no hope, expect to fail, and find it pointless to even try. The last nineteen essences deal with the everyday stresses and these will change from day to day depending what is going on in your life. For example, Star of Bethlehem aids bereavement, elm is for when you are overwhelmed, and walnut is particularly useful when starting something new.

I strongly believe that, as you can see, it is difficult to say that a certain remedy would be good for a certain thing. The last nineteen would probably help on the surface, but if you are soul searching, it would be important to find your type. However, your type, more often than not, can be well hidden!

Vine is one of the seven helpers. At its worst it can present as a tyrant, but at its finest it will be someone like Mother Teresa. Vine is about power, the ability to use it wisely, and the danger of abusing the gift of power. Children often battle with this dilemma when they bully. Centaury types are the ones that tend to get bullied.

Walnut is one of the nineteen 'backer uppers'. It's good for any sort of change, so will help with teething, puberty, menopause, a new school/job/house/partner or any situation that incorporates change.

It is best to seek a Bach Flower Remedy practitioner that can help you find a combination if remedies that will suit you best at the the time of consultation,

I always keep a bottle of Bach Rescue Remedy in my handbag. It's great for those demanding and stressful situations, especially in emergencies or if you receive sudden bad news. It is also great for children, as it calms them before an exam or performance. The Bach Rescue Remedy is a combination of five of the original Remedies: clematis, impatiens, rock rose, cherry plum and star of Bethlehem.

Australian Bush Flower Essences

(Information supplied courtesy of Australian Bush Flower Essences, all rights reserved.)

Ian White, who developed this range, is a fifth generation herbalist and grew up in the Australian Bush. As a young boy, his grandmother, like her mother before her, specialised in using Australian plants and would often take him into the bush. From her deep understanding, she would point out the many healing plants and flowers. He learned a profound respect for nature through her and went on to become a practitioner and a pioneer, working with and researching the rare remedial qualities of Australian native plants.

Australia has the world's oldest and highest number of flowering plants, exhibiting tremendous beauty and strength. Metaphysically, they have a very wise, old energy. People worldwide are incorporating the Australian Bush Essences to help with their own inner healing,

The Australian Bush Flower Remedies can help to give clarity to anyone's life, strength and commitment to follow and pursue goals and dreams. These essences are often ideal for the first layer of healing – working quickly on immediate problems that are preventing us from living our lives to the full. They also help us to develop a higher level of intuition, self esteem, spirituality, creativity and fun.

The more the essences are used, the more we are likely to experience greater awareness and happiness in our lives. So, everyone benefits... the individual, society and the planet.

There are a total of sixty-nine essences in the Australian Bush range, and each relates to a different emotional imbalance. Several may be combined together to suit someone's particular state.

For Old Soul Children, I would recommend the following:

Adol Essence: this combination essence addresses the major issues teenagers commonly experience. It enhances acceptance of self, communication, social skills, harmony in relationships, maturity, emotional stability and optimism.

Angelsword: taking this Essence allows access and retrieval of previously developed gifts from past lives. Angelsword protects from outside influences and entities, so one can receive clear information from one's higher self without interference.

Autumn Leaves: Autumn Leaves allows one to hear, see and feel communication from the other side and be open to that guidance and communication. It also further emphasises the sense of letting go and moving on in a very profound way.

Boab: this Essence is very beneficial in helping those who have had experiences of abuse or prejudice from others. Boab will also help clear the negative lines of karma between people. When used in a spray, it can be very effective in clearing negative energies. Boab can help break the chains that have been around human consciousness for thousands of years.

Bush Gardenia: this essence helps to turn the individual's head to reconnect and see what their partner is doing and feeling, and to discover what is needed to bring them back together. It is not only for romantic relationships, but also for family relationships, such as sibling rivalry. This essence is especially helpful for hormonal teenagers.

Crowea: this essence is for Old Soul Children who worry too much and, generally, for people who are feeling 'not quite right' with themselves and are just a little out of balance. In fact, this is an excellent essence for people who are not really sure of what it is they are feeling and always have something to worry about, without having specific fears. This purple flower has five petals with a prominent raised centre. Five in numerology relates to the emotional centre and the integration of emotions.

Dagger Hakea: this essence is for people who feel resentment and bitterness and hold grudges against people that they have previously been close to, e.g. family members and old lovers. It can also help with the unity of step families and to help a child to cope with divorce.

Fringed Violet: Fringed Violet is used for treating damage to the aura, where there has been shock, grief or distress, e.g. from abuse or assault. This is because it releases shock from the body. This remedy maintains psychic protection and is excellent for people who are drained by others or unconsciously absorb the physical and emotional imbalances of others.

Pink Mulla Mulla: Pink Mulla Mulla is for those who have suffered a deep spiritual wound long ago, often in their first incarnation, where they felt abandoned by spirit, which has led to a deep scar on the soul and psyche. It works on the outer causal body, clearing sabotage and the fear of spiritual abandonment once more that is stopping spiritual growth. On an emotional level, Pink Mulla Mulla is for those who put out prickles to keep people away. They tend to be quite isolated and unable to resolve a hurt, wrong or injustice, which can be felt very deeply. This impinges on their attitude to those around them and can make them suspicious of people's motives, allowing them no rest. They are often on-guard against people hurting them again; they may protect themselves by saying hurtful things to others. What they say to those around them does not always reflect how they really feel; it is merely a way of keeping people at a safe distance.

Tall Yellow Top: this remedy can help Old Soul Children when they feel that they are not connected to Mother Earth's energies, or if there is no feeling of connection or sense of belonging to the family, school, self, etc. Often, as a consequence of this alienation, the head or intellect takes over from the heart. Some may have been in this state for a long time. Tall Yellow Top will often need to be used for longer periods, sometimes for up to 6-8 weeks without a break. It is important when in this state to reach out to others for support. Be patient with the results from this essence if it appears to be a little slow in acting. The results are well worth waiting for.

Aromatherapy

Aromatherapy oils were used by the Greeks, Romans and Ancient Egyptians for bathing, massage and other areas of their daily lives. The oils contain healing powers of the plant from which they were extracted and have no side effects when used. Aromatherapy connects the past with present day and the essential oils bring a wide range of health benefits. They are, however, very powerful, so should always be very diluted when used for children.

Essential oils are safe to use in the home. I always use Clove, Tea Tree, Eucalyptus, Lavender, Chamomile, Sandalwood and Frankincense, in our family lives. They are very versatile and can be used for lots of different things.

Clove oil is always kept in our house to help with instant pain relief from toothache and sore gums. It's great for when your child is teething, and is a natural, fast-acting anaesthetic. It's much too strong to apply onto a baby's gums, so you will need to blend one drop of clove oil with two tbsp of olive oil or vegetable oil. Use a cotton bud or your clean finger to massage the mixture into the gums. I have also found that massaging Rescue Remedy into their gums is very good for teething.

Olive oil is also great to use when your child has a build of ear wax. At bedtime, pour warm olive oil into the affected ear and let the liquid work its way down into the ear. Put a cotton wool ball into the ear so the pillow does not become stained. Repeat this treatment for three days and the wax will come out on its own.

I always add a few drops chamomile and lavender to the children's bath after they have had a hard day at school, to help them relax. Lavender has many practical uses and has become known as the 'mothering oil'. Lavender has soothing and relaxing properties and is safe to put directly onto the skin to relieve pain from burns or sunburn. In addition, a few drops of lavender oil on your child's pillow will induce sleep. I make up my own lavender water and use it in the iron to give my clothes a fresh scent. It can also help with bruising if you add a few drops to a cold compress and apply.

Chamomile is one of the oldest herbs known to mankind. The Greeks named it 'ground apple'. 'Kamai' is the Greek word for on the ground and the word 'melon' (meaning apple) is used because of its distinctive smell.

Chamomile is great for colic and digestive orders. Chamomile tea helps to take away stress, anxiety and tension and, not forgetting, it helped to calm Peter Rabbit's stomach and soothe his nerves when he ate himself sick in Mr McGregor's garden.

Sandalwood has been used for at least four thousand years and is one of the oldest perfume materials. A truly powerful oil with psychological properties, it can help with balancing emotions. I use it at home and burn the oil or use it as an incense to repel negative influences and unwanted spirit guests. It also acts as protection for the family, and the high vibration and magical properties help spirits to cross over to the other side.

Tea Tree oil has been used in Australia by the Aboriginal

tribes for thousands of years. It can be used for a variety of health conditions, including: acne, skin wounds and burns, bacterial infections, such as impetigo, and nail and other fungal infections, such as ringworm. Tea tree oil has anti-bacterial, antiviral and antiseptic properties and is great for cleaning cuts and grazes. It's great to put directly into your shampoos and conditioners and is a must in giving head lice their marching orders.

Eucalyptus is great to use directly onto bites, as it will relief the itching. It is also great as a decongestant to relive respiratory problems; pour boiling water into a large bowl and add a few drops of the oil, then drape a towel over your head to create your own home own steam inhalation tent. Alternatively, a few drops on your child's hanky will help them to feel less congested.

When our whole family has the flu, my husband and I tend to burn eucalyptus in oil burners, as it is a powerful antiseptic and also analgesic to purify and energise the air, and to soothe mind and body of aches and pains.

Frankincense is used mostly in catholic churches and is associated with the highest spiritual aspirations, so it helps all of us to connect to the part of ourselves that's eternal and divine. It is also good for depression and calming the mind, without leaving you drowsy. It helps us to break away from the past and move forward, so it is a bit like Walnut in the Bach Flower Remedies.

Homeopathy

Homeopathy is not only a healing art, but is also extremely scientific. The founding father of homeopathy was Samuel Hahnemann (1755-1843), a German physician, who developed the basic principles of homeopathy in the late 1700s.

It has its roots in the law of similars. This law states that if a substance causes a particular set of symptoms in a healthy person, then that substance can cure that same set of symptoms when someone is sick in that particular way.

Homeopaths find out about the particular healing power that

a substance has locked inside it by conducting, what is called, a proving. Homeopathy is a way of treating illness, which uses the body's own abilities to make itself well, based on the principle of 'like cures like'. Homeopathic remedies trigger the body's ability to heal itself by stimulating a precise reaction in the body against the symptoms. The body naturally reacts against attempts to make it behave differently, so homeopaths give a medicine (called a remedy) which, in healthy people, is able to cause a set of symptoms which are the same as the symptoms being treated in the patient. When the body reacts against the remedy, it reacts against the symptoms too, and the patient gets better.

Homeopathic medicines are not toxic and are, therefore safe, and without side effects. All mental, emotional and physical conditions can be treated in this way. The majority of people who consult a qualified homeopath, experience better health as a result, and an increased sense of well being.

Homeopathy is individualised, so an appropriate treatment would depend on the child. All of the remedies could help a child, but no one remedy will help all children. Old Soul Children and spiritually aware children do very well on homeopathy too, but the best thing to do would be to visit your local homeopath and get them to prescribe for your child and their particular circumstances.

Other Things that May be of Use to You

If your Old Soul Child gets the winter blues, which is commonly known as Seasonal Affective Disorder (SAD), walks on cold, sunny, winter day will help reduce the symptoms. St. Johns Wort is a herbal, mild antidepressant that helps to increase the serotonin, yet it can also increase the skins sensitivity to sunlight.

I swear by echinacea, as it strengthens the immune system and helps you fight off bacteria and viruses. It can be bought in most health foods shops.

Good old vitamin C tablets are great to take once you get the sniffles and can be found naturally in oranges; however, strawberries, blackcurrants, potatoes, tomatoes and salad greens are also an excellent sources of vitamin C.

Weleda

In 1921, Weleda was founded in Switzerland. Rudolf Steiner, a renowned philosopher, and his pioneering colleague, a Dutch medic called Dr. Ita Wegman, worked with a group of doctors who believed that you cannot apply simple mechanical ideas alone to understand illness; health is a balance not just of bodily function but also mental and spiritual health. New ideas were developed to look at wider connections with the kingdoms of nature and evolution to understand our life, our feelings and our thoughts. Weleda was established in the UK shortly after, in 1925.

Out of this approach to life, Steiner (1861-1925) formalised his ideas and called this way of thinking Anthroposophy, which means 'study of the wisdom of man', and stated that it was a way forward in gaining knowledge about ourselves, and in seeking to unite the spiritual element in the human being with the spiritual element in the universe. The concepts of Anthroposophy are now used worldwide in Steiner Schools, agriculture (biodynamic or Demeter), medicine and many areas of the arts.

Weleda's motto, 'In harmony with nature', implies research into the structures of life and nature, as well as insight into the processes of the human soul and spirit. Weleda develops and sells complementary medicines, nutritional supplements and natural body-care products, but not makeup.

Their aim is to help everyone, old and young, to restore health and maintain wellbeing. They are committed to doing this naturally, ethically, safely, without animal experimentation and without damaging the environment. This is not a marketing ploy, but a way of life, and is deeply rooted in all aspects of company business. These beliefs affect every decision made at Weleda.

All Weleda products are aimed at enhancing self-healing

processes of the human organism, and to do justice to human needs in an integral manner, which are perfect for Old Soul Children and their families.

Conventional medicine is directed at killing germs, addressing symptoms, suppressing processes of illness and replacing missing substances. Anthroposophic medicine goes one step further by integrally focusing on human needs, offering medication and therapies that help the organism defeat illnesses by its own strength whenever practicable and meaningful. Weleda remedies are based on the knowledge of the affinity of man with nature, and a holistic view of the human organism as more than just a physical body. They guide the organism towards health, showing its healthy functioning, and helping the body to overcome the disease.

Their baby range would be the first step in helping your Old Soul.

Made with organic calendula flowers, the Weleda baby range provides a baby's skin with all the care and protection it needs from the day they are born. The calendula flower plays an important role in Weleda's baby care products and provides the basis of the range. For centuries, this medicinal plant was treasured for aiding the healing process of small wounds, red, inflamed skin and skin infections

Due to its immune strengthening and antiseptic properties, calendula also protects the skin against infection.

Weleda Bath Milks: for all the family, old and young, to help people relax or awaken.

Weleda Body Oils: again, for all the family, to create a warming and relaxing mantle around us and revitalise us.

Weleda Elixirs: nutritional supplements to support us at times when we need a little extra help.

Aknedoron Purifying Lotion and Cleansing Lotion: for teenage, problem skin (our skin is often a reflection of inner problems, physical and emotional).

Dermatodoron Ointment: a licensed medicine for eczema.

Massage Balm with Arnica: relieves muscular pain, stiffness and cramp (useful if you get very tense).

Chamomilla Pillules: this children's remedy is great for colicky pain and fractious infants that won't settle.

Fragador Tablets: relieve occasional nerviness and tension from day-to-day stress and strain; for days when you feel you can't cope and feel unravelled.

Avena Sativa Comp Drops: a gentle calming effect by day, aiding relaxation at night to promote restful sleep; for days when you feel wound up tight.

Bath Milks

Even everyday essentials can work holistically on body and mind to revive your senses, nourish your skin and nurture your soul, leaving you refreshed from top to toe. Weleda's bath milks harness the therapeutic properties of aromatic essential oils and disperse them throughout the warm water to gently envelop the body, to relax and calm or awaken and invigorate.

Elixirs

Weleda's organic elixirs are designed to provide specific health and nutritional benefits and maintain general wellbeing. They are rich in natural vitamin complexes and other active ingredients with valuable health-giving properties.

Birch can help us rediscover our vitality. Blackthorn invigorates and fortifies to help us keep up with demanding times at school or work, during growth phases, pregnancy or breastfeeding, or in later life. Sea Buckthorn is rich in vitamin C to help the body maintain its natural defences.

Weleda make a conscious decision from the outset to avoid artificial ingredients and use only raw materials from the natural world. For example, naturally occurring minerals, like sodium chloride or honey, precious plant ingredients grown organically, or better still, biodynamically at their own farms around the world. By using essential oils in their body care products for their natural preservative properties, they avoid the need to use artificial preservatives such as parabens. Many Weleda bodycare products bear the BDIH kite mark (certified natural cosmetic), so you can tell at a glance the product is genuinely natural.

Wherever possible, biodynamic or organic ingredients are used. Biodynamic agriculture involves growing plants to the highest organic standards without chemical pesticides or sprays. It takes into account, not just the seasons, but also the rhythms of the planets. Crops are planted or harvested at the optimum time and the soil is enriched and revitalised with biodynamic preparations and natural fertilisers, so plants have a strong inherent life-force and a more potent effect when used in health products.

Taking into account the impact that growing their own ingredients, biodynamically, has on the surrounding natural habitat, Weleda have developed 15-acre herb gardens in Derbyshire, with the advice of the local Wildlife Trust, to protect the biodiversity (the delicate balance of wildlife). This conscious awareness is ingrained in all Weleda thinking, right down to the low-energy, recyclable packaging they choose.

Sometimes specific crops have to be especially cultivated for Weleda, as they cannot pick them from the wild, such as Edelweiss, which is a protected species. It takes years of expertise to cultivate healthy organic plants that retain all of their wild characteristics, active compounds and valuable therapeutic properties.

Where wild ingredients are used, such as rose hips of Rosa Mosqueta that grows in abundance at the foothills of the Andes, these are gathered by controlled, certified collection. This ensures that the natural habitat is not damaged or exhausted. The local community is equally protected by fair trade. Where ingredients are grown for Weleda, they work with local farmers, helping them to convert their conventional farms into sustainable organic culture.

Through these fair trade agreements, Weleda offers economic and social support to these communities. People are just as important to Weleda quality as the use of healthy organic plants. It is a vital part of the Weleda ethos to take responsibility both for their environment and co-workers in this way.

From a personal point of view, these products are the step forward in nurturing your Old Soul Child, as Weleda recognise that we are all individuals.

Steiner Schools

Steiner schools are based on the philosophy of Rudolf Steiner, who founded his first school in Germany in 1919. There are now over nine hundred around the world.

Many parents/guardians who have home schooled their children have turned to Steiner Schools when they have placed their children back into education. The reason for this is that they feel that state school system does not provide the sort of holistic approach provided in the Steiner philosophy.

In Steiner schools, children learn to be valuable members of society in a positive and supportive manner, rather than trying to ensure that they all fit a rigid framework. Steiner schools have their own comprehensive and distinctive curriculum and teaching methods for pupils up to eighteen. This curriculum is based on a pedagogical philosophy that places emphasis on the whole development of the child, including a child's spiritual, physical and moral well-being, as well as academic progress. There is a strong emphasis on social abilities and the development of pre-numeracy and literacy skills. Formal learning begins later, as is the case in many more educationally successful European countries (Finland and Norway in particular) and learning takes place through the medium of creativity and artistic qualities, done in a very creative and artistic environment.

Steiner schools have a long track record of successful

outcomes. The schools do not select pupils according to academic ability and social inclusion is fundamental to the ethos, although in the UK this has been hard to achieve without State support. The Steiner Waldorf Schools Fellowship is currently addressing this problem, and hope that under this Government's Diversity Agenda schools with a different curriculum will be able to apply to enter the maintained sector. Pupils at Steiner schools take GCSEs and A-levels, but they do not sit other national tests, such as Sats, which may be one of the reasons why Steiner schools are not state-funded in the UK. The government would have to bend the rules to allow them to opt out of the national curriculum. But with the government increasingly encouraging schools to take more control over how they are run and what they teach, and with moves towards giving parents more choice of different kinds of schools, it suggests that this move might be supported.

Steiner Education respects the essential nature of childhood and enables each pupil to develop the abilities and confidence needed for life. In pre-school and primary school, the education provides a solid foundation of faculties and experiences, which the secondary level can build on. At this stage, qualities such as emotional maturity, good judgement, creativity and initiative, with a strong moral sense of responsibility, are cultivated.

The pupils learn about the world, society and themselves in a way with which they can strongly identify. The Steiner curriculum responds to the developmental needs of each pupil. It has proved adaptable over seventy-five years, in many different cultures, on all continents. This is because the curriculum is designed to develop faculties rather than merely delivering prescribed information: it is interdisciplinary and comprehensive.

The pupils enjoy continuity and personal commitment through their kindergarten teacher, during the early years, and between the ages of six and fourteen, from their principal teacher – the class teacher.

From fourteen to eighteen they receive the pastoral support of a class guardian. This longer term pupil-teacher relationship enables those responsible to follow and evaluate each child's needs through the important developmental stages of childhood and youth. Teachers are free to choose whatever material is appropriate to each individual situation and to shape and present it in a creative way. This enhances the teacher's sense of commitment and professionalism.

In a fast-changing and uncertain world, individuals are increasingly called upon to respond with initiative, flexibility and responsibility. As adults, former Steiner school pupils have proved themselves to be resourceful, creative and equipped to meet the challenges that life presents. They are in many senses 'world citizens'.

Individual subjects are developed from the youngest classes up to school leaving age in an integrated way, in accordance with the stages of child development. This helps the pupils through their school career, not only to follow the thematic threads, but also to develop their understanding of complex inter-relationships between phenomena. Devoting the first two hours of the day, for up to three or four weeks, to themes such as the geography of North America, mechanics, trees, money and finance, nutrition or the history of architecture, is an economical teaching technique, which helps focus interest and strengthens the memory. Practical life skills such as crafts, gardening, technology, and work experience on the land and in industry are complemented by a wide range of artistic activities, including music, drama, painting and sculpture.

Steiner schools are all self-governing learning communities. The responsibility for educational matters is carried primarily by the teachers, who work together in a co-operative way without a head teacher. All UK schools are registered charities with staff, parents and supportive 'friends of the school' working together with the legal association. Trustees are drawn from this body and are responsible for school governance, and an administrator manages to school's resources, usually assisted by members of the wider school community. This 'associative form of leadership' is committed to a process of working together in the best interests of the pupils. This way of working together not only provides a model for a caring and responsible community in support of the pupils, but is also an effective way of harnessing the gifts of all concerned to the well being of the school.

For many years, there has been a campaign, to get Steiner Education, into the UK maintained sector mainstream education, I can remember watching Melinda Messenger on *This Morning,* talking passionately about sending her children to a Steiner School. She talked about her son and about how he felt overwhelmed at the age of four because he could not hold a pencil properly, which really struck a chord in my heart. She uprooted her family from her native Swindon to move 100 miles away to Berkshire, so all three children would receive Steiner educations.

I thought that she came across very well, talked with such passion and made the ethos behind Steiner sound fantastic. Melinda Messenger made some very good points about needing to teach the child, not the 'National Curriculum'; I too feel it is more natural for children. However, a lot of people are opposed to their educational teaching and different beliefs. Could this be because this kind of different education is actually pressing their own 'fear' buttons, because they really do not understand what it really is about? To be honest with you, I have seen the lessons plans, and only wish that I could join in.

As a parent of three, Old Soul Children, I really do feel that Steiner education would benefit a whole range of kids, and maybe help parents with children that have ADHD.

Baby Mozart
Baby Mozart is a CD and DVD collection from the award-winning

infant-developmental media company, Baby Einstein, whose goal and philosophy is the satisfaction of a child's curiosity through sight and sound. In the main theatre section of this disc, you'll find lots of simple shapes, primary colours and favourite toys passing across the screen. The CD's are inspired by classical masterpieces. Tailored for little ears to help nurture a lifelong love of any music.

Designed to entertain and stimulate children from the age of 0-48 months, this programme provides an introduction to the music of Mozart, combined with interesting visuals.

Unlike the simpler earlier releases, this is focused on the works of Mozart, and so just like the Bach and Beethoven releases, all of the images are choreographed around the chosen pieces of music.

This release was named 'Video of the Year' by *Child and Parent Magazine* and is a wonderful expansion of the company's original ideas. It's a slight advancement in expectation of your child from the more basic initial releases, but has a video tutorial to help the parent understand how it all works.

Your child's brain will grow and develop more in the first three years of life than at any other time, and you can help to nurture that growth and development in many important ways; exposing youngsters to the melodies of the maestro can improve verbal ability, spatial intelligence, creativity and memory. In addition to this, it gets babies mesmerised for hours and you are guaranteed quiet time, so I would warmly recommend the whole series to any new exhausted parent!

Affirmations

An affirmation is a verbal, positive statement that we repeat continuously, which connects us to a goal we want to achieve. They can support our positive thinking, have a dramatic impact on our life's outlook and help us to make the big changes through our thinking. Affirmations really work and can help transform our lives.

When we say a positive affirmation, it gives us back our own power and we affirm to ourselves, the powerful message that we can, in fact, reach our highest potential.

Thoughts are like seeds; each one produces its own distinctive flower and fruit. It is the same with words; they can be creative, destructive, spiteful, or happy. When we understand and harness the energies of our mind, it can help us to master our own lives and that of our Old Soul Children.

What we say, what we do, what we feel, and how we react to situations, all have their origin in our minds. Our state of mind determines our daily experience, which can also limit our own success and create self-destructive thoughts and beliefs.

The energy of the human mind is like a muscle that needs to be exercised in a positive way. If negative thinking is created within ourselves, then it is amplified because we feed it with our own loss of inner power.

If any Old Soul Child is constantly reminded, on a daily basis, that they cannot do something, and that they are stupid, thick and useless, they will take on that belief themselves and incorporate it into their personal belief system. Self image will diminish and these thoughts will run systematically in their minds, leaving them feeling powerless. At their low ebb, feelings of guilt, anger and rage will take hold and they will also attract other negative personalities into their life. This will then become an endless cycle and your Old Soul Child may feel that they are faced with a 'no win' situation.

When we all are feeling unhappy, we see the bad side of any situation we are faced with. Some would say that their glass is half-empty instead of half-full. When faced, for example, with bullying, we can only see the bad, yet we need to find the cure. To every situation there is a cure in our life and we can find it. In the beginning, we may not want to and find it very scary to stick up for ourselves. When something negative happens to you, you CAN turn it around and there is always an upside to everything we face.

If we can change our patterns of thinking, it will help us develop a deeper understanding of our minds and we can let go of any emotional baggage that we may be carrying. We may be feeling so powerless about our pasts that we cannot have a

brighter future. Yet, if we give ourselves permission, we can bring the much needed improvement in our lives, for ourselves and our Old Soul Child.

If your Old Soul Child practises these simple steps, he/she will reap benefits in years to come. When they are a lot older, opportunities will come to them and new paths will open up, as their consciousness will continue to expand. Writing down just one affirmation a day will help your child and, if encouraged, a spark of light will ignite inside as they are encouraged just to do their best in all that they do. Affirmations will help them realise that they can do their homework or go to school and participant in new activities. They will help with self respect, release limitations and enable them to create the life that they really want.

Affirmations harness the power of positive thinking. As we focus our mental, physical, emotional and spiritual energies, it connects us with our subconscious mind and we begin to shift unwanted beliefs and feelings. We become conscious of what we create and begin to form healthy thinking and perspectives.

When sending positive thoughts and statements to the universe, this will be returned to us equally.

At first, there will be a great resistance, because of our own negative belief system. We battle against 'I can't do it' and 'I am not worthy'. This is normal thinking because deep inside we do tend to doubt that it will not work. The key is to trust yourself and ask your Old Soul Child to do same. As these negative thoughts come in, see them as hurdles that you can jump over and conquer. Tell yourself and your Old Soul Child to keep thinking and believing that you are going to achieve your goals – and you will.

For me, writing is a powerful tool to help me resolve issues and say all those things I feel that are stuck in my throat. I get to say what I really want to say and the end result is never what I would expect it to be. But that, for me, is truly experiencing the magic that writing brings me. Princess Diana wrote many letters to friends, expressing what she felt about situations, which helped with her own release of emotions, as she wrote them down.

Creating Your Own Affirmations

Writing down your affirmations helps you to begin to release the magic within you and gives you empowerment. All Affirmations should be positive and written in the present tense. From experience, avoiding the use of words like 'no', 'don't' and 'not', because an affirmation it is a statement of intention and if you find yourself with objections surfacing, you will need to restate the affirmation in a positive tense.

Use the words 'I am' instructs the mind that it is taking place now and relates that what you want is already accomplished. For example, 'I am happy now' supersedes 'I will be happy', because when we use the word 'will', we are, in fact, 'willing' something to happen, which may never occur. We also focus our mind on the word 'will' and give it energy, which increases our 'willing' for something to happen.

Help your Old Soul Child to get in touch with their creative skills and find pictures from magazines to stick alongside their goal. You can use candles, incense and music to create the right atmosphere, when you both go to work on your affirmations. The other major factor you need to consider, in order for it to work, is that you get into the feeling of having it NOW, because we are always living in the NOW. From past experience, many of my clients get stuck in the feeling of 'one day I will get this', and they have been waiting a long time for that one day, which never comes.

Get your child to repeat the affirmation three times a day to keep the process working and the universe listening.

These steps are essential in making the affirmations work for you and your Old Soul Child. Having positive mental energy is the key when harnessing the Law of Attraction. If you begin to tell yourself and your Old Soul Child that these do really work, you will start to believe in it. This will become a strong energy for both of you and when you believe it, you become it.

Creating powerful affirmations can be uplifting and help you both become and clear as you focus on your goals. As your repeat them to yourself on a daily basis, you become balanced and on the right road to create the life that you want.

The most famous affirmation, Emile Coue's – 'Every day, in every way, I am getting better and better." – satisfies all these rules. Louise Hay says, 'It is only a thought and a thought can be changed'.

It is a great idea to write your affirmations down and leave them lying around at home, where you will see them. Repeating them when you are looking at yourself in the mirror is also a very powerful thing to do, as it will make you believe in yourself.

It may sound strange, at first, saying to yourself 'I am beautiful,' or 'I am a good person', but the more you say, the more you believe about yourself and, as time goes by, it becomes second nature.

I teach all of my children that 'Down is never a permanent option'. In every cloud there is a silver lining and BELIEVING in yourself can make a difference.

Other Ways to Lift Your Old Soul Child's Self Esteem

Stick a photograph on your fridge or in their bedroom showing when they were happy. Every time they are feeling sad, tell them to look at the photograph. This will act as a reminder that they have been happy in the past and can be happy in the future.

Get your Old Soul Child to think about the people who have influenced and inspired them in their life.

Get them to surround themselves with positive people that

make feel good about life.

Get them to buy a notebook and write down their achievements to date. Encourage them to write down new achievements that they wish to aim for.

Magic Mirror – A Simple Protection Technique

I tell my children that life is like a magic mirror. What you reflect out into the world is what you get back. For example, if you do something that is not very nice, something will come back to you to tell you what you have done wrong. If you have done something really good, you will get rewarded in different ways.

This basic yet simple technique works really well and can be carried out anywhere. It is easy for us to grasp as we do not tie any belief system to it. It provides protection for you and it helps to build a shield when you are feeling most vulnerable or faced with a situation that makes you feel powerless. It does work; why not try it for yourself

Begin by finding a comfortable place in which where you will not be disturbed. Then relax, using any method you find works for you.

Try to visualize yourself standing in front of a large mirror and send the words, feelings or whatever you are feeling back to where it belongs. This will be deflected up towards the universe to be transformed into positive energy that will be re-used by the universe at the appropriate time. You will feel a positive shift in your body as you complete this.

Spend as much time as you need to build up this imaginary figure fully. A good idea is to set aside a particular time each day for the exercise and devote 10 to 15 minutes daily to it for a week or more.

Some of us have problems with visualization. If necessary, draw a picture of your shield with an image of you in the middle or create a three dimensional object representing your shield to help you to focus your energy on creating it. You can also simply write it down very specifically to help you to focus.

Melt Down

Ask your Old Soul Child what makes them get annoyed and angry; what really pushes their buttons. Then tell your Old Soul Child these easy steps:

STOP; TAKE A DEEP BREATH and WALK AWAY.

When you do this you are in control of the situation and it will make you feel much better and strong inside.

Magical Headphones

This technique can help your Old Soul Child if they are being bullied.

Get them to imagine, visualise and pretend that they are wearing headphones when the bully is talking to them. They can be their favourite colour and can be large or small. Tell your Old Soul Child that they are the only one who knows that they are wearing the 'magical headphones'. However, when wearing them, they can block out what the bully is saying, which really confuses the bully because they do not know that you are not really listening to what they are saying.

What Foods are Best for Your Old Soul?

Diet

My Dad always told us, as kids, that breakfast is the most important meal of the day, and he is right. I tell my three children that without food in our bellies, we are like cars without petrol and cannot get to the supermarket and back home. Any child that does not have breakfast or eat properly cannot possibly be able to function 100%, because their stomachs are crying out for food; as the saying goes: 'we are what we eat'.

Changes in the diets of Old Soul Children aid their spiritual, mental, physical and emotional care and are all important when they are growing up. Eating the right foods also can help with their spiritual connection and keep them grounded. Children grow up so fast that they need nutrition to run alongside them and a well balanced diet of love, exercises, compassion and emotional intelligence, maximises children's learning potential.

As parents, we are responsible for what we are feeding our children. A diet of junk food – seven days a week, 365 days a year – would clog up their inner souls and also their spiritual connection. Natural foods that still have Mother Earth's energies assist with their spiritual growth plan and aid their mental, physical and emotional health.

I know that when my children become unwell, it is telling me that they are working through their own issues naturally. As a parent, we are in tune with our own child's emotions, spirit, mental and emotional health and know them better than anyone else.

Home-cooked food is the best way forward. If you are on a budget and cannot afford organically grown fruit and vegetables, then why not grow your own. There are so many positive advantages to growing your own fruit and vegetables. Children get so excited when they see the first green leaves sprout and all their hard work in watering and caring for their home grown plants has been worth it. Children will benefit enormously from this, as it teaches them about where food really comes from (not just from a supermarket shelf) and encourages them to eat their own home-grown food.

Home-grown potatoes are simply the best for your Sunday roast dinner, and as fruit is loaded with fibre and many vitamins; we tend to make our own healthy cereal bars and nut and raisin mixes. We are mad about smoothies in our house; even hiding forbidden fruit makes the children want more of the same stuff. We freeze the leftovers (if any is left) for picnics and school packed lunches. Home-made soups are great for winter lunchtimes and you can also again hide 'forbidden veg' after you have whizzed it up in a blender.

I tend to have a holistic approach to diet, and my children like to experience different kinds of food for the very first time, without saying that they do not like it. I think about foods that will nourish their chakra systems, which also help their natural energies and enhance their immune systems.

You can choose any kind of food for your Old Soul Child, but when selecting, it is important to think about the colours you choose that reflect the chakra system:

BASE: Root Vegetables like carrots, potatoes, parsnips, eggs, beans, and any kind of meat and tofu which is rich in protein will help ground your Old Soul Child and govern the amount of physical energy that they have to play, run and walk.

SACRAL: Fruits like Strawberries, Oranges, Tangerines and melons will enhance creative expression and the amount of energy that they have available to pursue goals and daily life. They will also reflect our connections with other people on a physical, mental, emotional and spiritual level.

SOLAR PLEXUS: Pastas, cereals, cous cous, rices, sunflower seeds, milk and any kind of cheese and yogurts will boost self esteem and encourage inner love. This also reflects relationships in their life and their feelings towards the physical body and for others.

HEART: Broccoli, cabbage, spinach, celery and cranberries help with love and emotions. This Chakra opens up their own feelings of love and the connection to other people and the world that they live in. .

THROAT: Drinking plenty of water to keep hydrated, and

eating apples, pears, plums and apricots will help them to speak their own truth, needs and wants in life, and help them to accomplish their goals. It is also connected to their own self worth and accomplishments in life.

THIRD EYE: Grape and Pomegranate Juice, Blackcurrants, Blackberries and Raspberries helps awaken their inner senses and give them the ability to visualise through the power of their own imaginations.

CROWN: Drinking water will keep a personal connection to divine energies and the universe flowing.

As a therapist, I think that sometimes I am too careful about what I say and do in front of them because of the case of transference from parent to child. If a parent does not like a certain food, or has a fear of water, usually the child will mimic their behaviour, without the parent understanding what and where it has come from, and feeling that their child is becoming awkward.

Society has changed, and the emphasis on working many jobs to make ends meet is becoming, sadly, on top of our agendas. Bills keep increasing, yet our wages stay the same and people feel that they are in a 'no win' situation. Adults tend to over-eat, as we begin compensating for those emotional needs as well. So, surely, as a nation, we should be looking at our emotional health as well as our diet. Those couple of pounds that we are carrying around our bodies are, in fact, our security blankets as we are hiding from something that maybe, for whatever reason, we cannot or will not face, because we are not ready to or do not want to. This is what is happening with our children.

Negative emotions can send us straight to the food cupboards to indulge in chocolate or in a tub of ice cream and then we will be filled with remorse and regret with what we have just carried out. Others may binge and vomit and develop eating disorders.

Our children's emotional health and intelligence needs nurturing and is just as important as their physical health. This is one of the main contributors that children are facing when they become obese. Nine times out of ten, when emotional health is ignored, the same cycle is repeated over and over again.

In the United Kingdom, we really do tend not to talk about how we feel or what is troubling us and so our children do the same. We really need to get the emotional health right in helping us to lose those extra pounds that we have gained.

Serotonin is a hormone manufactured in the brain. When these levels are low, it may cause depression. People also believe that they are hungry and when they eat foods that contain high levels of sugar, they start to feel better and it releases happy chemicals to the brain. This is also because of low levels of Serotonin in the brain. Serotonin is a neurotransmitter, which means it is a chemical link between brain cell neurones. It is a vital chemical in how different parts of the brain communicate with each other. Serotonin can be found in antidepressants, like Prozac, which help people lift their low mood. It can be found naturally in foods like fruit, vegetables, beans and whole grains to help you boost your energy levels and also lift our mood. Fish, eaten three times a week, also helps to produce Serotonin. Exercising three times a week for twenty minutes can also be a good enhancer.

So, for children who feel emotionally starved, their levels of Serotonin will fall and to help them get a 'quick fix' they may turn to food to give them the comfort that they are craving.

We all want our children to have happy childhoods and become successful as adults. However, children are sometimes unhappy and misbehave because of what is troubling them and they cannot find the right words to really say how they are feeling. When their behaviour becomes out of the ordinary, we must not praise that kind of behaviour because it will tell a child that it is ok to behave in that way and so it will continue. The child may be craving extra attention because of their inner worries and troubles by being naughty, and if we rise to that behaviour it gives them the attention that they are seeking, because we are giving our own power to the situation. We need to recognise and praise the good behaviour, but ask our children what is troubling them when this kind of behaviour occurs.

Because our lifestyles are changing, some children are finding comfort in eating, as they begin to feel out of sync with life, resulting in carrying extra weight. For girls and women, this is usually influenced by the sacral chakra because they are trying to protect themselves from emotions of others. The sacral also looks after the sense of taste and appetite for our food. For boys and men it is the solar plexus chakra where the weight gain happens. This could be because of a lack of self confidence and self belief, or even the experience of a traumatic event. They may not be able to 'digest' what is really going on in their life and keep their true feelings of situations hidden in their stomachs. The solar plexus also stores their inner securities and the love for their own physical form. Some men are not in tune with their own feelings and close their hearts off to those around them, leaving them feeling isolated. In Men, if their heart chakra was open, it would help them to become in touch with their feminine side and if remained closed, their heart chakra becoming unbalanced. The saying, 'heavy on the heart' could, in fact, be true because they are not in touch with their own inner feelings, are fearful of love and find that they have not got the time to let it enter their lives.

Exercises and Aids for the Whole Family

Kites

Children of all ages get really bored and restless on rainy days. Why not help them to make a homemade kite for you to fly on a windy day? It can give your Old Soul Child a whole different meaning when you go and fly your kite, and creates fantastic memories to help you form a close bond. When it is a windy day, take your kite to a park and let the sylphs help you fly it.

Bike Rides

My mum would take my sister, brother and I on many bike rides when we were younger. We would pack up a picnic, go on adventures and come home tired but happy for our tea, and talk about our exciting day. When the sun is shining and there's not a cloud in sight, bike riding is a great way to get exercise, lots of fresh air and to spend time together as a family. It provides you with a low impact cardiovascular exercise that can be taken for pleasure or used to keep fit. There are many places to visit whilst riding your bike and it is a truly an experience not to be missed.

Swimming

Swimming is a great all-round exercise for you and your family. It benefits your heart and lungs and is a wonderful recreational activity for families, from water parks to the beach. When you swim regularly, it builds endurance, muscle strength and cardiovascular fitness. There are many psychological benefits to swimming, as it allows you to relax, like a form of meditation, and helps you to gain a feeling of well being.

Walks

Walking is a fantastic form of exercise and a great way of staying active. It can help the whole family to become stress-free and helps reduce depression, anxiety and stress. We got ourselves a border collie, named Max, to come with us when we are exploring the countryside and beaches. Walking helps you to feel full of energy and it gives you and your family more 'get-up-and-go' energy and allows them to feel more alert.

Skipping Ropes

Skipping is great exercise, which has a medium impact on our bodies. It helps to improve our cardiovascular fitness and improves our agility. Skipping ropes are cheap to buy and there are many benefits you can get from doing moderate skipping for 30 minutes, which is similar to jogging or riding your bike. For parents, you can skip to get fit, as it can be done anywhere, anytime. You and your Old Soul Child can start by seeing how many skips you can each do, when you take turns.

Karate

When children learn karate it can benefit them in many ways. It helps them to learn tolerance and respect for others, makes them feel more secure in their surroundings and helps them to develop self confidence. Karate can assist the overall health of the whole family, as it can help with enhancing coordination and balance, and sets the children up for a lifelong habit of exercise.

Yoga for Babies

Baby yoga offers babies quality physical stimulation, encourages neural development and complements infant massage. It helps to develop your baby's balance, coordination and sensory motor skills. The benefits of baby yoga will also help your baby's behaviour to become more settled and aids sleep. In addition, it helps parent and baby bonding and enhances communication, as well as helping with growth and muscle tone, and strengthening digestive, respiratory and immune systems. As a parent, it helped my children as babies, reliving wind and colic and helping develop their body-mind awareness. Massage benefits your whole family; it is one of the oldest treatments of applying hand pressure over the body to release knots and tension. It can relieve stress, headaches and helps with sleeping.

Marian Olphert

Marian, a bank clerk from Cambridgeshire, is married with a daughter, Georgina, who is now fourteen. Georgina is a likeable soul with an old head on young shoulders.

From a young age, no matter what the situation was, Georgina always had an inner-knowing that things would be OK in the end. Marian could read tealeaves and Georgina she wanted to learn too, so she could help people and make them feel better.

When Georgina was two, sitting on her Mum's lap, she pointed and said, "Oh look, Mummy. There's Baby Alex."

"What?" replied a startled Marian, and Georgina happily replied again. Marian became speechless and yet emotional because Georgina did not know that she had a stillborn baby boy that she named Alex two years before she was born.

Marian went upstairs and took Georgina to the spare room. Opening a drawer, she pulled out a photograph of Baby Alex to show Georgina what he looked like. She said to bring the photograph downstairs and put it with the others as he was part of their family. Marian did not do this before, because, it did not feel right.

Three months later, Marian began to notice that Georgina was seemingly having proper conversations with thin air. Marian would ask who she was talking to and she would reply that it was her friend Jamie. For months after, Jamie accompanied them everywhere and Marian was not even allowed to shut the car door until Jamie got in. Like most parents, Marian does not know where the name 'Jamie' came from, but they did everything together – played games, had tea parties. However, at times, Marian could not get Georgina in the car to take her to playgroup, because Jamie said she was not allowed to go. Like in the film, *Drop Dead Fred*, Georgina began to do naughty things, like drawing on the walls. When questioned about this behaviour, she would reply, "Jamie did it." Marian would say tell her that Jamie was not here, but Georgina would point to where he was supposedly standing and say "Yes he is, he is over there."

When Georgina was due to go to school, at four years and three months old, she became worried about Jamie going to school. Before school started in September, they went to the supermarket in the car and Georgina asked Marian to stop the car because Jamie wanted to get out. Marian pulled over and Georgina asked her mum to open the car door. Georgina said Goodbye and Jamie never came back. Jamie had stayed for a year and a half.

Chapter Five

Communication and the Wider World

Imagination is the highest kite one can fly.
Lauren Bacall

Crystals for Old Soul Children, Mandalas For Old Soul
Children, Mercury Retrograde, The uses of NLP in our
lives, Why are some people able to accept the concept of
ghosts with an open mind while others cannot?

Crystals for Children

For thousands of years, crystals have laid abundant in the earth.
Since ancient times, it was believed that crystals, gems and stones
had healing properties that promoted health and well being. The
Greeks and the Romans used them for health and protection, and
some were used as talismans because of their mystical properties.
They were also used to promote spiritual awareness by the rulers
of Ancient Egypt, in Atlantis to help with grounding and restoring
inner peace, and the Native Americans placed quartz crystals over
their eyes to help them have clearer visions whilst journeying. It
is also believed that Stonehenge was built by using the help of
crystals. Crystals are very popular today, both in healing and in
jewellery.

A child will innocently pick up a stone from the garden or a
shell from the beach, place it in their pocket and forget about what
they have collected until the time is right for them to connect with
it again. My son, Leo, is always picking up stones and telling me
that they have magic and want to be with him. I think, also, it
helps him to ground naturally to the earth's energies that support

him where ever he goes.

Old Soul Children of all ages have a great infinity with crystals. They innocently self-attune themselves without worrying what the crystal can really do for them. When children connect with crystals, they 'just know' intuitively which ones are right for them at that moment in time. Through challenges, children learn their own inner strengths and so choosing crystals helps them to respond to the crystal's healing energies in a positive way.

Bright and potentially creative children can often be hard to look after; yet nurturing these souls is very spiritual work. Crystals help Old Soul Children to ground and attune themselves to Mother Earth's energies. When they lose or misplace their crystals, it just means that the crystal has carried out the task of helping them with the particular issue they had at the time. Some children do get attached and may feel that they still need it, a bit like when a child doesn't wish to be parted from their favourite toy, blanket or clothing. So, when buying, make sure you buy a few extras for emergencies.

All kinds of crystals can act as good amplifiers to your child's needs. Just let your child pick and choose what they need at that moment in time. Old Soul Children are souls who are following a creative, yet spiritual, path. They find out about their purpose early on, and begin to use all of their unique gifts. With great humanity, these 'hidden talents' are remembered from previous lives and for these children it is easy to tap into consciously without forcing it to come to the surface. They are very aware of their spiritual connection and find that crystals work as natural amplifiers to enhance their own natural psychic and spiritual abilities.

Old Soul Children sometimes distance themselves from the physical world, because of what they are feeling around them. They can understand, in some ways, the environment they have chosen to grow and thrive in, yet get confused in the same way.

Crystals can help Old Soul Children connect with their own inner and outer worlds and also where they have come from.

The most important thing for any parent bringing up an Old Soul Child, is to blend all of the different aspects of life into one, which is very possible to do. With my own children, I help them work out what is troubling them with crystals. The crystals just seem to take away the anguish and the remorse or regret that they sometimes carry deep down within their hearts.

When your Old Soul Child picks their crystal for the very first time, they are also connecting with their own spirit guides, fairy and angelic realm. Please be assured, if your Old Soul Child picks up a crystal which seems unknown to you it is the right one for them at that moment in time.

As a child holds a crystal, they are connecting with the past whilst having a foot-hold in the present. The connection for any child with any crystal is that it makes them feel safe and protected. Crystals are sensitive to energies and so make a perfect partnership with an Old Soul Child.

When they are feeling unwell, a trip to any crystal shop can help. There are many different crystals to aid recovery on a more natural level (not that I'm advising not consulting medical professionals).

I watch my own children with anticipation in a New Age shop filled to the brim with crystals waiting to jump into their hands. They pick, choose, put back and keep what gives them a great calling and connection.

Children have an inner knowing about what crystal can help them at that moment in time, whether it's an Amethyst for spiritual knowledge, or a Carnelian for independence; the crystal will help them with their own inner healing.

When they hold their crystal in their hand, they can feel the energies in an instant – physically pulsating, tingling, vibrating and changing temperature. Old Soul Children can also feel the crystal emotionally and mentally and can think of many purposes of why they are drawn to it and how it can help them and others.

Crystals are fantastic accelerators for Old Soul Children, and these can help them to identify their truly spiritual selves and inspire them to reach for their highest potential. Here are some examples for the following areas: pregnancy, giving birth, babies, toddlers, teenagers and young adults.

Pregnancy

Bloodstone is a great crystal to use throughout the nine months, as it is very versatile and gives great grounding energy. It also stills the mind and brings us down to earth. The energy of Bloodstone can also help to guide you in balancing your chakras. If you are feeling tired, try Unakite, Rose Quartz for inner love, and Red Coral and Carnelian to help ground yourself and your unborn baby.

Giving Birth

If you are worried about choosing the wrong crystal for your unborn child, why not meditate to connect with the child's energy and ask what crystal would be suitable for your newborn. Moonstone, Amazonite, Aquamarine and any Agate crystal would be good energies for the new arrival, but the best of all would be using your own intuition.

A birthing crystal will also be an excellent choice to welcome your child into the world. Your intuition will know best what crystal is best for your new arrival. Here are some examples:

Aries	Clear Quartz/ Tekite/Hematite
Taurus	Chryscolla / Rose Quartz
Gemini	Peridot / Aquamarine/Black Onyx
Cancer	Mother of Pearl
Leo	Aventurine/Citrine
Virgo	Citrine/ Harkerite

Libra	Moss Agate/ Orbicular Agate/Green Aventurine
Scorpio	Snowflake Obsidian/ Rhonite
Sagittarius	Aquamarine/ Sodalite
Capricorn	Onyx/ Smokey Quartz
Aquarius	Amethyst
Pisces	Smoky Quartz/ Carrollite

If your child is going to be born on a day in which a cusp will occur, which means when a planet is about to move from one astrological sign to another, then it is best to take a crystal for each astrological sign with you to the birthing room.

Old Soul Babies

For a new born baby, you can hang clear quartz crystals in their bedroom window. This will act as a purifier, energy enhancer and protector, and will also help with nightmares. A rainbow effect can be created when the sun shines through the window, creating a home-made mobile. Rose Quartz and Clear Quartz can also be placed under the mattress whilst asleep in their cot, car seat and pram; this will aid better sleep and also acts as protection.

Old Soul Toddlers

Rose Quartz can help calm your child if they are experiencing the terrible twos. Red Jasper can also help to strengthen the immune system, and Tigers Eye can help calm fears when facing new challenges, like meeting new people or starting playgroup. Aventurine can also help with emotional issues

Old Soul Children and Teenagers

Hematite is great for teenagers with excessive hormones, and Tigers Eye could also be used to help protect them against negative influences. Amethyst is excellent in helping your child with spiritual awareness and intuition, and Clear Quartz can act as an all-rounder, helping them to find out who they really are. Rose Quartz is also an all-round crystal that works well in any given situation. As well as enhancing your Old Soul Child and Teenager's natural healing abilities, placing large Rose Quartz in all of the corners of their bedroom will help aid sleep, prevent nightmares and protect your child. In addition, placing or stitching a Rose Quartz Crystal into their school bag, helps when they are feeling uneasy on their first day at school. Tiger's eye can also help your child feel protected if they are being bullied.

Pink Carnelian helps unconditional love between parent and child. Its harmonious energy can help form a unique bond that can never be broken. No matter what experience parent and child have to go through, it encourages the relationship to grow in harmony.

Apache Tear can help with grief and also is a very good crystal to have in your pocket when you have to go to a funeral. This crystal can give general protection to the whole family, absorb the emotions and help spirits cross over to the other side.

Crystal hearts can be brought as birthday presents to help your Old Soul Child attune to the real magic of their special day. These crystal hearts affirms the love from an adult to an Old Soul Child.

Wearing crystal pendants or power crystal bracelets, or carrying a piece of any kind of crystal in their pockets will help your Old Soul Children and Teenager to feel empowered in every area of their life.

Crystals for Everyday Use for Your Old Soul Child
The following crystals can help your Old Soul Child to remain calm and relaxed, and allow them to express how they are really feeling about any situation. These crystals can also build confi-

dence, bring joy and can be used to enhance creative expression. These crystals can also work at all levels of mind, body, spirit and soul, and also increase spiritual awareness and concentration, by raising energy levels:

Psychic Abilities	Amethyst
Heals Emotional Pain	Aventurine
Helps with Fears	Yellow Topaz/Smoky Quartz/Emerald
Frustration	Moss Agate or Obsidian
Protection	Hematite
Success	Citrine
Intuition	Moonstone/Sapphire
Strength	Amazonite/Magnetite/Ruby
Communication	Blue Lace Agate
Inner Peace	Celesite
Helps with Food Allergies	Citrine
Inspiration	Green Tourmaline
Confidence	Garnet/Hematite/Tiger's Eye
Worries	Purple Fluorite
Enhances Memory	Clacite
Reduces Tension	Malachite
Self Expression	Lapis Lazuli

Place any of your Old Soul children's crystals on the windowsill in their bedroom, so the crystals can absorb the sun's natural healing energy. The energy from the sun and crystals will do two things: Firstly, it will cleanse and energise their bedroom, and secondly, when your child goes to collect the crystal, they will connect with the life force and feel invigorated. If the sun does not shine in their bedroom, you can place their crystals in a room where the sun does come into the house and then later in the day or early evening place them in their bedroom.

Chakra Crystals for Your Old Soul Child

You may wish to ask your Old Soul Child to use their intuition in choosing what crystal is right for them. If they do not feel drawn to the crystals given, they can choose a crystal or stone that they feel drawn to by using the appropriate colours, which correspond to each Chakra.

CHAKRA	CRYSTAL	COLOUR
Base	Red Jasper	Red
Sacral	Carnelian	Orange
Solar Plexus	Yellow Jasper	Yellow
Heart	Rose Quartz/Aventurine	Pink and Green
Throat	Blue Lace Agate	Blue
Third Eye	Amethyst	Purple
Crown	Moonstone	White

Crystals Chosen for Your Old Soul Child

The following crystals, chosen for your Old Soul Child, are suitable should they need guidance on their spiritual purpose, spiritual development and spiritual path in this life on earth – whatever stage they are along their path, whether they are part way through their spiritual journey or whether they are just beginning their quest. These eight crystals have been chosen, not because they have been lying in Mother Earth for an eternity, but because they are amplifiers to help restore and ignite your Old Soul Child to find their true soul path.

Turquoise: To help with friendship and enhance intuition. It helps strengthen the auric field and increases their healing energies, allowing a natural connection and communication to the physical world and spiritual realms.

Amber: Amber can help your Old Soul Child to feel more connected to the physical plane. Amber's soothing and light energy can help with past life issues and give insight into the present.

Jade: Use this for calming and relaxation, and to help bring about emotional balance. Use this energy to examine courage and the real meaning behind it; let it helps you to understand your dreams.

Flint: Caveman used it to light fires and so it can ignite your child's thoughts, ideas and dreams. It can also help your child when they feel disempowered in dealing with stressful situations.

Opal: This has a watery effect and can help with emotions. It can help release blockages and help to lift moods and raise feelings of self-worth. Opal can also give an Old Soul Child hope and happiness for future events.

Coral: Helps aid your Old Soul Child with clear communication and transfers knowledge from previous lives. It can also help with inner peace and wisdom. It is also a good protector and helps restore harmony in the event of emotional conflict.

Pearl: It can help your Old Soul Child restore faith in themselves and also in their surroundings. It helps them to focus on their school work and also helps them strengthen their own belief system.

Jet: Assists with grounding and also helps to prevent nightmares. It can also prevent Psychic attacks and is good for leadership abilities. It facilitates emotional balance, justice and protection, and dispels fear. It absorbs negativity and strengthens psychic awareness, regulating the body's natural energy flow.

Pendulum Power

Pendulums have been used for divination and dowsing, and have existed in various forms for thousands of years, coming in many varieties, shapes, sizes and weights. Ancient civilizations used pendulums to find water, oil and even gold. Today, however, many use the pendulum to guide them in finding the correct answers to important questions for their life. I used mine during healing work on clients and also for my own inner growth.

My first experience of a pendulum was when I was a child. I clearly remember my Nan, Phyll , using her wedding ring on a piece of cotton as a pendulum, to find out what child everyone was expecting and she was right every time. Crystal pendulums swing freely when children start to play with them; this is how they learn to use them.

To Make Your Own Pendulum
A homemade pendulum will work just as well as a classic one. A cork tied to a piece of string, or a stone from the garden, will give the same effect. My children and I like to make our own from an assortment of gemstone beads, which can be brought from New Age shops or on the internet.

Choosing a Pendulum
A child MUST choose the pendulum that they most have affinity with, as it will always work better for them and they can tune it to their own energy. Let your child try as many as they wish before they purchase one; the Pendulum will call out to them.

It is important to let them spend some time learning how it works properly for themselves. They may want to cleanse it by soaking it in Sea Salt, to free it from other energies.

How to Use Your Pendulum
With an open mind and in a clam and comfortable state, suspend any disbelief that you may have about the pendulum not working for you.

Next, you will need to establish which way the Pendulum will swing for Yes and No. Hold your Pendulum and place your other hand underneath it. Ask the Pendulum what direction is for Yes and which direction is No (ask these questions one at a time), and it will swing in a gentle way. It moves in a different direction for everyone.

When you have established which way the Pendulum is swinging and you feel confident to ask it questions, you have to make sure that the questions you ask are CLEAR and that the Pendulum can give you a Yes or No answer.

Make sure that you completely stop your pendulum's motion between questions so that you get a clear answer for each question asked.

You could keep a notebook to write down your questions and your pendulum's responses.

Please note; questions about personal wealth or next week's lotto draw may never be answered. This falls into the category of personal gain, and there is a huge difference between personal gain and personal improvement. Some Wiccans will use their pendulum for protection, cleansing and shielding. They will use it, for example, to ask about finding work, or making their wages stretch, which is completely different to the 'I want lots and lots of money' approach. It is down to an issue of personal responsibility in how you use your pendulum.

As a Pagan, I am aware of the Wiccan principle of the 'Threefold law of return'. What ever energy you put into the world (positive or negative) it will be returned to you, three times the power. So, if you need pennies from heaven and ask your Pendulum to tell you when they are coming, you may find your bank account empty for unforeseen financial purchases. Actions then need to be balanced or you may find things get out of control before getting back to normality.

How to Make Your Gem Essence

Gem Essence is a form of vibrational healing. This is where the vibration of something is used to help you heal. This form of healing contains essential properties that can help your Old Soul

Child harmonise their mind, body, spirit and soul connection, and they respond very quickly to it. It also stimulates the body's own ability to self heal and helps restore balance and harmony. Essences can be used on plants and animals and are suitable for any age.

Before you begin, it is important to find out the characteristics of the crystals you are using. Some crystals are known to be toxic and soluble and will crack in direct sunlight.

Place your chosen crystal in a glass bowl, fill it with clear mineral water and leave it for twelve hours or over night. Personally, I have found that, when I am making some essences, the time of day is not a critical factor in the preparation, but the intention is the most important thing to consider, alongside a calm and focused mind.

Next, put the gem essence water into a dropper bottle. When making these for myself, I use a combination of 50% brandy and 50% water, so that the essence is preserved and no bacteria will grow in the bottle. For my Old Soul Children, I tend you use an alcohol-free formula, which is a mixture of water and vinegar or vegetable glycerine.

Label the bottle (e.g. Amethyst Essence), date the mixture and use it within a week. It is best to make your essences as you need them; this will keep the vibrations and the water pure.

To Take Gem Essence

You can place between two and four drops directly onto your tongue. Alternatively, place two to six drops in a glass, add mineral water and sip slowly. You can also add them to your Old Soul Child's bath to help restore their whole energy field.

Use it also as an auric cleanser by placing a few drops into a diffuser sprayer; spraying their whole bedroom and the rest of house will change and maintain positive energy in your home.

How Gem Essence Works

Gem essences are excellent to promote inner healing. They can strengthen our positive qualities and help with emotional and psychological healing, as well as helping to break the negative cycle of past conditioning. As each crystal has a different healing effect, intuitively, you will know what physical, mental, emotional and spiritual aspect your child will need to help them dissolve any blockages or issues they may have. Let the magic of crystals work with your Old Soul Child and bring magic into your life every day.

Mandalas for Children

(created by George David Fryer)

Mandala is Sanskrit word and comes from the classical language of India and of Hinduism. It means 'circle' and 'centre'. Mandalas are a representation of the universe and act as a collection point for universal forces. They have been known to many ancient cultures throughout history, and were used for self knowledge and spiritual knowledge. Mandalas are very popular today in art therapy, and can be found in ancient Tibetan religious designs, Navajo sand paintings, and huge stained glass windows in medieval cathedrals.

Carl Jung believed the Mandalas are 'a representation of the unconscious self' and their symbolic nature can help as an aid to meditation and trance induction. Jung encouraged his patients to draw Mandalas to help them express their own inner feelings when they had trouble taking.

Every child is born an artist and when a child picks up a pencil for the very first time, between the ages of three and five, they naturally draw Mandalas. Drawing circles, sketching and doodling allows them to connect to their inner spiritual selves, at any given time, and also connects them to sacred symbols and awakens their own creative powers. Doing this on a daily basis helps them to gradually express their creative selves, whilst helping their feeling and intuitive skills. It also brings a lot of enjoyment.

Mandalas can be used as creative tools for anyone. When children are working with mandalas, they find that it is a relaxing, stress-free activity, which helps to soothe their minds.

During this fun activity, anyone can gain access to intuitive insights about themselves. However, for the Old Soul Child, colouring or even creating their own Mandala is an empowering experience, because they can really express themselves without being held back by fears of criticism. This also aids your child's positive self-image.

Using a Mandala as a meditation aid has proven to restore peace of mind, relieve depression, and inspire motivation. It helps to relax your physical, emotional, mental and spiritual health, and can ground you when you are feeling unsteady. Whilst meditating, it accesses the powers of healing, knowledge, and restfulness.

In my opinion, it is a fantastic experience for both children and their parents, whilst painting and drawing together. With my children, I encourage them to imagine a wish and to paint a Mandala whilst thinking of that wish. Sometimes my children even write their wishes, so that they will not forget about them. I really have to resist the temptation to walk around and see what they are doing, as I believe it is distracting.

Mandalas are never alike; they carry the child's own soul energy, which is unique to them and assists with their soul's unfoldment and development.

Personal symbolic colours, chosen by them, benefit them by connecting them to their inner child and creating inner peace, which also balances and restores their chakras.

Children find that there is no religious or cultural resistance to drawing them and the children have told me that, when they are working on them, it helps to take their mind off other things and gives them a chance to relax and let go of what is troubling them. Jade says that it helps to clear her mind so that it does not wander off, and it relieves headaches.

The different forms of Mandala will call for your attention to help your individual light shine. They are undemanding and contain many healing properties, which makes them accessible to people with widely varying skills: children, those with disabilities, the elderly, imaginative and the talented artist.

There are many colouring books that contain Mandalas, which can be found on the internet. Alternatively, you can create your own. The first hurdle to overcome is your belief of 'I cannot draw'.

Whilst drawing the circle, we begin to manifest our own creativity and are able to bring our vision and inner images into physical manifestation with colour, and the masterpiece that you create can be used as a meditation mandala for your daily contemplation. This will enhance personal power for you and your child and help to rediscover your creativity whilst having fun.

Mercury Retrograde

Mercury, the planet of communication, is named after the 'Winged Messenger'; the Roman God who was noted for his speed and swiftness.

Mercury is the ruling planet of Gemini and Virgo, and represents thinking patterns, ideas, methods, information, our mental outlook, and the way we think and communicate. It helps us to move from one thing to the next and find answers to those burning questions.

In Astrology, the planet Mercury is also known as 'The Cosmic Trickster', and will retrograde every four months, three to four times a year, lasting nineteen to twenty-four days. When a planet goes retrograde, it appears to move backwards through the zodiac, going contrary to its normal direction in the sky. It also, literally, moves closer to the earth and looms larger in terms of visibility. All of the planets, except the sun and moon, have retrograde periods. However, Mercury is most famous for them, which many people watch.

Many of my friends have reported 'Mercury retrograde horror stories': communications go awry, computers misbehave, arguments erupt, telephones break down, transportation is affected, cars do not run, and buses and trains are late. Everything comes to a grinding halt, and people are so frustrated because they are stationary.

It is wise not to make important decisions while Mercury is retrograde, as we will be clouded by misinformation. Mercury influences mental clarity and the power of the mind, so when in retrograde, we can make mistakes, which can make us feel foolish and inadequate.

Mercury retrograde affects people differently, depending on where it is in their personal birth chart. For me, personally, I abandon signing documents, having business meetings and travelling to new places until after Mercury turns direct in motion. I am not advising you not make any decisions in that period. However, from past experience, I have had to be prepared to change details later, as I always receive new information, which alters decisions made.

Retrograde Activities

During Mercury Retrograde periods, you and your Old Soul Child can take advantage of the three weeks to talk about what has occurred previously to you both, and to take time out to reflect upon and reconsider your experiences. One of the activities we do at home is to write down as many words beginning with RE as possible. In this astounding time, you can REview, REdo, REthink, REorganise, REhash, REconsider and REplan all areas of your lifestyle. If you are feeling stuck during Mercury Retrograde, then why not list all the words, with your Old Soul Child, beginning with RE and see what areas you can bring harmony to.

In its powerful but simple way, Mercury reflects back to us what we need to look at in our own lives and our own experiences. A change in the direction we are heading, allows progressive ideas to be mulled over before a commitment is made. Why not go on the internet and find out when Mercury goes retrograde. Any significant new endeavours, could then be planed around each retrograde, so that they succeed with effective planning, actions and decisions. When the retrograde arrives, you can then use it as a period of reflection, and plan what to do when Mercury goes direct again.

As for Old Soul Families, it is time to reflect on what you have achieved as a family and where you all want to redirect your new energies. Reviewing and deciding if you are ALL on the right yellow brick road of life will support every member of the family.

Old Soul Children and families can be deeply affected by the subtle changes that Mercury retrograde brings; affects everyone individually. Those who are born when Mercury retrogrades have an easier time and thrive when it revisits their own signs again. Below, is some information, which was given to me by my guides,

Running Bear and Camarius, on how Mercury retrograde affects your Old Soul Child:

Aries Child

When Mercury retrograde is placed in their sign, they can become impatient, irritable, quick-tempered and very headstrong. They will lack physical and emotional energy and run out of patience with others. We need to teach them to take three deep breaths before speaking or acting impatiently.

They can get carried along with their own verbal, one-sided viewpoints, and fail to listen to the other side. They will make snap decisions and opinions and will become verbally and mentally restless.

It becomes a verbal war; they forget to communicate as knowledge becomes their power, which corrupts their thinking. They then become very impatient and highly impulsive.

Taurus Child

With a Taurus child, stubborn thinking is increased in their own thoughts of how their world should be. They tend to rush about, not take time when learning new things and feel that plodding along is what they should be doing. They will begin to question everything that comes their way in those three weeks. They feel uncomfortable in surroundings that are not common to them and will not go to new places to meet new people. They are like a 'bull in a china shop' if approached from the wrong angle, as their stubbornness becomes an irrepressible force that will not shift.

If they are working, they become lazy, lethargic and dissatisfied rather quickly, and may find themselves unemployed because of losing interest during the Mercury retrograde period. They find it difficult to manage their material and monetary worlds during this period, which makes them feel unsteady and unstable.

Their tempers, angers and aggression are displayed openly to loved ones because they feel safe in their surroundings. Sarcasm is often used when speaking, as they are feeling low due to their lack of self esteem in retrograde period.

Gemini Child

A Gemini child will become even more restless and highly-strung, and their curious nature can lead them into trouble. They become fidgety, missing vital points in schoolwork and lacking in concentration because their minds crave more and more stimulation

As this sign is the symbol of twins, they will see issues from both sides, which also gives them double worries. They will distrust others and become agitated very quickly. They stick to their own decisions and will oppose others in making them for them.

As Mercury rules Gemini, their own nervousness is heightened more and they become inconsistent with everything in their life. They will reflect that they need more changes in their lives and take every single thing that happens to them very seriously. Life, for them, is dull, and they become fickle in every aspect, throwing tantrums if they do not get what they want.

Cancer Child

A Cancer child will become easily distracted in their achievements, which leads them to take things too personally. As they are open in their surroundings, this could lead to them feeling depressed and unable to lift their mood. Feeling insecure of their own abilities, they have a tendency to become deceptive with their own frustrations.

They become more overly sensitive and emotional, very moody and lazy, and pay less attention to detail whilst studying. They are unmoved and less sympathetic to those they love when Mercury is in retrograde. They retreat into their own shells, becoming unsociable, sulky, self-pitying and difficult to live with. They are tactless when approached, and can easily corrupt their environments to get their own way.

Leo Child

A Leo child will become extremely creative, tending to get wrapped up in their own projects and shut out the rest of the world because they are only interested in their own ideas. These projects tend to fall apart because of becoming single-minded and not sharing the keys to their successes.

They tend to get trapped during Mercury retrograde because, previously, they tend to put all of their eggs into one basket, which leads them to being inflexible with everyone that they meet. They keep their fears to themselves because they do not want to experience humiliation and criticism, which may lead to them coming across as arrogant, which they will simply hate.

Interaction with others becomes a thing of the past, as their excessive temper flares up at the slightest thing that does not fit into their lives. Pride may often go before a fall, as their attempts to control their lives and other people's fails every way they try.

Virgo Child

When Mercury retrograde is in their sign, they tend to become very critical, finicky and fussy over the smallest things. They complicate matters, not just for themselves, but for everyone, as they begin not to trust easily and to project this onto others.

As they are born perfectionists, they tend not to take care in their school work and do not completely finish tasks. There is no sign of their high expectations of themselves, as they begin to turn molehills into mountains.

They find faults in others, which can be very critical, whilst they are feeling vulnerable. Their distrusting nature can make them seem cold, distant and very good at losing their cool when confronted with obstacles.

Libra Child

During Mercury retrograde, a Libra child will become more weak-willed and introverted, as they weigh up every aspect of their own life and also of others. They can show extreme rage when their buttons are pressed and become impatient of routine. Sulking every waking moment, they become indecisive when decisions have to be made and their temperament seems to change every five seconds.

Scorpio Child

Mercury retrograde will make a Scorpio child more aggressive and forceful in situations that they feel afraid of. They become very emotional, secretive, intrusive to others and tactless. They also begin to become irresponsible by not finishing what they have started. They can appear to be withdrawn from their environments and vindictive towards others when not getting their own way.

They do not reason with others, and their persuading powers fail to impress others to let them have their own way. Because Scorpios become more sensitive during Mercury retrograde, their pride allows them to be easily hurt and attack their opponents with insults.

Never giving up, their suspicious outlook is heightened, at this time, because of their own insecurities, and the belief that there is a reason behind everything.

Sagittarius Child

A Sagittarius child will lack confidence because of missing vital information and their minds will become scattered. Their natural strength will become out of balance and they will shift into becoming quite outspoken and judgemental.

They can become less forgiving and too demanding of their peers. They will flare up at the slightest mistake and fail to see their own. They work at faster paces and rush their school work, making mistakes, which they will not look at along the way.

Their desire to be freer is the main drive that keeps them going during Mercury retrograde.

Capricorn Child

Capricorns tend to build a fortress which is magnified during retrograde periods; they feel insincere about themselves and are unable to reach their own goals. Impractical and unrealistic risk-taking is increased, and they become reserved in themselves when Mercury retrograde is taking place.

They seem to come across as depressed individuals because their own unhappiness is buried deep down inside. A pessimistic nature helps them to spread doom and gloom for themselves and others. Giving up on life, this can become overbearing for others in their company.

Pessimistic, fatalistic, miserly and grudging of others; their mood swings create unhappiness for everyone that comes along their path. Worry and anguish are held onto, as they are unsure that letting go is the best thing to do.

Aquarius Child

When Mercury is in this sign, the child's thinking is more introspective. They tend to think about issues which are out of their comfort zone and become the rebel to all causes. Becoming detached from their environments and friends, during periods of retrograde, they feel lonely and become absent-minded when wanting their own way.

They are happy to spend time on their own and come across cold, aloof and unemotional in most situations. They demand more of others, which becomes unreasonable and then they get disappointed quickly when let down and find it hard to forgive. Their anger can be fierce; they cannot see their own faults and even transfer them onto others.

Pisces Child

A Pisces child will become secretive, careless, unimpressed with everything, unsympathetic and indecisive during Mercury retrograde. This sign tends to be more uncompassionate and feel down on their luck, which becomes a curse.

They tend to also feel uncreative about their lives and feel vulnerable with life lessons, because of not knowing what road to take. They become concerned with their own problems rather than others.

Egotism takes over and they mislead others in what they want them to believe in. They are often seen as dreamy throughout most of their life, but this period often is a time for them to become more introspective. This comes across as pessimistic, impractical and fearful because they are feeling emotionally restrained.

To find Mercury in your birth chart, I would recommend that you find an astrologer. Derek Hawkins is a psychic working intuitively through the medium of astrology. In interpreting the birth chart, he is able to advise, inform and empower people. Standing in your own birth chart does have a profound effect on you, which gives insight into your own unique personality. Contact details can be found at the back of this book and I recommended that this is a great way to be introduced to the art of astrology.

NLP – Neuro Linguistic Programming
(A huge appreciation and thanks to Gemma Bailey in helping me write about the true concept of NLP and what it can do for you.)

NLP stands for Neuro Linguistic Programming. NLP is a set of psychological tools which can help improve how you think, behave and feel.

Neuro Linguistic Programming means the following: 'Neuro' relates to the brain and the sensory information coming into our nervous system. 'Linguistic' refers to language and other non-verbal ways that we give meaning to the sensory information we receive. 'Programming' describes the patterns and systems we run to achieve our outcomes.

NLP was developed by Richard Bandler and John Grinder in

the early 1970s. I think it's important to use the word 'developed', as they didn't actually 'create' something new, just identified something that was already in existence. They wanted to know why and how some people were masters at influencing and changing human behaviour. When they identified who these people were, they set about modelling them to find out, specifically, how these people were so effective.

NLP is an art and a science. It teaches us techniques and strategies that help us to communicate and use our thoughts more effectively. NLP reminds us that whatever we focus on in our environment (by way of seeing, hearing, smelling, tasting and touching) has an impact on the thoughts that we create. These thoughts affect the way that we feel; our feelings affect our behaviour and reactions and our behaviour and reactions will influence the results we achieve in our lives. The developers of NLP modelled others who were excellent within the field of therapy, language, psychoanalysis and anthropology to learn the ways they consistently achieved positive results and change.

NLP and hypnotherapy are very interlinked. Both teach us about ways of achieving and terminating trance. Trance is a very useful state that we enter into at varying depths, at different points, during our usual daily lives. For example, when we 'zone out' when driving. They both help to create changes in the unconscious part of the mind, which is the part of the mind responsible for generating and maintaining habits and instincts – the things that you do without having to think about doing them – such as breathing. Hypnotherapy usually involves the client being in a deep, relaxing trance state during which time, directions for change can be given that are more readily accepted by the unconscious part of the mind.

NLP tends to be more interactive, and does not usually require a trance induction. Instead, the client may be asked to make adjustments to the thoughts that they have. For example, if they have a fear of something and constantly recall a threatening picture related to that fear, they may be asked to change elements of the picture that will help to reduce the fear, such as changing the picture from colour to black and white. NLP also uses our language and our bodies in different ways to alleviate the effects of problems. So, if something makes you feel depressed and your body sinks down, you would be encouraged to sit up and breathe deeply. If you find yourself saying that something is 'difficult', you would be encouraged, as an alternative, to say that it is 'not easy'; this creates the possibility of achievement within your neurology, instead of feeling that there is no point in trying.

NLP is based around 'presuppositions', which are convenient beliefs that I recommend all parents live by. How many times have you heard your children say, "I can't do it!" and felt totally frustrated? One of the presuppositions of NLP is that 'there is no failure, only feedback'. If you can teach your children to live by this belief, you will increase their motivation, willingness and determination, which will lead them into making greater discoveries and increase their levels of perseverance. Remember though, that children learn by example, so you have to be a leader and set the example you want them to follow.

In terms of how NLP can apply to other areas of life; it is fast growing in business due to the techniques that facilitate effective persuasion and communication; it is also used in education, so that teaching can be customised to meet individual learning styles. Athletes can also benefit from the strategies that enable them to achieve a peak state in quick, simple steps. Anyone, who ever communicates with another person, can benefit from learning about what NLP has to offer.

Children are egocentric creatures because, on the whole, they depend on others for their survival. Therefore, all Old Soul Children can benefit from NLP by becoming more aware of others, as well as discovering who they truly are and who they want to be. We all want our children to have a positive impact on society and our community, and we want them to be balanced and happy. However, as adults, in the western world, we find that life seems to become more stressful and complicated as we evolve. NLP can teach them how to perceive problems as challenges, how to communicate their needs, how to access good feeling, and many more useful skills. If your child lacks useful thoughts and emotions, then NLP could be very beneficial.

NLP should be integrated into teaching training and used in schools, as it would be very useful for teachers to learn ways of teaching that appeal to a greater majority of their class. As an example, some people learn best by hearing instructions on what they need to do, some prefer to see it being done and others like to get on and do it. Teachers should be taught in all of these learning styles, instead of teaching in the way that feels most comfortable to them. Their most comfortable teaching style might only appeal to half of the class. We often hear in the news about the lack of respect from children in schools, and teachers being fearful of their pupils. There are ways of using your body when gesturing that send off unconscious signals to those you are communicating with and if your signals say 'You make me feel uneasy', then we can begin to understand how teenagers and children begin to overstep the mark at times. NLP can teach us different ways of using our bodies that command greater respect and say 'It's time to be quiet and listen to me.' In NLP they use something called 'The Feedback Sandwich', which is basically stating what is good, what could be better and overall what was good. When this is used in training/learning, it keeps the focus on improving, instead of what was wrong. As we tend to get more of what we focus on, pointing out all of the things they were done wrong is not necessarily beneficial; it can lead to de-motivation. When the corrections that need to be made are sandwiched between what was good, it keeps motivation high and sends the signal that the achievement was valued. This would help with raising your Old Soul Child, as we can be completely unaware of our behaviour and place expectations on our children.

NLP can help parents to discover ways of empowering their children to become better leaders and decision makers. It can also help babies, toddlers, teenagers and young adults to communicate clearly, which would mean that a lot of arguments would cease to exist and many problems would disappear.

NLP can help children become more confident, but confidence doesn't necessarily mean happy, or motivated or understanding or unfearful. We want our children to be well-rounded emotionally, so that they do not experience peaks and troughs in their emotions. NLP can provide ways of increasing positive emotions that children can be taught to use when they feel that they need a boost. Also, remember that anything one child says or does is likely to get mimicked by many other children. Wouldn't it be great if it was your child setting a positive inspiring trend?

NLP is a good way to help with parenting your Old Soul Child and can show you new skills to improve the way you influence your own child. As a parent of three Old Soul Children, I know that my behaviour and the way I communicate with my children will influence them, not just in those five minutes, but that it will leave a huge impact on them for the rest of their lives. Children do as we do, not as we say. If our behaviour contradicts what we tell our children, they will mimic us. So, if we want our children to excel in all areas of life, the best thing to do is to use all areas of life as positive examples that our children can model. There are many times that my children will push the boundaries, to see how far they can get before I make them stop. This is a vital part of their learning journey as they mature into young adults and if your child is strong willed, they may not be sure where those boundaries might me. They can take the risk of speaking out about what they know. Children do this because it show's they are capable of being comfortable in their own power and feel safe in their own environment. Just keep the boundaries firm and remember that, once they are really secure, you can relax occasionally for a treat or for a fun day.

When a child has decided to have a tantrum in the middle of the supermarket, restaurant or even at home, never scream back at them. Just keep your own manner calm, but containing. If you scream back, you just feed the battle of wills. Have respect for the growing will of the child but help them to temper their power. Part of this phase is that they are actually afraid of their own power and need help in handling it.

Children have a natural resilience, which helps them bounce back from situations that they have to face. If you let your child express everything and share their feelings of upset, then they will not have lasting effect on them and they will not suffer from ingrained trauma. What also helps with Old Soul Children's self-confidence is for them to that it is the world that is wrong, not them. Of course, if a child gets continual messages that they are not doing very well, then they will lack confidence, and begin to believe that message. However, as parents, giving them love and affirmation, you can override that, particularly if you explain that it is not wrong to be different. A good lesson for them to learn is not to believe in all that the world seems to say, but as a family you can take your own stand and belief system against it.

If you appreciate your Old Souls Child's point of view, then you are halfway to helping them move forward and experience new and wonderful things in all areas of life.

NLP is fantastic for families with children that have Attention Deficit Disorder or ADHD, as it is commonly known. I have met countless numbers of parents who feel powerless, as the society that they are living in are not supporting the family and not finding ways to help their child to master their own emotions.

NLP4Kids is a programme that was founded by Gemma Bailey and Kay Gill in 2007. It is used for teaching NLP to children in an experiential way, such as by doing role-play and games. The knowledge has been simplified and is very covert in its teaching. For example, if a child believes that they are unable to do something (such as achieve a particular grade in school) a suitable, role-play activity could be to have them pretending to be their teacher, or someone who believes that they are capable of achieving. You would then ask the child, who is acting as 'teacher', how he/she knows that the child will succeed and what evidence she has. The child will answer these questions as if they really are the teacher, saying things like, "Oh, I know he can get an A because he really knows a lot about his subject and he revises a lot." In doing so, the child will be accessing positive internal resources that will put them in a better state for actual achievement. I really do feel that this programme can help so many children and I urge parents to book on these wonderful courses.

NLP is a must for our Old Soul Children who are living in this ever changing world.

Why are Some People Able to Accept the Concept of Ghosts with an Open Mind, While Others Cannot?

Some people dismiss the spirit world as jiggery-pokery. Others wait in the firm belief that loved ones, who have passed over, will be in contact one day.

I firmly believe that, after ten years of research, children's imaginary companions are a sign that your child is open to a whole other magical dimension of life because they have a natural doorway, connecting to the spiritual realms. Parents, in today's society, really need to help their Old Soul Children to open up to the magical worlds, so that their worldly experiences are accepted in everyday life and not frowned upon.

Natural mediums, sensitives and clairvoyants are able to hear, see, perceive, feel, sense and communicate with the spirit world – giving their clients evidence that the door to spirit contact can remain open into adulthood because the magic never died. I, for one, never listened when told that ghosts don't exist. I still see spirit guides, angels, people that have passed over and the faerie kingdom on a daily basis, but this is maybe because I have an advantage – I was born on Halloween.

Halloween is when the veil between dimensions is at its thinnest. On Samhain, the spirits can slip back to visit the world that they resided in before their death. Many traditions around the world maintain that, if you are born on this day, you have a natural ability to see spirits of any kind.

But what about the Old Soul Children? Why can they connect?

When a child is born into this world, they are un-programmed and as they grow up, their minds are open to endless possibilities. Their connection is still strong because they have not forgotten where they come from, and consciously know that other dimensions exist, which amalgamate into our world. Old Soul Children are more receptive to spirits because they do not have years of social conditioning and do not have reams of information going through their thought processes like an adult.

To the Old Soul Child, impossible things can happen and they go with what they feel without thinking of logical answers or feeling fear. Old Soul Children are also not afraid to say what they think. However, when we tell other adults of our experiences, some believe and some are sceptic. The reply may be "You must have been imaging it!" Or "Have you had too much too drink?". If society reacted in a less negative way, and were more accommodating, would we all be more accepting and more creative in our thinking?

Adults search for answers to questions with logical thinking to give them reassurance, which sometimes they cannot find; adults will convince themselves that there is logic and it only has to be found. Old Soul Children, however, are more open to ideas than adults, because they are not set in their own belief system. As adults, we are not even aware, of what higher realms are all about!

The spirits that come and play with your child could, in fact, be children, adults or animals that are missing their earthly connection, family members and friendships. We must also consider the spirits that are new to crossing over, and get stuck because they have not finished their earthly business. Most of the Old Soul Children that I have interviewed, always believe that their friends are living people.

Old Soul Children see more than adults for one simple reason... no one has told them that they aren't supposed to see things like that. As we grow up, we are all shaped by the beliefs of our parents, family and then our society. Until that point, however, we are free and unbiased. We really need to make it easier for them to accept that what they are observing is perfectly natural and not to be afraid. In today's world we are raising Old Soul Children who are more spiritually awakened than we are. This is because, when they are in the Interlife, planning their next incarnation, their spiritual needs became a top priority and decides the types of Soul Path Lessons they need to enhance their own spiritual growth.

Father Christmas, the Tooth Fairy, Bogey man, Jack Frost and the Fairies at the bottom of the garden are an important part of childhood. When the time comes, where adults tell them that they do not exist, some are left heartbroken; others refuse to believe it and never stop believing. However, some adults still tap into the magic and spirit of these tales, which can remain in our hearts and minds forever.

As explained in Chapter One, it seems that children, up to the age of eight, are receptive to spirit contact. After this time, the tangible, concrete world of logical strategies and mathematical equations sets in. As the child challenges what they know, starts to perceive and test boundaries, questions their parents and, importantly, absorbs their peers' perspectives and opinions, some faculties may get lost or hidden away?

From the age of ten, Old Soul Children start wondering if what they see if real, or just their imagination. A spirit will continue to try and get their attention, but this confuses and scares the Old Soul Child, causing them to shut down their connection with the spirit world, and their natural abilities cease.

It is truly important to support your Old Soul Child and tell them exactly what is going on, explaining that they have a 'special gift'. This is so crucial, as I feel that not talking about it will make them feel that something is wrong with them. If an Old Soul Child has got no family support, they may feel that they really do have something to fear. From experience, the age of the Old Soul Child is very relevant here, because the doorway to spiritual awareness maybe close to closing down and their spirit family do not want to close that door.

With my own Old Soul Children, Jade, Amba and Leo, I have been very open about it from the start and now they have developed a deep interest in all spiritual things, but there is no pressure on them, if they wish to drop it for something else.

Its like Piccadilly Circus at home, especially when I know that I will always have a houseful of spirits and that they are around more often than I think they are. Leo always says that a man is walking through our house. Could it be the spirit of a man coming to say hello or walking in his own time and crossed over into ours? Our dog, Max, will even lay in his bed growling at things that I cannot see and our four cats will hiss and their fur will stand up on their backs, while looking again at things I cannot see.

Sit down with your Old Soul Child, and keep reaffirming that what they are seeing is OK. Take time to sit down with your child. Ask them simple questions about this friend and you might be surprised about what they will tell you. A lot of times, you can verify this information by asking questions about the house at the local council offices, your neighbours and searching the internet.

Old Soul Children are, generally, laid back and do not have worries about their education or what they are going to be when they grow up. They just go with the flow, which really does wind up past generations. Frequently, such children are misunderstood and those who do not understand their special abilities trample on their sensitivities. Today's schooling, for example, is based on Victorian values, which drastically need updating. By writing this book, I aspire to broaden other people's awareness and inspire parents to empower their children to reach for the stars and beyond.

Many parents struggle to bring up a positive Old Soul Child in today's ever-changing world, as they have their own set of spiritual values, which challenge the old ways of doing things with new thinking. However, parents wishing to nurture the special nature of their child should use boundless exercises as Old Soul Children often learn more from experience than from intellect) to spark their imagination and help them to become grounded on the earth plane.

Old Soul Children are born positive, which needs to be encouraged for them to be the best that they can be. As they grow, they are not bothered about material wealth or designer names, and are just happy connecting with Mother Nature.

I saw my own daughter, Jade, when she was eight, struggling with the concept of 'seeing things'. During the time, she was at a different school and the talk of ghosts was banned from playground discussion because it frightened other children. It also upset teachers, because of their own belief system, years of conditioning and their own inner fears. This situation is extremely difficult for children who really do have spiritual gifts that need to be nurtured on a daily basis. Jade would come home from her old school feeling that no one would ever understand her or they think her mad for seeing things. At that time, Jade spent most of her school day alone and told me what happened when she came home from school. In one serious incident, when she was being bullied, Jade was tied to a tree in the playground. She was terrified of what might happen to her next, but then her Great Grandfather, John, appeared to her and said that help will be on its way. As we are a sensitive family and feel deeply for what happens to each other, this reassured us that her spirit family were always looking out for her at this most distressing time.

Jade does seem to be having the problems of an Old Soul Child who is aware of more than the moment and the present image. With my help, she will be able to grasp the concept that 'seeing beyond the veil ' is a natural gift that people really do have, which, in time, will help other people.

Chapter Six

A Collection of Your Stories

David Wigzell, Amba Holmes, Leo Holmes, Amanda
Britton, Nina Hawthorn, Tansy, Lucinda Bender, , Stephen
Rose,Whisk, Kirsteen Black, Liz From New Zealand, Becky
From Cardiff, Billy, Carly Smith, Grandma Jessica and
Windy Blow, Will, Martin and Darby, The Imaginary Cow,
Becky, , Jennifer, Adam, Sue Price, Jenny Kenny, Joanne
Patterson Mary Day, Ada Odell, and Nanny Ghost

The most beautiful thing we can experience is the mysterious.
Einstein

Since my research began, ten years ago, it has taken me on many
wonderful journeys in the search of stories about children and
their imaginary friends. I could fill another three books with all
the amazing stories that I have heard. This chapter contains just
small sample of your stories.

David Wigzell

David Wigzell contacted me after I appeared on a BBC Southern
Counties Radio phone in, regarding my research. At the time of
his stories, he lived with his family in the Taunis Hills; a little
north of Frankfurt, in a town called Oberusel, and was teaching in
an American International School.

When his two daughters were young (Eliane, now thirty-five,
was about three, and her younger sister, Sophia (known as Sisi)
was too small to do anything but feed and burp), they each had an
imaginary friend, one a baby and one a husband. The details are
quite amusing.

As David's wife called him 'Dave', this became the generic term for all husbands. For example, Eliane would ask "Is John, Mary's Dave?" rather than "Is John, Mary's husband?" She also announced that she would have a Dave of her own one day and subsequently, every now and then, she would tell them what her Dave was doing, what he did for a living, etc. After a while, they noticed that Eliane hadn't mentioned him much lately and eventually, David said, "How is your Dave?" She shrugged, and said casually, "Oh he's dead." And that was the end of him. David adds that he was not too sure if she really understood the concept of death at this time.

Sisi's imaginary friend also arrived at the age of three. She adopted a baby into the family and they had to be careful not to tread on it, or sit on it. On one famous occasion, they were having a picnic in the forest and to reach their favourite spot, David had to drive up a long muddy track. On the way back from the picnic, Sisi suddenly screamed, "We've left the baby!" She became very distressed and nothing David could say would persuade her that the baby would be waiting for them when they got home. David finally took pity on her obvious distress and had to back the car several hundred yards up the track to the picnic spot (since turning the car was impossible and going forward and turning at the bottom of the track was met with more distress, as Sisi thought the whole family was going home without the baby). Back at the picnic spot, David held the car door open while the baby climbed in, and all was well.

The baby quietly disappeared, but a few years later, when she had actually started school, Sisi had some imaginary animals that lived in the bottom of the wardrobe in Dave's bedroom. They were called the 'Grabbly Things'. They had five legs, were about the size of small rabbits, and were made of pink plastic. Sisi would hear them around the house saying, "Come on, grabblies," in the most affectionate terms. Eliane went along with this, even pretending she could see them too and David says there were times when he almost saw them himself.

Sisi also had imaginary houses. She would lay claim to an area of the floor, not always in the most convenient place in the room, but usually in the corner, and it would be marked out with a few small objects. She would sit in the middle of it, and woe betides anyone who stepped into it. This pattern lasted much longer that the imaginary friends – up to about seven years old.

David said that the games the girls played as kids were quite imaginative; pretend games figured largely. Neither were interested in competitive sport, in the least; both liked to sing and dance. Both were very intelligent, but he had no success trying to teach them to play chess, although other board games were popular.

My Daughter, Amba

In November 2002, I was pregnant again, which sadly ended in a miscarriage. Amba was running around in her nappy and, for no apparent reason, she wanted to go upstairs and took Eric by the hand. I decided to follow them upstairs and Amba walked into Jade's bedroom and climbed up onto the rocking horse. Amba began to look at the window, and started to wave. Eric asked "who are you waving to, Amba?"

"The man, Dad," Amba said, and waved even more.

"There's no one there," said a puzzled Eric.

I stood behind Eric and whispered, "Don't tell her that there is no one there, just go along with it and see what happens."

Amba continued to wave, and then said, "Man gone now."

"Where has the man gone Amba?" I asked.

"Gone home," Amba replied and then went to play with her toys.

A few days later, the girls and I were getting ready to go to school, when Jade came running into the bathroom and said "Mum, Amba's saying the man is in the cupboard. Shall I let him out?"

"Yes, why not." I replied and walked toward to doorway. As I did that, Amba shouted, "Man's out now," and I felt someone walk past me, leaving a cold breeze behind them.

My Son, Leo

My son, Leo, seems to be more spirituality aware than the girls were at his age. There have been many times when he has left my husband feeling that a cold shiver has run down his spine. Leo talks about his other mummy, and that she lives very far away and, when quizzed, he starts talking about the tractors we have seen earlier or the shops that he has been to. For Leo, it is just a natural thing for him to talk about without getting worried about it.

We went to Scotland for Christmas in 2006 and it seemed that something or someone had hitched a ride with us and joined us on our holiday. Leo began staring into corners and Eric thought that it was freaky because it was as if someone was there. Eric became more worried about Leo, because he could see it and Eric could not. For Eric, however, it has got easier over the years because he has got used to the kids saying things and it no longer 'spooks him out'.

When we came home, Leo would wake up, on a regular basis, and tell us that the man had woken him up.

Jack and Harry entered our lives when we went to Ireland in September 2007 and have been with us ever since. Jack and Harry are brothers and they play with Leo a lot. Leo often talks about London where Jack goes to work.

We went to Ireland for our family holiday in September 2007 and decided to go out for dinner on the first night. Some of the restaurants we went to were packed and the last one we found had one table left with six chairs. We all walked to the table and began looking at the menus. Jade went to sit down on a chair and Leo shouted "Jade, don't sit on Jack!" So, she had to move to another chair.

The waitress began to look for Jack, and asked, "Where is Jack, as there are only five of you?"

Leo replied, "Jack is sitting there," and pointed to the empty chair. The Waitress looked stunned and said, "Can I take your order?"

On that holiday, Jack came everywhere with us and we were informed that Harry had gone back to work. Jack also came home with us to England and made several appearances. On 30 October 2007, the day before my birthday, Leo awoke up crying uncontrollably and said " Nanny Phyll here, Nanny Phyll here". At 2.00a.m. and half asleep, I said "Nanny Phyll is at home and we would speak to her in the morning." Leo happy with that, climbed back into bed. The alarm clock went off and I grumpily pulled myself out of bed and the getting ready for school run had begun.

7am arrived and the telephone began to ring and I let Eric pick it up. I remember clearly, using the vacuum cleaner at that time, and Eric just stood in front of me with a blank expression on his face, handed me the phone and said "It's your mum." "What does she want" I thought, placing the telephone to my ear. I could hear my mum crying and she informed me that Nan had in fact passed away. I was totally stunned as none of us had seen this coming.

I gathered my things together and drove behind my parents to my Nan's house. On arriving, I noticed other relatives and as I entered the room where she passed away, I began to send her Reiki to help with her passing over to the other side. I looked down and noticed a photograph on the floor; I picked it up and turned it over. My emotions came to the surface and I just allowed the tears to flow, I was looking down at a photograph of my three beautiful children with my Nan. Leo came by my side and gave me a hug and said "Nanny Phyll came to say Hello and went home again". I looked at my son, smiled and knew that she had come back in the early hours of that morning to say goodbye.

A year after Nan Phyll's passing I decided to meet with a medium called Amanda Britton. The session began and Nan came through singing congratulations regarding the publication of this book. My grandfather connected with her my dad's side with the name of John. Tears began to fall down my face as she went on to describe him and told me his favourite hobby was collecting coins.

My breath was taken away, when she told me that my Irish grandfather was known by several names and one of them being Jack when he was younger and that Leo knows someone called Jack. I began to cry uncontrollably as this was the confirmation that I needed. I knew then that Jack was in fact my Granddad and he had come to help Nanny Phyll cross over when it was her time.

Amanda Britton

Amanda Britton is a modern day spiritualist medium with over seventeen years of experience with a genuine gift and is based in Bedfordshire. I first met Amanda who is from the North East of England at Biggleswade Spiritual Centre.

Amanda's down to earth genuine approach to her work is shown through her demonstrations of mediumship and private sittings that she is able to prove that communication with loved ones in the spirit world is possible and that life is eternal. As a Spiritualist Medium, her job is to provide evidence of survival after physical death and serves spiritualist churches throughout the United Kingdom.

Amanda encountered her first spiritual experience at the age of three, when her Great Grandmother appeared in her bedroom. Great Grandmother Jane said "tell your dad that I've come to visit." This was met with disbelief from her parent's.

However, not long afterwards she appeared to Amanda again and stated that if they didn't believe, to tell them that the porcelain lampshade in her own bedroom that had cottage designs on the very top - this was out of her view and belonged to Jane. Her dad was very shocked when she told him about her reappearing and what she had said.

Throughout childhood years, she played regularly with spirit. One game Amanda played was being the teacher and the spirit children her pupils, lining them up in the hall way. She distinctly remembers one of the children being called Denise, who would come to her in her dreams.

Nellie her other Great Grandmother passed to Spirit, when she was nine years old. Whilst burning some of Nellie's unneeded belongings at the bottom of her garden she appeared to Amanda and her brother, and said "I have gone nowhere, I am still very much alive watching over you."

Incidentally her brother was also aware of spirit from an early age, which really perturbed him to the point, that he would not go up to bed unless Amanda went at the same time.

Throughout the adolescent years, Amanda was a very sensitive child, and easily picked up peoples emotions and feelings and continued to be interested in all things connected with spiritualism.

In her early twenties, she attended Durham Spiritualist Church, after being coaxed there by her brother. This was the push she needed to get through the front door and informed that a healing appointment was waiting for her. Amanda recalls her first encounter with spiritual healing was out of this world, and said "she felt that she literally went out of this world for a good forty minutes."

The Spiritual healer informed Amanda that her spirit door had been opened and became very confused as to what she meant but thanked her. From this experience she had an overwhelming urge to visit the church regularly. After attending a few services, the medium gave her a message and said that, 'one day I would work for spirit".

Amanda was invited to join the church development circle and consciously followed the spirit world teachings and gave messages every week in the Spiritualist Church.

Amanda felt her own self confidence was the biggest downfall.

Her step-mother passed to spirit and felt she pushed her whole heartedly to do platform work. This continued to happen and kept being pressed forward by feeling that she was put me into a corner, especially when the booked medium did not turn up and she was the only one who could take the service.

Amanda's Great Grandmother Nellie was a medium and paternal Grandmother used to read the tea leaves. Amanda recalls one time walking into her sitting room and Nellie announced that her brother Jack who had passed over had 'been for a visit. Family witnesses say that she would often sit down and chat to him which seemed a perfectly natural occurrence to the family.

Her paternal Aunt Audrey is aware of spirit too. Before Amanda announced she was pregnant with Anna, Audrey she saw her husband, Amanda's uncle from spirit and he appeared with a child in his arms, all wrapped up. He said "We are sending Amanda a baby girl" and she has asked to see her, but he said not till she comes to earth. Her Aunt has heard spirit externally, calling her name. When Anna her daughter was born the midwife commented that she had been looking around the room as she was being born. She said, "She has been here before". As a young baby she was extremely aware of her surroundings and weighed people up.

Aunt Audrey's youngest son told her when he was three, "I am glad that you are my mum and I am glad that dad is my dad and that Paul is my brother". He stated that he had the choice to which family he belonged to.

Her mother was very spiritually aware, but did not have the self confidence in her own abilities to develop her gifts further to help others. At fifty-two years old, she had to have her leg amputated. Just before the operation she stated to Amanda that Uncle Jim and her Mother had visited her from Spirit.

This seemed to encourage her Mother to overcome the obstacles that having a limb removed can cause and amazed the family with her determination to carry on as normal.

Her Mother did speak about her Father especially when the Yorkshire Puddings were out. Her Father her father would tell her "Why don't you put brown sauce on those Yorkshire puddings?" and she would laugh because that is something he would do on a frequent basis when he was alive!

Amanda's father was a big disbeliever, until Step Mother passed to spirit. She appeared in the bedroom to let him know that she was all right. He has smelt her perfume, things are regularly moved around the house, and fragrant powder appears on the dado rail in the hall. When Chris was alive she used to say that one day she would prove to him that there was eternal life. This she has certainly done! Since then her Father has had more spiritual experiences and has become more intuitive.

Amanda has three children and her two sons have both had spiritual encounters and have mediumistic abilities. Her daughter is very much like Amanda when she was growing up, even thou she has not said anything that she too is mediumistic aware.

Amanda feels that she is still learning and reaching forward with her work and has the greatest respect for the spirit world and knows without a shadow of a doubt that the work she does, could not achieve without them. Learning to trust the spirit world whole heartedly is the key to being a successful medium.

Nina Hawthorn

My dear friend Nina has five grandsons and one granddaughter. Her daughter, Yvonne, began to notice that when her daughter, Meg, was about four or five months old, in familiar surroundings, she would become transfixed, and stare into space for long periods of time. None of Yvonne's three boys displayed this kind of behaviour and Meg is more sensitive and aware.

Also, when Meg was placed in her cot or bouncy chair, she would always cry with frustration, at being placed where she did not want to go. Yvonne would walk away and make dinner and

Meg would continue to cry. Meg would then begin to gurgle a lot and start to laugh, as if someone was in the room with her. Yvonne would investigate, but as she walked over to Meg, she would stop. As soon as Yvonne left the room, Meg would begin laughing and chuckling again. Every time Yvonne came back, Meg would stop and then start again when she walked away.

When Nina used to babysit, as she would hold Meg, her eyes would fix on something for moments at a time and she would smile to the corners of the room. When she did this, she would say "Hello Nan", which was Nina's mum.

Yvonne said that it was her strong mother's instinct that lead her to believe that someone was definitely looking after Meg.

Nina did not feel a presence but felt that there was definitely someone entertaining Meg. It was almost as if Meg was the only one that could see and hear and the rest of the family were not meant to.

Tansy

When Tansy was little, she had three imaginary friends: Green Giant, who was covered with prickles and lived in a castle in Spain, a small boy called Christmas and his friend, a little girl called Alouetta.

Tansy does not know where they all came from, they just appeared one day. They faded out when she started at primary school, aged about five.

She does not remember playing with them like with real physical friends and was just aware that they were around and helped her along.

They were not a secret, as she used to tell her mum and her friends at school all about them. However, Tansy does remember a girl, slightly older than her, making a bit of fun of Christmas, saying, "Oh, does he just pop up like a jack-in-a-box at Christmas, then?"

That incident made Tansy feel suddenly very sad and hurt. All of the exuberance of sharing a special, magic story with contemporaries seemed to shrink and hide in her. She did not talk so much about them after that. Tansy felt that she had to protect them from the brutal, physical world that they had all come into together.

One day, if Tansy has children, she hopes that they will come back and play again. A little bit of her still misses them.

Lucinda Bender

Jennifer Cigler, a customer representative, who worked for the *Washington Post*, contacted me about her imaginary friend, Lucinda Bender, who was very mischievous.

Lucinda would draw on the walls with crayons and cut her baby brother's hair and Jennifer would get blamed for her tricks. Her parents still like to remind her that whenever they went out to dinner at a restaurant, her dad would always have to request an extra seat for Lucinda Bender, or else should throw a fit! The waiters would always ask if they were waiting for another member of their party and Jennifer would curtly inform them that Lucinda was sitting there!

Stephen Rose, 39, Kent

Stephen first had an experience with an Angel coming forward to him when he was a child. His parents had decided that he was old enough to be left alone, but he wasn't so sure. He was a bit annoyed and frightened, so he eventually asked for someone to help. They answered his prayers and sent an angel. He isn't sure who she was, maybe Mother Mary, or some other ascended being of light, but she was there for him. He remembers where she appeared in the room by the window, surrounded by a shimmering silver and white aura and she just glided towards him. He was enveloped in a cloud of light and love. She took the negativity away and he wasn't frightened anymore. He was upset with his mother and father at the time, as he had been blamed for something he hadn't done. She said that she would always give him strength and that we are never alone.

As Stephen described it, "She held my hand, mopped my emotional brow, and healed me in a way which is difficult to describe. She lifted all the worry, fear and emotional pain in an instant and replaced it with a feeling of being held so completely and utterly loved it is impossible to convey the contrast between how I had felt and how I now felt. She did tell me that my mother wasn't able to understand the situation and nor was my father. I so wanted my Mum to come to me, but she explained that wasn't going to happen. She told me that I was a lovely boy and I would be a lovely man and heaven would not sit ideally by and ignore a request from someone, anyone like me - young, innocent and in need of help."

He does remember that his thinking was logical and her delivery was humored and understanding. The strong sense that he got was that she knew what she was talking about, but he had never trusted anyone outside of the relationship with his parents as much as he trusted them, and in the moment that they were letting him down, here was this presence telling him to be calm and accept their fallibility. He remembers thinking / knowing that healing was possible.

"I remembered reasoning that there was life after death. My father had given me the two alternatives. There were those that believed that God was a man on a fluffy cloud and there were those that believed that there was absolutely nothing. Well now I knew a healing spirit; an angel, she was very real and beyond physical, more powerful than flesh and bone, warmer than sunlight and able to take away pain. In my worst emotional moment as a child I experienced something so special and I believed in the power of good over bad. And that meant there was something, something in the bible and other holy books and scriptures, something after death, something more than what normally perceive. I didn't believe in the white haired Father

Christmas look-alike, but I did believe that absolutely-nothing-after-death wasn't a reality either. I sat and meditated and tried to imagine nothing, and I realized that as I imagined the complete darkness, there was still something there, it was me watching the darkness and I would not cease to be. I'd met an Angel, and I can remember the warm glow that gave me."

That experience set his view of life up and he trusted spirit and the angels as he knew they were around.

Later in life he had pretty much written the experience off as 'one of those childish things". By then he ran a company, and being practical believed having one's feet on the ground is essential for success. He had moved away from spiritual matters and, like most people got stuck into the cut and thrust of life. That was until he was on holiday in Barbados with his family when he was actually given photographic evidence of the existence of angelic beings.

"We were all sitting on the balcony, and I was asking for  healing help for my daughter, at the time. I found out later that my Mum had also been asking for healing for my Step-Father. My wife took a picture of my mother. Mum was pulling a face as the shutter clicked, so she took another shot immediately afterwards. When the photos were viewed we were stunned to see a figure of light right next to Mum. In the second picture, taken in exactly the same spot, with the same exposure and settings, there was nothing. In the past My Step-Father was a professional photographer, and he couldn't explain away the light in the photograph. Mum was certain it was an angel, and both my wife and Step-Father were blown away by the picture. I knew I had definitely received a wake-up call. I remembered my childhood experience and realised that something spiritual was trying to come into my life."

Both Stephen's Step-Father and daughter got better after this angel appeared.

He decided to follow his childhood dream of becoming a healer he started learning Reiki healing, and during one practise he felt very strongly that the Archangel Michael was with him. His hands were guided into a set position, palms together like in prayer, with the thumbs against the heart chakra.

"I felt uplifted and blessed, but wanted confirmation that it was real. It seemed so outlandish to think that 'the' Michael would come to me, just like that. But, my brother, Chris, is an experienced medium and when I spoke to him he told me something incredible. He said that 'Dad' had come through to him, and had kept repeating the name Michael three times. I had my proof! I believe that Michael was showing me a very old hand position known as the Gassho position, which literally means to place the two palms together. It is a gesture of respect, humility and reverence and it is used to concentrate the mind and to express the total unity of being. It is seen as a connection between mind, body and spirit, promoting calmness. What was different was the book, which appeared between his palms. I believe what Michael was showing me was that as a goal it was a very pure one, and as a means to an end, it would provide a connection with the infinite, specifically represented in this case by a book."

Stephen and his brother Christopher have gone on to become reiki practitioners and teachers honouring their childhood experiences. For more information, please go to www.reikirose.co.uk.

Whisk

June, now forty-eight and living in a small town called Burntwood in Staffordshire, had an imaginary friend when she was a child. Her mum tells her that she was about two and a half when Whisk first came to visit her. He then appeared to her on all sorts of occasions.

She was four when she started school, and remembers Whisk being about her height, but he was an old man with a white beard and white hair. June cannot remember if he had glasses but he wore a little dark Mac and a hat.

June must have been five when we were on the bus on their way to visit her grandmother.

June says that the last time she remembers seeing Whisk was when they were getting off one of the many buses they had to catch. Her mum dinged the bell to stop and they made they made their way to the exit and had her baby sister in a cuddle seat, was holding other sister by the hand and was waiting for me. Before they would get off, she called out to Whisk to hurry up and he caught up with her and was never seen again.

Her Mum tells her that she was quite sad when Whisk stopped coming to see her. Two years ago, on her first visit to Ireland, she saw a picture of a leprechaun and the memories of Whisk came flooding back. The picture was identical to Whisk and June now believes that he was really there and that he came to keep her company until she started school.

June's Grandson was also about two when he started to talk to someone called Rose. This was the spirit of his father's grand-mother and he only used to talk to her when visiting his paternal grandparents. He would often babble and laugh at someone, that no one could see and stand at the bottom of the stairs shouting, "Wose!" This only lasted for a few months.

Kirsteen Black

From a very young age, Kirsteen had two imaginary friends: Boddid and Shabby –miniature people who lived in her bathroom cabinet. Boddid was a boy and Shabby, a girl, and she believes that they were brother and sister. Today, she can still picture them very clearly in her mind; Boddid was bald and Shabby had straight black hair to her shoulders.

Kirsteen does not think these imaginary friends were ghosts, as they were so small; they were really just her entertainment.

She did have very strange experiences from around the age of ten to fourteen; quite often, when she would go into the shower room or take a shower, she would get an eerily, cold, shivery feeling overcoming her whole body.

Kirsteen would feel the blood draining from her face and would start to hear monotone voices speeding up and getting louder and louder. They were all jumbled up and she could not make sense of what they were saying. She was not afraid of them, but often left the shower room in a state of shock and particularly remembers one time, her auntie saying, "What happened to you? You look like you've just seen a ghost."

Kirsteen told her auntie that she thought she had seen a ghost, but no one wanted to believe or listen, so she put it out of her head until the next time it happened.

Kirsteen learned to block out the voices and think of other things when the feelings would start. She could control them better as she got older and does not remember them being much of an issue later in her teens.

Liz from New Zealand

Liz contacted me after reading and immensely enjoyed my article on imaginary friends. She was delighted that I was writing a book on this subject, which has fascinated her for a long time – all her life, in fact!

My own name cropped up in her research for the novel that she is working on, which I am looking forward to reading when it is published. She is working to gain an understanding of imaginary friends from all possible perspectives and of the function they fulfil in the lives of the very young.

Liz was born in Bangor, County Down, Northern Ireland: a seaside town, twelve miles from Belfast. Her dad was always away in the army, probably in Palestine when her imaginary friends (who were earth spirits) first appeared. This was when she was about two and a half to three years old, in 1953 or 1954.

Her mother worked all day in Belfast and returned home each evening, and days were spent with Granny in a two storied, grey stone house facing Bangor Bay.

This special time involved the companionship of three 'friends'. The energy that she felt came from a main source that she named Eire. It only occurred to her many years later that this is the Celtic name for Ireland. However, she must have heard the grown ups talking about Eire, as her family had experienced, first hand, both sides of the troubled times of the early twentieth century (she had a great uncle in Sinn Fein and her maternal grandfather shot by the IRA), and the spirit of Eire would have been in the air that they breathed.

Eire was accompanied by two other 'friends', named Washy and Orchid. However, Eire was the main one. Liz had an overwhelming sense that Eire believed that she could do anything, and felt totally supported by this feeling. Eire was very strong, dependable and very funny. Liz wonders if this was a connection with the universal spirit referred to in Sanskrit/theosophy as 'Atman' (meaning 'un-manifest'), 'the source' or 'summerland'.

Liz remembers being in a nest of long grass with these friends and feeling completely safe in their company. This was an intense early childhood experience. The feeling of joy was complete, blissfully happy and peaceful.

When the family moved to Belfast, she was enormously excited to have friends of her age for the first time. Eventually, she went to school and adored the company of real friends for a few years, before her family migrated to New Zealand in 1959.

Sometimes, she thinks of the happy times she had as a very young child, before the connection with her invisible companions appeared to cease. There was some loss in the migration process and the subsequent family break-up in New Zealand.

Many events have intervened in the interim, but now Liz seeks to know more about the experience that was pure and uncomplicated. She feels that there is a lot more to know and intends to keep unpicking and prodding; the book that she is writing relies on her doing this and successfully making a closer link with this spirit of the imagination, which appeared to leave. However, Liz wonders whether it really did ever really leave.

Becky from Cardiff

Rebecca contacted me after seeing an advertisement in a magazine, asking for experiences with imaginary friends.

She now lives in Cardiff. However, when she was living in Stow Hill Pontypridd, with her mum and dad, she had imaginary friends, who she now remembers vividly and has fond memories of the way she felt about these childhood companions.

These were not your conventional imaginary friends. Little Miss Piggy was a little girl, but looked very much like the character from *The Muppets*. However, she was not nasty like the character, but nice. She also had a mini robot that she could actually see. The robot was silver and metal, and looked like a cross between the Tin Man from *Wizard of Oz* and a 1950's children's toy.

They were both about the size of a baby/small Toddler. Never naughty, they used to go everywhere with her: in the car, in the bath, at the dinner table and to bed. Her mum remembers Becky shouting at people, including family and friends, telling them not to sit on certain seats because her friends were there and they would to squash them. When adults ignored the pleas and sat down regardless, she would be heartbroken until they got up and let Miss Piggy and Mini Robot move. She did not understand why nobody believed that they were really there. At the time, even her mum did not believe her. Becky's mum now wishes that she had, because she is becoming very spiritual and realises that, as a child, she was very psychic.

When Becky's mum fell pregnant, Becky knew that she was going to have a baby brother, even though her mum never had a scan. It was around the time of her brother's birth that Robot and Piggy became less frequent in her life. She still misses them.

The house that they lived in at the time used to give Becky the creeps; she was constantly having nightmares and waking up soaked in a sweat and vomiting. Her mum would hear noises at night and thought that she was out of bed when she was sleeping. In the morning, the bedroom would be a mess, as if someone had thrown all of her toys around.

Becky always had a feeling that someone was watching. Even before she knew what spirits were, she felt that she was aware of things that no one else was aware of. Throughout her life, she has had dreams about people and things that have come true; she once woke up in a panic because she was convinced something bad had happened to her Brother. She rang her mum, who told her that, at the exact time she woke up, her brother had been involved in a car crash. Luckily, he was OK.

Becky would dream as a little girl that she would marry a black man. She met her husband, Les, eleven years ago and told friends that she was going to marry him, even though they had not even spoken to each other. She did not see him again for a year. The first night they met, after that, they spoke about children and marriage and have been together ever since.

With regards to spiritual abilities now, she still has dreams that come true, hears voices and has senses about things. Becky does have some spirit activity in the house and, from time to time, sees and hears things.

In the future, she wants to improve her natural abilities. Her mum is also finding ways to harness her abilities and is attending a spiritual healing class.

Billy

Karen first heard about my research when I spoke at the Vision

Showcase, which was being held at the Leeds Marriott Hotel in 2006. Karen was at the showcase in her capacity as a holistic therapist, offering aromatherapy, reflexology and hypnotherapy.

Billy, her ten year old son, over the years, has had imaginary friends and also discussed lots of things with her that he should not really know. For example, he was able to recall his granddad, who died before he was one. Billy was born on Karen's father's seventieth birthday, and six weeks later, they learned that her father had terminal cancer. He passed away before Billy's first birthday.

At about two years old, he surprised Karen by asking her when he would become small again. On probing, he told her that he used to be a tall lady and wondered when he would become small again. He seemed a little worried to talk about it, but he did say that he used to be a girl and would often want to wear his sisters dresses.

Billy had an imaginary friend at their old house until they moved. It was a girl that would not enter the house. Karen began questioning and was informed by Billy that the person was called Sonia and looked just like one of their neighbour's daughters. Karen went to speak with the neighbour and was told that she lost a daughter at birth but named her Sonia. Billy also spoke about angels on the rooftops.

Billy does have a lot of nightmares which disturb him, but through the use of different essential oils (mainly Frankincense and Tea Tree) this has improved.

Karen's sister has a daughter who was the youngest child in UK to be diagnosed with Narcolepsy. She has many more experiences that Billy.

When they moved house, she described, in detail, a little girl who had been killed on a train track near their home. It was later found that there used to be a train track there. As she often drifts though out the day, they feel that she is more of a target to spirituality. She has mentioned voices and has horrific nightmares.

Karen believes that imaginary friends are ghosts reaching out to your child.

Carly Smith

Carly Smith contacted me after reading my story about connecting with angels in the *News of the World* Sunday magazine in 2005. She was very interested in my experience with angels and decided to visit my website.

When she visited my website she clicked onto the imaginary friends' link, as this was also of great interest to her; as a child, she had an imaginary friend for about eight years and still remembers everything about him. His name was Lazy Johnfants and he lived at 7 Drears Road. Her parents say that from the moment she began to talk, she was talking to Lazy Johnfants, and continued to do until she was eight years old.

He went everywhere with her: ate with her, went to bed at the same time, and always played with her. Carly's mum thought she was misinterpreting his name and was trying to say 'Lady Johnson', but she had no idea who she was.

When Carly used to speak about Lazy Johnfants, it was as though he was a real person. Walking down the street, she would hold out her hand as though she was holding his.

She does not know what he looked like, or even if her friend was male. She also does not know where he came from, and does not remember when, all of a sudden, Lazy Johnfants stopped talking to her.

Carly read that an imaginary friend could be a grandfather or grandmother who have died before a child is born. Her mum's mum died of breast cancer before she was born, and now, at twenty-four, Carly believes that Lazy Johnfants was her nan looking over her as she was growing up.

Grandma Jessica and Windy Blow

Helen Palmer, who lives in North Manchester, told me these two wonderful stories:

Molly, her daughter, is now nine and will be ten in June. When both mother and daughter were younger, they both had imaginary friends.

When Molly was six months old, her grandmother was diagnosed with ovarian cancer. As time passed, her grandmother started undergoing treatment and various operations and Molly would talk to her friend, Grandma Jessica, in her bedroom and everywhere. As her grandmother's cancer went into remission Grandma Jessica went away.

When more treatment, such as chemo, was required, Grandma Jessica came back. Her partner's mum would take Molly for walks and Molly would tell her where Grandma Jessica lived; she would point down the street near her other daughter's school. There was nobody in the family called Jessica. In fact, on both sides of the family, the term 'nana' was always used rather than 'grandma'.

When they used to ask her questions, she would say that Grandma Jessica had lots of children: Green Baby, Pink Baby, Orange Baby and Blue Baby, but then Blue Baby died. Helen recalled to me that, "A three year old saying that a baby had died was hard to take and the way she talked you'd really believe her."

Grandma Jessica had pink hair, she drove a pink car, and lived in a big house with a pink door, but then, in November 2002, Grandma Jessica went away and never came back. At the same time, her grandmother lost her battle with cancer.

Helen's imaginary friend was the opposite. She was called Windy Blow. When she was four or five years old, the family lived in South Manchester opposite a big park. She grew up in an old Victorian town house and lived on the top floor. Windy Blow used to come up through the dumbwaiter (a small lift used to move food or laundry between floors) with a lady in a brown dress and had brown hair cut into a short bob.

Windy was naughty and used to make Helen put toilet rolls

down the toilet and take the labels off tins so no one would know what was in them. Her mum, when making tea, would go mad as she'd think she was giving them beans but when she opened the tin it would be rice pudding or fruit cocktail!

Helen actually remembers the lady in the brown dress, as she used to give her chocolate fingers when she had the measles. In the past, Helen asked both her mum and dad who she was and they said that nobody came to see her when she had measles. However, to this day, Helen is sure that she came to see her.

Will

Helen Barker contacted me after reading my article on imaginary friends, because her two year old son, Will, talked non stop about a child called Georgia, who is three, lives in his bedroom and plays with his toys.

One morning, when they were taking the middle son out to school, Will shouted upstairs, "Come on Georgia we're going," then he said, "Oh, Georgia sleeps." On returning home he got really excited, as they pulled up in the car saying, "I can see Georgia now." They went into the house and he said, "Oh she's up now." Helen asked Will to show her where Georgia was, and he took her by the hand and led her into the living room. He then looked really surprised and said, "Georgia's hiding."

Will also told Helen that Georgia's mummy sleeps in her bedroom. Neither the family nor the childminder knew any one called Georgia, so they were really intrigued to know where the name had come from.

Like me, Helen miscarried twice in the six months before she got pregnant with Will and part of her wants Georgia to be one of those babies – making her husband think she has definitely lost the plot!

This, however, is not the family's only experience of imaginary friends. Her daughter, Amelia, who is now thirteen, had an imaginary cat called Echo. This went on for months, until she saw a medium who told her that Echo was, in fact, her granddad.

The medium advised her to speak to Amelia about it and she would tell her something about Echo that would show her that it really was her granddad. She asked Amelia about Echo and she said he was her friend and he was not like other cats because he had a leg missing. Her granddad had his leg amputated a couple of years before he died. After that, she did not mention Echo again and for a while became quite embarrassed about it if anyone asked her about the cat. Now, of course, it's her party piece and she tells everyone!

Martin and Darby

Deborah was looking at my website, as she is very interested in anything spiritual and also has an intuitive part to her.

Her son, Martin, is now twenty-one years old and is the eldest of her three children. He had an imaginary friend when he was around three years old called Darby. Darby would come with them on outings and even sit at the table with them whilst they ate. Also he/she would sleep under Martin's bed. This went on until Martin was around six and a half years old. After this, we heard no more about Darby.

Deborah was very interested in the idea of imaginary friends being grandparents, as her husband's mum died when he was just nine years old. Apparently, her husband's mum really adored children, but could not carry children naturally so she adopted him. She would have had more children by adoption but fell ill. Deborah believes that Darby could have been her, coming along at a time when their second child was born a daughter. Incidentally, she would have loved a daughter. Martin has a small recollection of Darby and Deborah is now convinced that it would have been his grandmother coming along and helping out in the best way she could from the other side.

The Imaginary Cow

Grace contacted me about her mother. When her mother was a child she had an imaginary cow as a friend and she insisted on taking the cow everywhere. Her gran, it is said, was at her wits end and was unable to persuade her mother that there was no cow.

During a family holiday to the seaside they all got fish and chips for lunch and were sitting on the promenade eating (cow included), when an elderly, rather overweight, gentleman sat down next to them. Her mother instantly burst into tears. Her gran was forced to ask the man to move to the next seat, as he was sitting on her daughter's cow and it was being squashed. He, of course, thought she was completely insane and moved on.

Becky

Becky contacted me and wanted to share these experiences:

She has four small children, aged six, five, three and seven months. When her five year old was younger, he would often wake in the night saying that there was a man in his room and, on other occasions, it would be a little girl. This went on for about two years, but he soon became really frightened by it and it began to stop. Now, he never talks about it.

Her three year old had an imaginary friend and called Milo, and told her that he died in a fire. He told Becky how he died in such a way that she does not think a three year old could make it up.

When she was pregnant with him, she went to a clairvoyant, who told her that she was having twins, but would lose one who would play with her son, which now seems a good explanation. The clairvoyant told her many things, all correct, and she really believes that loved ones, who have passed, do come and visit through dreams.

She does not discourage her son from talking about his friend, and they even threw a pretend birthday party for him, which her son was thrilled with.

Jennifer

Jennifer lives in Kentucky and has three boys: William, three, Tyler, eight and Gage, ten. Her middle and youngest children both had imaginary friends, who were both named Jason. Jennifer made it clear to me that her youngest had never been told of Tyler's friend.

When Jason was her middle child's friend, she described him as a mean little boy who would knock him off his bike or take it from him. Eventually, they put the bike in a room to keep Jason and her child from fighting over it. When they got the bike out the next day, the bike had a broken reflector on it and Tyler said that Jason had done it.

With William, Jason also tries to get to him to do naughty things, which is out of character for William because he is a well-behaved child.

Jennifer is told by William that Jason dislikes his Sister, but likes Jennifer because she is a good mother to him. She originally thought that it may have been her children using their imaginations, but when William asked her some questions about Jason, it left a cold shudder down their spine. He said that Jason's mother had the same name as her and that is why Jason likes her name. Jennifier strongly believes that Jason is a ghost and that he has attached himself to them and not their house.

Jennifer also explained that she too could see ghosts and spirits. Most come to her in dreams, but some are not so friendly and plague her with horrible nightmares.

Adam

Adam is now seven and a half. When he was very young (just able to talk), he used to say that his grandpa would visit him in his bedroom and, as both of his granddads were alive, his mother, Janice, just humoured him. This went on for a few years; he would describe his Grandpa and tell her about his life and was curious about why she could not see him.

Adam also told her some disturbing things about his 'other mother'. She used to beat him and starve him, so he had to go and live with grandpa on his farm. This really upset Janice and she hated his other imaginary mother. He told Janice, however, that she was his best and only mother now. These events all stopped about eighteen months ago and, when questioned, Adam states that he cannot remember.

Sue Price

Sue shared her experiences of imaginary friends when she saw my advertisement in Cygnus magazine.

She has a daughter, Emma, who is now seventeen, but was about three years old when they moved into their present house. Underneath the stairs was quite a big cupboard and she would often hear Emma talking to somebody there. When questioned, she told her she was talking to her friend Amy with a black face. This happened quite regularly and she would just chat away in her childish manner.

Sue found it interesting when she told her that she had met Amy's father. Sue asked what he was like and she said that he had a black face as well and funny hair. She said that he didn't talk like them and that she couldn't understand him.

She told her that he lives far away. Sue can only remember the one incident which involved the father, but Amy with the black face was a regular visitor. If Emma wanted to talk to her she would open the door under the stairs and call her.

Jenny Kenny

Jenny shared these tales about her and her sister's childhood stories:

Jenny was friends with an old man who she used to play real cards with on the landing upstairs and he used to cheat. Her older sister, Alison, was friends with a brother and sister who had died in a fire. When Alison was around three years old, she must have sat next to the coal fire just a bit too closely and their mum warned her to move away. Alison replied to Mum, "I know, because otherwise I'll burn like those children and pointed to the corner of the room." She then went on to describe how they'd died in a fire and how their skin was all crinkly now and melted off – much to their mother's amazement.

Joanne Patterson

Joanne read an article about my book and thought I might be interested in her daughter's imaginary family. (Or is it?)

Joanne's four year old daughter has always said that she has a past family, ever since she could only say a few sentences. She refers to them as her old family and has old parents and siblings.

When she first told Joanne about her old mum, she thought that she had been dreaming. However, she was able to go into some detail about them. Her old brother even comes to visit her and stays in her room. She comes out to tell Joanne that Sam has dumped his suitcase in the middle of her room again and made a mess.

Mary Day

From the age of three to five, Mary remembers having a friend that would visit her. She recalls her very well: what she looked like and how she dressed. Her mother used to worry about it as she would often catch her playing with her friend.

Mary recalls being asked who she was talking to and being surprised that no one else could see her. Her name was Manina, or so Mary thought, but as she got older, at the age of eleven, her grandmother talked about a daughter of hers who died at the age of ten. They did not have any photos to show her but when her grandfather was alive he was an artist and drew a picture of her. The only one her grandmother had. The resemblance was uncanny and she was told that her name was Caterina. Mary often wondered what happened to her!

Her son Tom, who is now twelve, also had an imaginary friend when he was younger. His name was Sam. He doesn't talk about this anymore, but when she separated from her partner four years ago, he was hearing voices that really frightened him. They were saying some nasty things that made him really scared to be alone in his room. He now says that he hears voices now and again, but he doesn't really talk about it. He says that he can control it by asking them to leave. Mary believes that Tom is spiritual and will try and help him develop the very special energy that he has. At this moment in time, Mary is developing her own spiritual side.

Ada Odell

When my Nan Ada was alive she was always partial to a cup of tea before any task was carried out accompanied with her favourite cigarettes. An eccentric woman, who would often inform me she would see people out of the corner of her eye and they would disappear again, which was always followed by laughter. When I was growing up, I often would not understand what she was explaining to me and did not know that Nan Ada was in fact seeing spirit, until I was much older to under the concept of spiritual beings.

A new family moved in Nan's old house after she passed away. They have a young girl who kept asking her mum for a cup of milk or tea and a biscuit for the lady. This went on for several months and the mum did not understand why. It was only when the little girl told her mum that the lady was called Ada, that she contacted my uncle, as she knew that was her name. The mum went on to explain that her daughter would sit on the stairs for hours and talk to Ada!

I can remember clearly as a child, sitting on the stairs at home with my sister and brother, Nan drinking her cup of tea looking out of the high window and telling us what she could see along the road, whilst we ate our biscuits.

Was our Nan Ada playing the games with this little girl, like she did with us? Or was she walking through her time line as a spirit and popped in to say Hello! One will never know!

Nanny Ghost & Connor

Bernice Harrison's mum passed away in 1994. When Connor was about 2 ½ he started to get visits from her mum. They had a picture of her on the living room wall and even from a new born he would stare at it, Bernice thought it was her imagination that as a baby, as he would stare so intently at her picture. Until her mother- in- law noticed it too and commented on how strange it was.

As he grew into a toddler he stopped looking at her picture, as he had a new sister Jessica to annoy and other distractions and Bernice kind of forgot about it.

One day, she was in the kitchen. Connor was about 2 ½, he was supposed to be using the bathroom upstairs. Suddenly she a heard scream and rushed to him and found him sitting on the top step of the stairs. He had blood dripping from his nose and he was crying uncontrollably. He was in quite a state and couldn't tell her straight away what was wrong. Eventually after a lot of comforting, he calmed down and told in his own way what had happened. Connor had gotten hold of his Daddies' razor and was trying to shave like he'd seen Daddy do and showed Bernice using actions to explain what he had done. When suddenly, a face jumped out at him and it scared him so much that he cut himself and dropped the razor. She cuddled him and calmed him down and obviously, gave him the "you don't touch Daddy's stuff" lecture. At first she wasn't sure, but told him that it was nothing to worry about and that he shouldn't be scared, no one could hurt him.

Connor has never been one to have nightmares so when he

wakes up at night crying it is unusual. This happened on a few occasions and he would tell Bernice that there was someone in his room. He wasn't scared as such, just crying as a child does when they've been woken up unexpectedly. The last time it happened was about 6 months before they moved house. Connor woke up again only this time he had quite a conversation with his "ghost". He said that she was a lady and that she wore a yellow hat and that she didn't like milkshake but she did like chocolate orange. When asked who he thought it was, he said it was "Nanny Ghost" and he pointed to a picture of her, the one on the living room wall. Bernice tells me that her Mum would never have worn a yellow hat, she did however have blond hair and quite often wore it in a way that a child might have thought it was a hat.

That's when she decided to get in touch with me. If her son was being visited, she wanted to know how to handle it and make sure that Connor was understood and not scared by it. I talked to Connor and confirmed that is her Mum. I told Bernice that her Mum had been trying to get through to her, but she wasn't listening so she was going though Connor to get her attention. Well, it worked!

Connor has had no more visits from her. He is nearly nine now and is still a sensitive boy and has only just started to sleep without a night light. They moved into a very old house and quite a few "paranormal" things happened. For the first few months it seemed as though the house was testing the new comers. Kitchen cupboard doors would open and slam shut for no reason, plants would shake and the leaves would move as though someone had walked into them, keys and remote controls are regularly moved and recently a diary has gone missing.

Four weeks after moving in, Bernice fell on the stairs and broke her ankle. For eight weeks she had no choice but sit on the sofa. It was during this time and Bernice realised that they were sharing their new home with "someone". She would catch glimpse out of the corner of her eye, although to this day she is not sure who it is, she feels certain that it is a woman. The family have never felt threatened by any of this; in fact to Bernice, the home has a warm and friendly atmosphere. It seemed to her that once "they" realised that the family were staying, they stopped or rather quietened down, but every now and again they still get doors slammed and what sounds like pots being banged together. Yet Connor didn't really seem to notice any of this; it was only his new bedroom he hated and for two years said that he it was scary and he wanted to go back to his old one.

Connor seems to have lost his Nanny Ghost for the moment; maybe she will come back one day.

Chapter Seven

Child Prodigies and Famous Personalities

*Without leaps of imagination, or dreaming, we lose the excitement of
possibilities. Dreaming, after all, is a form of planning.*
Gloria Steinem

The Dalai Lama, Famous Child Prodigies, Ruth White,
Robert Louis Stevenson, Princess Margaret, Lita De
Alberdi, The Brontë Family, Robin Gibb, Kurt Cobain,
Beyonce Knowles, Dorothy Virginia Margaret Juba, Lucy
Maud Montgomery, Films on the Big Screen: *Harvey, Bogus,
Heart and Souls, Drop Dead Fred, Pete's Dragon*, Children
Televison Programmes: *Tweenies, Arthur, Charlie & Lola*,
Dave Mill, Julia Donaldson, Mike Meyers, Allison DuBois.

The Dalai Lama

'Dalai' means 'ocean' in Mongolian, and 'Lama' is the Tibetan
equivalent of the Sanskrit word 'guru', meaning 'spiritual teacher'
or 'monk'. The Dalai Lama is the head monk of Tibetan Buddhism
and can be traced back to 1391. Most Tibetans believe that the
current Dalai Lama is the reincarnation of his predecessors. There
have thirteen Dalai Lamas, with the first having been born in 1351.
They are, in turn, considered to be manifestations of
Avalokiteshvara, or Chenrezig, Bodhisattva of Compassion,
holder of the White Lotus. Thus, the current Dalai Lama is also
believed to be a manifestation of Chenrezig; in fact, the seventy-
fourth in a lineage that can be traced back to a Brahmin boy who
lived in the time of Buddha Shakyamuni.

Upon the death of a Dalai Lama, the high Lamas search for a

young boy who was born around the same time as the death of the current Dalai Lama. It can take around two to three years to identify the next Dalai Lama.

Senior High Lamas receive information during meditation or through a dream, which helps them to identify the location of where he may be found. A young boy may also begin talking to parents and siblings of a previous life, and request to be taken to where he/she once lived.

If taken, the child may recognise people and objects, a rosary or damaru that belongs to the previous Dalai Lama; this is considered the main sign of the reincarnation. The young boy is then brought to the monastery to begin his training and education as a monk, which is carried out by the other Lamas.

Lhamo Dhondrub was born in 1935, to a peasant family in Takster, which is a small village in Northeast Tibet. In 1937, when he was two years old, he was appointed as the successor to the 13th Dalai Lama, who died in 1933. Regents ruled Tibet while he trained and he was installed on 22 February 1940, taking the full name Lobsang Yeshe Tenzin Gyatso.

The Dalai Lama has travelled extensively, meeting with many political and religious leaders and founded more than two hundred monasteries. After a failed uprising and the collapse of the Tibetan resistance movement, he fled Tibet in 1959, and today, his Holiness, the fourteenth Dalia Lama, lives in exile in Northern India. He describes himself as 'a simple Buddhist monk' and is a man of peace. In 1989, he was awarded the Nobel Peace Prize for his non-violent struggle for the liberation of Tibet.

Famous Child Prodigies

Can we create a child prodigy or are they born that way? Are they simply miracles of nature? Can these Old Soul Children start remembering skills from previous lifetimes and memories that help them to become child prodigies in their current lifetime? Are they born with prior knowledge and skills for them naturally to be able bring hidden talents to the forefront?

Yet, some say that a child prodigy is a result of pushy parents, pursuing their own dreams through their children, rather than allowing their child to have a 'normal' childhood.

As past life regression is used for adults to explore life events and relationships from previous lives, could these young prodigies be reawakening their hidden talents that were soul fragments from a past life, which, in fact, split off and reunite in their current lives?

This ancient soul retrieval technique is practiced by the core Shamanic community and is a powerful healing technique: The Shaman would journey to the Lower World to retrieve the soul and return it to the person, restoring wholeness, health and wellbeing. When Old Soul Children reincarnate that lost soul part returns with him, without doing any Shamanic soul work and these children rediscover the magic of life and have a sense of aliveness and a desire to try other things.

A child could also been drawn to a particular object, like a piano, that draws out their natural talent. When this happens, they get caught between lives – their past and the present. Sometimes they cannot fathom what connection to follow because both needs are great. However, Old Soul Children do not feel that they are not getting into the same situations time and time again, as there is always a nagging feeling inside them to make most of their talents. They let go of any negative karma, whereas an adult may hold onto it, which holds them back in their current life.

Unlocking their creative talents is what their soul path mission is about, whilst they explore their current incarnation. These young prodigies are fascinating, but adults find them intimidating when both worlds meet. In the adult world, these children are often ridiculed, neglected and misunderstood because adults are either fearful of the situation, threatened that the child knows more than them, or they are simply jealous.

Through this experience, the Old Soul Child begins to question their existence in this strange adult world and then become fearful of the situation that they in, because a child feels lost in the adult world.

Child prodigies challenge our thinking about education and the place of children in society. They have the ability to learn very quickly and throughout the world's history, there have been the appearance of well-known young child prodigies with amazing talents. Here are some that have gone on to contribute their natural raw talent to the world:

Famous Child Prodigies or Do They Have Past Life Memories?

Wolfgang Amadeus Mozart could play the harpsichord at three. Before he reached his fifth birthday, he could master complicated scherzos in just half an hour and had started to compose his own works. As a young child, he could play pieces of music from memory, having heard them only once. When he was six, he was playing before the Bavarian Elector and Austrian Empress and his father was taking him on concert tours to show others his son's talent.

William James Sidis (1898-1944) was born to Russian-Jewish immigrants. He was reading and spelling at two and invented a new table of logarithms at eight. He could speak six languages by the age of ten, and at eleven, he was enrolled at Harvard University and began to deliver lectures on mathematics. His father pushed him further as his talents became more and more obvious and Sidis was denied any free time during his childhood. He grew deeply bitter and resentful towards his father. He graduated from Harvard at sixteen and lost all interest in Mathematics. Despite his talent, he did many clerical jobs and died from a brain haemorrhage at 46.

Carl Friedrich Gauss told his father, at the age of three, that he saw a mistake his father had made on the complicated payroll; he was right. He also taught himself to read. Whilst at school, the teacher tried to keep the children busy by adding up all the numbers from 1 to 100. Gauss did it in minutes.

Gifted child artist, Wang Yani, from China, painted at a nearly-adult skill level at the age of five. As a child, she produced a prodigious number of works, at one point finishing 4,000 paintings within the space of three years.

Frederic Chopin composed his Polonaises in G minor and B flat major 9 when he was just seven years old, and Franz Schubert began composing before the age of twelve. Juan Caramuel y Lobkowitz, as a child, liked to delve into serious mathematic problems and published astronomical tables when he was just ten.

Five year old, Arran Fernandez, become the youngest person to pass a GCSE exam. Ruth Lawrence, who now is in her eighties, went to Oxford University at the age of twelve to study Maths.

Marie Curie (1867-1934) was born in Warsaw, Poland and taught herself to read Russian and French. At the age of four, she would freak people out with her incredible memory, as she was able to recall events that happened years before.

Vanessa Mae began playing the violin at the age of five and was soon making regular TV appearances. She earned £36 million and in 2007, becoming the wealthiest British entertainer under thirty.

Could karma also play a part in a child prodigy's life? Could they, in fact, make contrasting choices in the Interlife to clear old karma until they get it right? Maybe these choices were to use their karmic gifts to challenge others that also have karmic lessons and for everyone to learn from a different perspective.

Conscious of their ethereal abilities and imaginary friends when they were younger, these personalities now use their spiritual experiences to help others find their own inner guidance and connect to the subtle energies.

But it is not just healers that have been influenced. A whole manner of people have experiences of imaginary friend: writers, singers, even royalty:

Ruth White

Ruth White was born in 1938: the year before the Second World War began.

Since early childhood, Ruth was aware of a shining presence with whom she could communicate and who was always with her. At first, she thought this being was an angel that looked liked the ones found in her Bible picture book. She could also see nature spirits in the garden, in parks, in streams and in the trees that lined the road where she lived. At first, Ruth thought that everyone could see her angel.

Ruth also saw colours around people that often changed according to mood and their emotions. To Ruth, these visions were normal and she was surprised to learn that not only did her parents not see what she saw, but also that they became angry and anxious at what they saw as her 'fantasies and lies'. She soon learned that if she wanted to continue to enjoy her private world, it was better not to speak of it. Throughout her childhood, Ruth's inner world was very active and the being by her side always helped and supported her along the way. However, Ruth did, at times, tried to shut the extended vision out, in order to conform to what seemed to meet general approval.

Ruth's childhood in the war years was uneasy and deprived. She had an early awareness that she was different from her parents and brother, which sometimes caused difficulty living together.

Ruth was born with very little sight in her right eye, which was assumed to be a lazy eye. Ruth spent some years being forced to wear an eye patch over her good eye in order to make the 'naughty, lazy eye' work. It was not until Ruth was eleven that it was discovered that the right eye was neither lazy nor naughty, but physically incapable of much sight because of scaring on the retina. During a rapid growth period from age twelve to fourteen, her left eye became more and more short-sighted and during puberty there were fears from her specialist that she would lose her sight.

Ruth had a passion for languages and she wished to study them at University, but eyesight problems prohibited reading and doing close-work by artificial light. Ruth was advised to take up gardening as an occupation, which she found undesirable, and decided to train as a teacher.

Miracles Began

At teacher training college, Ruth met Mary Swainson, a Jungian psychotherapist and inner-brother of the spiritual and esoteric order, known as the White Eagle Lodge.

With Mary's help, Ruth understood her experiences better, put them into context and developed a strong channelling relationship with her discarnate teaching guide, known as Gildas.

Gildas readily answered the questions that Mary and Ruth put to him and, very early on, explained that he was not an angel, but a guide. Guides have already incarnated and reincarnated on earth many times, and may or may not do so again. Angels have never incarnated and never will; they are manifestations of divine energies and they help and protect us in many different ways.

Gildas

Gildas is a discarnate teaching guide, dedicated to helping individuals in incarnation, by giving a wider spiritual framework in which to see life's problems and opportunities by teaching about other realms and dimensions.

The last incarnation of Gildas was as a monk in fourteenth century France. He is now part of a group on the other side, which is involved with teaching and healing work, and building a bridge between the planes. Gildas offers knowledge about the wider spiritual dimensions of his experience and offers Ruth's clients a clearer and broader perspective of life on Earth and the problems and dilemmas that we encounter.

Ruth believes that, before incarnating this time round, she

made an agreement with Gildas to be a channel for his work.

It is now fifty years since Mary helped her to discover and develop the means of communicating with him. Gildas is always near to her, just as he was when she was a child. Rather than seeing him as a shining being or as a monk, Ruth senses his presence as energy, sees his colours and smells his fragrance. It takes only a few moments to make the slight shift of consciousness that enables her to receive his communications. Ruth no longer writes his words by hand, but speaks them into a tape recorder or types them into her computer.

Today

Over the years, Gildas and Ruth have built up a working relationship. He is a friend and colleague. When they do work together, such as workshops and writing books, they design them together. Ruth says that Gildas plays his part and Ruth hers.

Ruth draws on her own experiences and training and it is amplifies by Gildas' perspective. Subject matter is often put forward by Gildas. Much of Ruth's knowledge has been informed and trained by Gildas.

Ruth explains that it is exciting to have such a presence always near her, but it also brings responsibilities.

Gildas' teachings have been translated into several different languages and many people now come to her so that she can channel Gildas' wisdom for their lives and dilemmas.

After a marriage break-up, as a single parent, Ruth re-trained in counselling and psychotherapy. She decided that this was a step forward in the right direction to support her understanding and practise of channelling, and to help others to integrate similar spiritual experiences and beliefs into normal living.

Ruth now has a busy practice as a spiritual teacher, channeller, writer, counsellor and transpersonal psychotherapist (U.K.C.P.). Ruth has a postgraduate diploma in counselling and guidance from University of Reading and is a founder member of 'Training for Supervisors' at the Centre for Transpersonal Psychology, London.

Robert Louis Stevenson

Robert Louis Stevenson was born on November 13, 1850, in Edinburgh, Scotland – the only son of respectable middle-class parents.

Throughout his childhood, he suffered chronic health problems and he spent much of his youth bedridden. To amuse himself, whilst in bed, he created his own world of friends and playmates which adults could not see. However, to him they were a real and an essential part of his loneliness and he wrapped himself in fantasy as a child.

As an adult, Stevenson's interest in children's imagination, and his own memories of his invalid childhood, may have been stimulated by the success of his boys' adventures in the mid-1880s. This was to feed his fertile and vivid imagination in creating his great books of high adventure and heroism such as *Treasure Island* and *Kidnapped*, which are still very popular today.

Robert Louis Stevenson credited his 'little people' or 'Brownies', as he called them, for much of his literary output. Could Stevenson have been, in fact, connecting to the middle realm where fairies reside? If so, they bestowed their luck onto him, whilst he wrote using and weaving their magic in his own stories.

Stevenson was very bright and a gifted storyteller, and one of the many books he wrote was called *A Child's Garden of Verses*. A copy of a wonderful poem in this volume, *The Unseen Playmate*, can be found at the front of this book. I used to read these poems as a very young child. On rereading them, I had not realised just how many of them stayed with me, especially the one just mentioned.

Princess Margaret

There is little information to report, but Princess Margaret is said to have had an imaginary friend called Cousin Halifax. If ever there was mischief and her nanny asked what had happened, the deed carried out would be placed on Cousin Halifax.

Lita de Alberdi

Lita de Alberdi is an accomplished spiritual teacher and author. Lita is the UK's foremost light body and channelling teacher. Lita's unique approach to energy is the result of more than twenty-five years of study, from psychology and sociology, to yoga and meditation.

Lita developed contact with the higher realms from a very young age. There were many things in her awareness and Lita happily contacted me about her friend:

Lita's friend was called Mudder and she was a little girl like herself. Mudder arrived when she was two and left when she was four and a half. She left to go on holiday and never returned.

Lita, an only child, remembers that Mudder caused great consternation in the household, as her father was always sitting on her and getting very irritated by her presence. Mudder had a chair, food and so forth, which drove her father quite mad. Her mother was more sympathetic.

Lita was an only child and very psychic; there were many beings in her awareness from a very young age and Mudder was one of many, but Mudder was different in that she related to Lita and was a real friend to her.

The Brontë Family

During their years at their parsonage home in Howarth, West Yorkshire, England, Charlotte, Emily, Anne and their brother Branwell were all home-schooled. The Brontë family were plagued by catastrophe, by the deaths of their mother and two older sisters Maria and Elizabeth. This made the remaining children form an intense and close relationship.

In 1826, their father, Reverend Patrick Brontë, gave Branwell a box of toy soldiers. Branwell allowed his sisters to choose a solider, which inspired them to write hundreds of poems, stories and a series of plays (*Young Men, Our Fellows* and *Islanders*). Branwell, the artist in the family, decided to redraw and amend the map of Africa, which led them, as children, to create an imaginary island set on the African Coast with a city named 'The Great Glass Town'. Different characters were developed in their brand new world. They all wrote their accounts in tiny handwriting on minuscule notebooks, so that it would be illegible to their Aunt and Father. The only way it could be read was with the aid of a magnifying glass.

Charlotte left for Roe Head School at thirteen years old, and the Great Glass Town was abandoned. At home, Emily and Anne went on to create the imaginary island of 'Gondal': a land covered in mists and moors. It was ruled by Queen Augususta Geraldine Almeda, who strongly believed in the power of justice.

Charlotte returned home and, with Branwell, they created 'Angria', a country near Gondal. Two Dukes inhabited Angria and their love affairs and battles were the main themes of the stories. The imaginary worlds of Angria and Gondal were influenced by real people and real places.

These two imaginary countries lasted until 1839 when Charlotte wrote a farewell letter to Angria. Emily never abandoned her imaginary world; it was so meaningful to her that she spent many of her hours writing about them and maintained the script into her adult years.

Having such rich imaginations as children helped them to create many stories which have secured them a rightful place in the literary world and thousands are still enjoying them today. Charlotte Brontë is best known for the wonderful *Jayne Eyre*.

She also wrote *Shirley*, which was published in 1849, followed by *Valletta* in 1853 and *The Professor* in 1857. Anne Brontë wrote two novels, *Agnes Grey* in 1847 and *The Tenant of Wild fell Hall* in 1848. Emily Brontë's haunting and breathtaking classic novel *Wuthering Heights* was published in 1847. The only works that Branwell Brontë ever published were a handful of poems in Yorkshire Newspapers.

The Brontës created Paracosms, which are imaginary fantasy world with much added details. However, could they, in fact, tap into earthly energies and spiritual realms, which gave them so much inspiration and benefited them all in having a clearer connection with their environments? As they connected with the energies around them, you can clearly see it gave them empowerment to use their own natural wisdom and intuitions freely.

Children often create these worlds between the ages of eight and ten, as they create stories either through writing or playing with others. Like the Brontës, children will create Paracosms similar to their own worlds, either fantasy or alien, involving other humans and animals. They are usually filled up with names, places, history and tales from their own fertile imaginations.

Robin Gibb

Robin Gibb is a Singer and Songwriter. He is best known as a member of the singing and song writing trio, The Bee Gees, who became one of the most successful musical acts of all time.

Living in Oxfordshire with his brothers, at just four years of age, Robin Gibb described, in great detail, the previous occupants of the house: a couple called John and Mary and their young child, Elizabeth, who never grew up.

He gave accurate descriptions of the family, including the length of the dresses, which clearly defined the period in history they came from. From the confidence he gave to his parents in describing the couple, investigations into the history of the house took place. They discovered that a couple called John and Mary Rose had, in fact, lived there with a daughter who died in infancy.

The description of the clothes that the couple were wearing, matched the era they were discovered in, exactly.

Kurt Cobain

Kurt Donald Cobain was born on February 20, 1967, in Hoquiam, Washington, USA. After his second birthday, his imaginary friend, called Boddah, just appeared: a ball of energy that his family went along with by setting a place for him at the dinner table. Like most parents, they raised concerns about his new friend. His Uncle was posted to Vietnam and his parents told Kurt that Boddah had to go as well, but he did not believe it.

In the film *Kurt and Courtney*, Cobain's Aunt Mary talks about Boddah. Mary plays a recording of Cobain talking to Boddah when he was three years old. It was set up to echo and Kurt asks, "Is that voice talking to me? Boddah? Boddah?" In watching the film, you can hear Kurt say, "Where's Boddah?" And "Boddah did it." And then he giggles before saying it again.

Cobain was a bright and active child and, at the age of four, he was prescribed Ritalin for hyperactivity. Courtney Love openly said that Ritalin was the cause of Cobain becoming addicted to heroin.

At seven, his life changed when his parents divorced. He became withdrawn and found it hard to speak to his parents because he felt ashamed and resented them both because of what happened. He did not want to see any of his friends at school anymore, yet craved the classic family security that he desperately wanted. As he grew into a rebellious stage, he found himself moving from one relative to another and also becoming more depressed. He also battled chronic bronchitis and intense physical pain due to an undiagnosed chronic stomach condition. This was one of the reasons that Cobain relied so much on drugs, because they helped his pain and this is not an attempt to justify drug use.

Cobain enjoyed singing from the age of two. His interest in music kept him going when his parents divorced and he decided that he wanted to be in a band at the age of twelve. His uncle gave him his first guitar at the age of fourteen. This inspired him to begin to work on his own material.

During High School, Cobain met Novoselic: a devotee of punk rock. Cobain tried to persuade him to form a band with him and gave him a demo that he recorded with his earlier band. Finally, after months of persuading, Novoselic agreed to join Cobain. After forming various bands, they found themselves interviewing drummers and eventually found David Grohl. And thus, Nirvana was born. The trio shot to fame in 1991 with their debut hit *Nevermind*. However, Cobain struggled with the amount of attention the band received.

On April 8, 1994, the music world stopped in disbelief, as thousands of fans around the world were left devastated. Kurt Cobain was discovered with a shotgun blast to his head. He was twenty-seven and the suicide note (a one-page note written in red ink) was addressed to Boddah. (Full text transcripts of the suicide note can be found on the internet.)

In the note, Cobain spoke of the great empty hole he felt had opened inside, turning him into a 'miserable, self-destructive death rocker'. He also expressed his terror that Frances Bean's life would turn out like his own, as she reminded him of how he was when he was younger. Calling Love 'a goddess of a wife who sweats ambition and empathy', he implored her to 'please keep going' for their child's sake.

Courtney Love read the suicide note out at the funeral. His closest family broke down in tears because they knew just how much his imaginary friend meant to him.

Even after his death, the music of Nirvana still resonates with fans, old and new. The fans still debate about his death, and firmly believe that Cobain did not commit suicide because the suicide note contained two different forms of handwriting.

Beyoncé Knowles

Beyoncé Giselle Knowles was born on September 4th, 1981, in Houston, Texas. She is an American R&B singer, actress and songwriter in the group Destiny's Child. It is hard to believe that this talented young lady had no friends at school, but she was one of those kids that the other kids just did not like. As she did not have anyone to play with, she created imaginary friends. Her mum would go to her school at lunchtimes and she would witness Beyoncé pushing an empty swing, acting like there was somebody on it.

Dorothy Virginia Margaret Juba

Dorothy Virginia Margaret Juba was a Supermodel in the 1950s and was reputed to be the highest paid Manhattan high fashion model of her time, earning $75 an hour. She was born on December 11th, 1927 in New York City and passed away from Liver Cancer on May 3rd, 1990. She was 63 years old.

Half Irish, half Polish, Doe (as she was known to her family) was brought up in Jackson Heights, Queens. In 1937 she was bedridden with rheumatic fever for one year. Her mother kept her at home for a further seven years so that she would be able to recuperate; this limited her contact with the outside world. In fact, her only connection with the outside world was through the telephone, through which she spoke only to other invalid children that her tutor taught.

To overcome her loneliness, she took up painting and, whilst she convalesced in her overprotective mother's care, Dovima became her imaginary playmate. The name was constructed from the initials of her names: Do-Vi-Ma.

Juba was discovered by an editor from *Vogue*, whilst she was waiting for a friend for a lunch date, who worked in a building full of advertising agencies and fashion magazines. The next day, she did her first photo shoot and never looked back. When she began modelling, she used the name of her imaginary playmate, which catapulted her to fame and she became an overnight success. Before her modelling career started, she wanted to go to art school and train for six years to become an illustrator.

In her career, she was on all of the covers of fashion magazines and worked with all the top photographers.

Dovima formed a close bond with Richard Avedon, a photographer who created the famous photograph, *Dovima with Elephants*, which was taken in August 1955. In the picture, she is wearing an evening gown created by Dior and is surrounded by circus elephants.

Lucy Maud Montgomery

Lucy Maud Montgomery was born in the village of Clifton (now called New London), Prince Edward Island, on November 30th, 1874 and died in Toronto on April 24th 1942 of congestive heart failure. L M Montgomery, as she was publicly known, wrote the international best seller, *Anne of Green Gables*, in 1908.

Her mother died of tuberculosis when she was just twenty-one months old and her father decided to return to Cavendish, Prince Edward Island. Maud, as she was known to family and friends, went to live on her maternal grandparents' farm, which became the setting for her books.

Having already brought up six children, her grandparents accepted the responsibility of bringing her up, but were deeply religious and not affectionate towards her. They also resented Maud's passion for her missing father. In her first volume of *The Selected Journals of L.M. Montgomery* (1985), she referred to herself as an 'emotional orphan' who was cut off from having a loving environment, despite growing up with adult family members.

Maud was an only child, very sensitive, extremely bright and had imaginary pals (a young girl Katie Maurice and a woman called Lucy Gray) living in the glass door of a cabinet to keep her company. She also gave names to plants and trees, including a geranium named Bonnie and a path in the country she called

Lovers' Lane. Her first written works were about her pets, hymns, poems and drawings of her imaginary friends.

From the age of nine, Maud kept a daily diary which was written in every day until she died in 1942. It became her best friend and everything was recorded in her personal confidant, from the weather to her feelings and even town gossip.

Storytelling was in the youngster's blood. Maud came from a literary family: her uncles, William and James, wrote poetry and her great aunt, Mary, often told stories from her childhood. Her Grandfather also loved to share stories with the rest of the family. Maud dreamt of being a writer and wrote her first poem, *Autumn*, when she was nine. At twelve, she wrote a poem called *Evening Dreams*, and when she was 16, she sent a poem to the local newspaper, *The Charlottetown Patriot*, but it was never published.

Like many writers, Maud used many of her own experiences to write *Anne of Green Gables*. Both Maud and Anne were orphans and they both had red hair, freckled faces, pointy chins, and loved to talk. Anne, like Maud, also had imaginary friends and talked to her plants. *Anne of Green Gables* is about Anne Shirley, who lives at the end of the nineteenth century in Avonlea on Prince Edward Island. Marilla and Matthew Cuthbert decided to apply for a boy from the orphanage to help with work on their farm, but the orphanage makes a mistake and sends the Cuthbert's a girl: Anne, who is bright, hard-working, caring and sociable; emotional Anne is a wonderful role model, with her fiery temperament and endless chatter. She immediately falls in love with Green Gables, and her adoptive parents find that they haven't the heart to send her away.

In the book, Anne was constantly searching for 'kindred spirits': people with whom she felt strongly connected, which echoes Maud's own loneliness whilst growing up, which every child and adult can identify with.

Anne of Green Gables is a touching story that has all the essential elements of real life and it became an instant success. The book sold more than 19,000 copies in five months and the publisher begged Maud to write another 'Anne' book.

Anne of Green Gables has been translated into seventeen different languages, and made into plays, films and a television series. During her writing career, she published twenty-two novels, an anthology of poetry, about 450 poems and 500 short stories.

In addition to these examples, Polar Explorer Dave Mill created his imaginary friend, 'Nobody', at the age of thirty-four, as a survival mechanism during a solo walk to the North Pole. This was to preserve his sanity on expeditions.

Prize-winning children's author and creator of *The Gruffalo*, Julia Donaldson, played with 'Popski' as a girl and years later joined in with her eldest son's imaginary friend's adventures, which later were used as inspiration for a series of stories. When she was growing up in London, her sister Mary and her would create imaginary characters and mimic real ones.

Funny man Mike Meyers used his imaginary eagle friend to keep him entertained during the endless hours in the studio, recording the voice for *Shrek the Third*. He admits he 'creating' many pals to keep him company in the lonely sound booth.

The concept of imaginary friends has hit mainstream media and has been portrayed in many ways: cartoons, books and films. Below are some examples:

Films on the Big Screen

Harvey

This classic, Pulitzer Prize-winning stage play, Harvey, was made into a classic film in 1950, starring James Stewart. James Stewart gives a fine performance, which became one his most popular roles. He plays the middle-aged, eccentric, wealthy Elwood P Dowd, who strikes up a close friendship with a six foot rabbit (Harvey) that only he can see.

Harvey is a Pooka, which, according to Irish folklore, is a mischievous shape-changer who can enter through locked doors and windows and be here, there, everywhere and anywhere.

In the film, Stewart is an alcoholic whose drunken antics are tolerated by most of the citizens of his community apart from one person: his snooty socialite sister, Veta. Veta is determined to arrange a wonderful marriage for her daughter, Myrtle May, to a respectable man. Concerned about Elwood's mental health, she begins to plot to have him certified to Chumley's Rest Sanatorium. This happens, but the staff come to think that the flustered sister is crazy; they let Elwood out and lock Veta up instead. Elwood and Harvey set out to straighten out the mess.

Dr Sanderson, the owner of Chumley's Rest Sanatorium starts to see Harvey and wants to take him away from Elwood. He convinces Elwood to take a serum that will stop him from seeing the rabbit. Veta is told the news by a cab driver and rushes back to halt the procedure.

Harvey is a great light-hearted comedy family film. There are many twists and turns in this much loved classic; one that simply cannot be made nowadays. James Stewart steals the show. His natural performance and overflowing good nature makes it impossible not to like him. This film explores issues such as kindness to others and imaginary friends, but ultimately it is about one family's plight with sanity, love, separation and protection. Also, there is a happy ending!

Bogus

Bogus is an enchanting film about seven years old Albert, played by Haley Joel Osmet. Albert's single mother (Nancy Travis), a Las Vegas circus performer is suddenly killed in a car accident.

Albert is sent from Las Vegas to live with his mother's foster sister, Harriet Franklin (Whoopi Goldberg), whom he never knew existed. Harriet struggles to get used to Albert – this strange little boy who just seems to talk to himself. But what Harriet does not know is that Albert has brought along a friend called Bogus, who is played by Gerard Depardieu. Bogus becomes a teacher, playmate and guardian angel for Albert and Harriet.

This film is an enlightening experience of imagination and trust. Whilst you watch this film you discover the magic of how it feels to be a kid again and grow to learn that magic really does exist. This film is well directed and the screenwriter has portrayed the situation accurately, because it is true to the experiences of the children that I have interviewed – their imaginary friend is also their guardian angel.

Norman Jewison

Norman Frederick Jewison was born on July 21st, 1926 in Toronto. Today he is a film director, producer and actor.

His parents used all of their time running the family shop and he was looked after by his two elder aunts. Jewison's childhood was not an unhappy one, and he had dozens of imaginary friends. Some were big, some small, some were twins and he even had triplets that helped him to conjure and create his own imaginary world, which was filled with people, places and games that took him to magical places.

One of his aunts, a schoolteacher, taught Norman to read at an early age and he learnt, early on, about the power of imagination. Jewison, a father of three and grandfather to four, produced and directed *Bogus* and feels that it is one of his most personal films to date.

Heart and Souls

Heart and Souls was made in 1993, starring Robert Downey Jnr and Elisabeth Shue. Harrison, Penny, Julia, and Milo are four earthbound ghosts that all have unfinished business in this world before they can move onto the next.

In 1959, they all board a bus that later crashes and all of them die, but do not go to heaven right away. On that night a boy is born, they become guardian angel-like ghosts, visible only to the boy. When it becomes obvious that they find themselves permanently trapped on earth, they become Thomas' imaginary friends until he is eight years old and they do not understand why they are still attached to Thomas.

Milo, Penny, Julia, and Harrison begin to seriously interfere with his life and his surrounding, but Thomas grows fond of them. When people begin to think that Thomas might have something wrong with him, they decide not to let Thomas see them anymore. This devastates him, so they decide to withdraw, to make Thomas life more stable.

Twenty years later, Thomas is grown up and very discontented when it comes to letting people into his life. The quartet is still with him, even though he can't see them. One day, they appear to him to help Thomas bring some order into his life.

However, the quartet also have their own personal ghosts to lay to rest before they can enter heaven.

They stay by his side until Thomas helps each one to resolve and complete the one major issue they wish they could have resolved before they died. The challenge begins, for each of the ghosts, to overcome inner obstacles, and have the guts to follow their hearts, leaving them empowered to enter heaven in peace.

Hearts and Souls makes you smile and this feel good film is not only heart-warming, but also well-executed. With excellent acting, it tells us, in a humorous way, not to miss our opportunities.

Pete's Dragon

An early film of children's imaginary friendships is the classic, *Pete's Dragon*.

This was first realised on November 3rd, 1977. Directed by Don Chaffey, it is a live-action/animated, musical feature film from Walt Disney productions.

Pete is a nine year old orphan escaping from his brutal adoptive parents, the Gogans, who use him as a slave. His only friend is a cartoon dragon named Elliott, and they both success-fully escape to Passamaquoddy, a small fishing town Maine, and live with Nora, a lighthouse keeper, and her father, Lampie.

Elliott is sought for medicinal purposes by the corrupt Doctor Terminus who believes the dragon can bring them riches.

The element of a Power Animal protecting young Pete from harm is the main theme throughout and helps him to find true happiness. Priceless memories come flooding back when I watch this film, as I truly believed that Elliot was always with me on my travels to school and chased the bullies away.

Drop Dead Fred

In *Drop Dead Fred*, Phoebe Cates, plays Lizzie Cronin: a recently separated young woman, who manages to lose her purse, her car, her job and her husband all in one day. After moving back into her mother's home, she makes a strange discovery: in the back of her old wardrobe is her old jack-in-the-box, covered in the tape her mother had put there to lock in her imaginary friend, Drop Dead Fred. Opening the tape, who should pop out? Not jack, but Drop Dead Fred (Rik Mayall).

Now Fred is appalled to find that 'Snot Face' is all grown up and that she even 'did it' like the pigeons. Fred is still as mad as ever, and is out to cause as much mayhem as possible. No one can see him except Lizzie, who still gets the blame after all these years. She is terribly unhappy, so Fred sets out to help her get back on the right track and rebuild her shattered life.

The mischievous, gladioli-hating, Drop Dead Fred also helps Lizzie to cope with her pushy mother (the 'Mega Beast'), which places Lizzie in many embarrassing situations. Lizzie's mum, Polly, becomes very disturbed when Lizzie mentions that he is back and is responsible for all the things that are going wrong. In true Polly style, she seizes the moment by taking Lizzie to see a Psychiatrist. Lizzie finds her inner strength, with the help of Fred, and says goodbye to her husband and also her mother.

Drop Dead Fred is an absolutely fantastic film and is a classic piece of comedy. The hilarious portrayal of Fred by Rik Mayall is fantastic: brilliantly funny and also amazingly touching when it's needed.

Fans of the BAFTA Award winning, cult comedy, television series, *The Young Ones*, will be aware of Rik Mayall's brand of comedy. British audiences know him very well for his portrayal of the angry, squat-dwelling Rick, and as Alan B'stard in the BAFTA Award winning, *The New Statesman*, which also won a 1989 International Emmy Award.

Anthony Fingleton

Samantha, the oldest daughter of *Drop Dead Fred*'s screenwriter, Anthony Fingleton, had an imaginary friend – this was the inspiration for the film. Samantha's friend was called Sarah and became an important member of the household. Whenever water or milk was spilled on the carpet, Samantha would blame Sarah.

Fingleton and Carlos Davis (his co-writer) agreed that this would make an excellent idea for a television series, and developed the idea to feature a young woman whose imaginary friend came back into her life during a time of crisis. Whilst thinking of ideas, Davis had lunch with a friend who told him a story that she was writing, about her five-year old daughter's imaginary friend, whose name was Drop Dead Fred. Davis and Fingleton went on to turn the idea into a feature film.

Donna

Donna, now thirty-one, recalls that her imaginary friend appeared when her brother, Stephen, went to school and got new friends. Stephen did not want to play with her much after that. Donna had John Henry for years. Donna's mum recalls that John Henry was still around from time to time when Donna started school. Donna just remembers playing with him in all weathers. At Christmas, he would go away for a holiday but would always come back from

Father Christmas with presents for her. The trigger for Donna remembering her imaginary friend was watching *Drop Dead Fred*.

Children's Television Programmes

The Tweenies
The Tweenies (Jake, Fizz, Bella and Milo) are bright and colourful characters, and cover certain appropriate issues for young children, including imaginary friends. The show also includes a story time, which I like because the more books are seen by children; the more likely they are to read them themselves. In one episode, called *Pretend Friend*, Jake has an imaginary friend called Douglas. Fizz and Bella are practising a new dance – the Tweenie Beat – but Jake can't seem to learn it, so Douglas helps out.

Arthur
Arthur is an animated series that is aimed at children between the ages of four and eight. Based on the children's books written by Marc Brown, the series chronicles the adventures of Arthur, an eight year old aardvark. DW (short for Dora Winifred) is Arthur's little sister and loves to bug her brother. In one episode, Arthur is embarrassed by DW's imaginary friend, during a trip to the amusement park with his friends, which is the last straw for him.

The imaginary friend, Nadine, moves in with the family and she follows DW everywhere. In the episode, everyone has to be careful where they sit, or what they say, because Nadine is very sensitive.

Watching this episode would provide a very good opening for parents to talk to their child about their imaginary friend, because the heart-warming tale does, in fact, show that children's imagination should never be ignored.

Charlie and Lola
Charlie and Lola are children's picture book characters, created

by the brilliant Lauren Child. The books, which were made into a hit children's TV series, focus on Charlie and Lola's imaginations, as they learn how to get along, behave and live their young lives happily. The best known imaginary friend to young children is Soren Lorenson, Lola's imaginary friend: a little grey boy who becomes her confidant and security blanket.

Medium

Allison Dubois was the inspiration for the hit NBC drama television series, *Medium*. Allison Dubois was just six years old when her great grandfather contacted her from the spirit realms and gave her a message, which needed to be passed on to her mother.

He told Allison that he was okay and that he was still with her.

From an early age, she knew that she was different to other children and struggled to make sense of her dreams and visions of dead people.

At ten years of age, she was visited by people who told her that she would help lots of people when she was a lot older. She did not understand at that time, but when she became an adult, she understood that these people were, in fact, her spirit guides. Contact from her guides continued during her teenage years.

She was born on January 24th, 1972 in Phoenix, Arizona, USA. Her parents divorced when she was a baby and she has one older brother, Michael. She grew up knowing that both of her parents loved her and played down her natural talents.

She attended Arizona State University and majored in political science (she minored in history). In her senior year, she began interning at the District Attorney's office. Her natural abilities were put to great use when she began to assist law enforcement agencies across America in solving crimes.

For four years, Allison completed a variety of tests regarding her psychic abilities in conjunction with the studies of mediums and psychic phenomena at the same University. These were validated, scientifically, by Harvard-trained psychologist, Gary Schwartz, and caused much controversy.

Today, Allison DuBois is world renowned as a psychic. She has an amazing writing gift, and has written three bestselling books: *Don't Kiss Them Goodbye, We Are Their Heaven* and *Secrets of the Monarch: How the dead can teach us about living a better life.*

If you are mourning the death of a loved one, then her books will give you reassurance that people on the other side are with us all the time.

In her first books, Allison tells us how she juggles normal life – raising three spiritually aware daughters who have inherited her gift, whilst using her natural psychic abilities to help others. It also shows that you can, in fact, blend the spiritual and physical worlds into one, creating harmony where you go, in giving messages to people that have crossed over.

Allison is educating others throughout the world to have a better understanding of psychics and mediums, which I know she will be successful in completing.

Useful Websites

Below are some links to websites you may find of interest

Intuitive Children ~ www. intuitivechildren.co.uk
Website dedicated to the support of Intuitive Children and their families. Tips on how to empower your child, increase their self esteem and help them trust their inner wisdom. Contact Kylie with your stories and find new ways to raise your Intuitive Child/Old Soul Child. Sign up to our newsletter.
Email: enquiries@intuitivechildren.co.uk

Kylie Holmes ~ www.touchedbyanangel.me.uk
Intutive Angel Therapist, Writer, Past Life Regression Therapist. Empowerment Workshops & Tools as you explore your Spiritual Journey. Choose from: Working With Angels, You & Your Guide and Writing From Your Soul. Sign up to our newsletter.
PO BOX 210
St Neots
PE19 6YA, England
Tel:+44 (0)870 780 8413
Email: kylie.holmes@btinternet.com

Australian Bush Essences ~ www.ausflowers.com.au
45 Booralie Road,
Terrey Hills, NSW, 2084, Australia
Tel: 02 9450 1388
Fax: 02 9450 2866 International Tel: 61 2 9450 1388
International Fax: 61 2 9450 2866
E-Mail: info@ausflowers.com.au
Practitioner Help line: consulting@ausflowers.com.au
Essence Help line: consulting@ausflowers.com.au

Ann Brady www.reikiann.com
Reiki Master & Karuna Reiki Master
Offering Reiki training to individuals from all walks of life.
Email: annbrady07@aol.com

Delphi Ellis ~ www.thenewpath.com
Holistic Consultant. Specialist in Dream Analysis. Award
Winning Dream Expert as seen on The Wright Stuff, GMTV and
Radio 1Xtra.
PO BOX 1144
Bedford
MK42 7ZH, England
Tel: +44 (0) 7833 958432
Email: delphi@delphiellis.com

George David Fryer ~ www.psychicartist.co.uk
Spirit Guide drawings, Spiritual Images,
Past Life Portraits, Mandalas & Workshops
Email: psychicaritist@f2s.com
Email: psychicartist@mac.com

Keith Beasley ~ www.algarveowl.com
Teaching Reiki without rules and help with unlocking your inner
wisdom.
Email: owl@algarveowl.com

Michelle Shine ~ www.michelleshine.co.uk
www.homeopathyworkedforme.org
Using Homeopathy to treat the person and not the disease.
Michelle treats both adults and children for a variety of
complaints that include both physical and emotional problems.
Tel: +44 (0) 20 8959 8855
Mobile: + 44 (0) 7956 207556
Email: michelle@michelleshine.co.uk

Ruth White ~ www.ruthwhite-gildas.co.uk
Spiritual Growth, Counselling & Psychotherapy
Karmic Growth, Channeling & Guidance
www.ruthwhite-gildas.co.uk
Email: tigerruth@ruthwhite-gildas.co.uk
Tel: +44(0) 1273 584060

Leda Sammarco ~ www.ledasammarco.com
Writers Coach, that can help you to unleash your creative
potential.
Tel: +44 (0) 7930 568 516

Bully Defenders ~ www.bullydefenders.com
Anti Bullying Website that can help Parents, Children and
Teachers that are affected by any form of Bullying.
Email: enquiries@bullydefenders.com

Bullywatch ~ www.bullywatch.org
Bullywatch is an organisation based in Yate, Bristol, UK, that
started up in 2001. There aim is to support those who are being
bullied by giving them someone who will listen to their issues and
help them try to resolve those problems.
Tel: 01454 318753
Email: bullywatch@hotmail.com

Weleda ~ www.weleda.co.uk
Anthropsophic and Homeopathic Medicines and Natural
Bodycare.
Weleda UK Ltd
Heanor Road
Ilkeston
Derbyshire
DE7 8DR

Queries: Contact Weleda Direct
Phone: 0115 944 8222
Fax: 0115 944 8210
Email: weleda.direct@weleda.co.uk

Steiner Schools www.steinerwaldorf.org.uk
The Steiner Waldorf Schools Fellowship (SWSF) represents 35 Steiner schools, 51 Early Years settings, 4 Early Years training and 8 Steiner Teacher training courses in the UK and Ireland. It is the home of the European Council for Steiner Education bringing together some 630 schools in 22 countries and it is a partner in the Alliance for Childhood. There are over 958 schools, 1600 Early Years settings and 60 Teacher Training centres worldwide.
Steiner Waldorf Schools Fellowship Ltd
Kidbrooke Park
Forest Row
East Sussex
RH18 5JA, England
Tel: +44 (0)1342–822115
Fax: +44 (0)1342–826004
E-mail: mail@swsf.org.uk

Gemma Bailey www.gemmabailey.co.uk &
www.peoplebuilding.co.uk
Offering Hypnotherapy Services and NLP
Email: infopeoplebuilding.co.uk
Tel: 0845 8377531

Helen Wozniak www.glassmandala.co.uk
& Hema Vyas Helping individuals reach their full potential and find happiness. Specialised in many area's including, inter-personal relationships, Psychoneuroimmunology, and advanced training in Emotional Intelligence and Past life Regression Therapy.
Email: hema@glassmandala.co.uk

Derek Hawkins www.derekhawkins.com

A Psychic working intuitively through the medium of Astrology. In interpreting the Birth Chart, he is able to advise, inform and empower people. His aim is help people to be better understand themselves and the various layers and complexities which make them who they are. Email: information@derekhawkings.com

Emma Stow Astrology www.emmastowastrology.co.uk

Emma Stow has studied conventional western astrology, esoteric astrology and energy coaching. She is primary concerned with individual potential and contribution as it relates to personal and global evolution. Email: info@emmastowastrology.co.uk

Angela Tarry www.auraenergyphotos.co.uk

Angela Tarry is well known as the aura expert. A trained Psychotherapist and Colour Therapist, Angela has been taking Aura Photos for over 14 years. Email: angelatarry@aol.com
Tel: 01903 539 621

Ninny Noodle Noo www.ninnynoodlenoo.com

Ninny Noodle Noo which stocks a range of *heirloom and quality* toys, including beautiful hand-crafted Ostheimer toy figures, toys from Spiel & Holz, Kinderdram, Erzi and Haba, Barefoot Books, organic children's clothes and toiletries.
Email: dottyspots@ninnynoodlenoo.com

Reiki Rose www.reikirose.co.uk

Stephen & Christopher Rose are Reiki Practitioners and Teachers honouring their childhood experiences.
Email: *info@reikirose.co.uk*
Tel: 01580764640
Fax: 01580761667
Mobile: 07718342077

Do you have a story to tell?

If you have a story about Children's Imaginary Friends or anything else that you feel Kylie may be interested in. Please visit the website www.touchedbyanangel.me.uk www.intuitivechildren.co.uk You can contact her by email: kylie.holmes@btinternet.com or you can write to her at PO Box 210, St Neots, Cambs, PE19 6YA.

BOOKS

O is a symbol of the world, of oneness and unity. In different cultures it also means the "eye," symbolizing knowledge and insight. We aim to publish books that are accessible, constructive and that challenge accepted opinion, both that of academia and the "moral majority."

Our books are available in all good English language bookstores worldwide. If you don't see the book on the shelves ask the bookstore to order it for you, quoting the ISBN number and title. Alternatively you can order online (all major online retail sites carry our titles) or contact the distributor in the relevant country, listed on the copyright page.

See our website **www.o-books.net** for a full list of over 500 titles, growing by 100 a year.

And tune in to myspiritradio.com for our book review radio show, hosted by June-Elleni Laine, where you can listen to the authors discussing their books.

mySpiritRadio